Edited by
Joe L. Kincheloe
and
Shirley R. Steinberg

# Thirteen Questions

## Reframing Education's Conversation

PETER LANG
New York • San Francisco • Bern
Frankfurt am Main • Berlin • Wien • Paris

**Library of Congress Cataloging-in-Publication Data**

Thirteen questions : reframing education's conversation /
edited by Joe L. Kincheloe and Shirley R. Steinberg.
   p. cm.
   Includes bibliographical references.
      1. Education—United States—Aims and objectives.
2. Educational change—United States.
I. Kincheloe, Joe L.    II. Steinberg, Shirley R.
LA217.2.T48        1992        370'.973—dc20            92-3894
ISBN 0-8204-1925-7                                              CIP
ISBN 0-8204-1924-9 (pbk.)

∞

© Peter Lang Publishing, Inc., New York 1992

# Thirteen Questions

PETER LANG

New York • San Francisco • Bern

Frankfurt am Main • Berlin • Wien • Paris

# Contents

To Ian, Meghann, Chaim and Bronwyn

# Preface

Independence Day 1991 evoked a variety of emotions as we watched from our rural South Carolina vantage point. Parades in both urban and rural locales marked by flag waving spectators cheering Patriot missles, A-10s, and B-52s, were out-of-synch with the evolving vision of America we have nurtured for the last quarter of a century. Celebrations of freedom which honored the "free" Kuwatis and the absence of bloodshed in Operation Desert Storm failed to mention the 150,000 Iraqi men, women, and children killed in the hostilities. As we watched CNN, NBC, ABC, and CBS and read our Gannett newspapers, we heard or saw virtually no reference to alternate perspectives on recent American history. It was assumed that all among us held the same viewpoints as to the meaning of the way Independence Day was celebrated and we all possessed the same vision of what the "New World Order" should be.

It was this absence of diversity, this equation of dissent with some pathological psychological constitution that especially disturbed us, that confronted us with our roles as critical, democratic educators. We pondered how discussing the power dimensions of information access in our education classes evoked such puzzled and sometimes hostile reactions from many of our students. We empathized with them, understanding their lack of exposure to people like us. Indeed, we were the people their ministers, their coaches, and some of their high school social studies teachers had warned them about. How could they see our calls for critical reading of the text of American foreign policy as anything but unpatriotic, anti-Americanism? They had never heard such perspectives before.

This is the central idea of *Thirteen Questions: Reframing Education's Conversation*: Many students have never heard a different perspective. As we survey the educational literature which addresses these thirteen questions, we find an alarming homogenieity of perspectives. Many leading publishers simply don't consider viewpoints similar to ones expressed in this book—"not marketable," "too dangerous," "too far ahead of the times." Thus, students are subjected too often to blandness and one-dimensional texts on education.

The only language of educational reform they hear is business mantras of the Reagan-Bush variety. Focusing on measurable results, more testing, corporate partnerships, business-funded model schools, and teacher accountability, the language of right-wing educational reform excludes questions of social justice and civic courage.

But hope persists, oppositional voices can still be heard. Courageous teachers still inspire students despite accountability-based, evaluation procedures that work against them. They are heroic, and will live forever in the good works of their students. In addition to our brave teachers, we would also like to thank our editor, Michael Flamini, for his vision of what could be in educational publishing. Barbara DeLorenzo and Brenda Stitler deserve special thanks for their typing. We are especially indebted to our contributors who we consider a special and extraordinarily articulate group of scholars. We hope their visions are as inspirational to our readers as they have been to us.

Joe L. Kincheloe
Shirley R. Steinberg

January 1992

# Introduction: The Questions We Ask, The Stories We Tell About Education

## Joe L. Kincheloe

The questions we raise, the debates in which we engage about education are ultimately questions and debates about the stories we choose to give meaning to our lives. In our autobiographical stories we become heroes or heroines who act on particular understandings of why we are here, what demands our attention, and what is insignificant (Postman, 1989, p. 122). In our stories about what constitutes a good society, an ethical act, an authentic way of being human, the sub-story of education takes shape (Giroux and McLaren, 1989, p. xii). In the last decade or so a dramatic debate has developed over the nature of the social and educational stories. Unfortunately, too little of this debate has filtered to the public or even to the pre-service or in-service teaching of teachers. The traditional stories (sometimes called the meta-narratives) are under attack and the "rancanteurs" who grant shelter to the old stories have retaliated with an elaborate re-packaging of their tales.

Sensing that the old stories were threatened by the faithless, conservative politicians and theorists rode to power on their skillful depiction of a good vs. evil struggle. The modernist story of progress, characterized by a faith in traditional science, time as money, a cult of reason, an idealized notion of freedom framed within a decontextualized and vague humanism, and the superiority of the Western tradition, formed a tentative alliance with a fundamentalist Christianity and its Puritan vision of a Christian "theocracy on a hill" (Giroux, 1991, pp. 7-8). Education became one of the primary battlegrounds for the conservative forces, as a veritable "battle for the mind" took shape around issues such as school prayer, textbook content, government support for private Christian schools, the evaluation of teachers, phonics, the curriculum, and school management. The conservative story has certainly established itself as the dominant narrative, but it is not without opposition and internal tensions. This book examines thirteen commonly posed educational questions of our era and provides tenative answers based on stories that differ from those of the conservative power holders.

In the process of answering these thirteen questions the authors confront the many dimensions of narrative composition: How do we choose our stories? Upon what criteria do we base our decisions about what type of society our schools should work to create? How do we decide what we need to know or not to know? What is the nature of the process which certifies certain information as valuable school knowledge? How do we apply the knowledge gained in schools to our own lives and the larger society? In order to tell coherent, convincing stories and to formulate answers to these questions we must develop a system of meaning. For our story to be compelling, the system of meaning must be just, optimistic, empathetic, and democratic.

We begin the construction of our system of meaning with critique and then move to a positive assertion of a socio-educational vision. Our critique is grounded on the concept of postmodernism in that it questions Western reason and its social, political, and educational effects. It questions the Enlightenment and Marxist stories with their obligatory "heroes" and the supposition of their privilege to historically situate, define, and judge other stories without applying such analyses to themselves. Our postmodern critique contends that the Grand Narratives of Western Civilization, with their stories of progress, expansionism, and the success of science, have presented us with unexamined notions of knowledge, truth, objectivity, and reason. We argue, such definitions can be exposed as forms of social power, a victory of a particular narrative's way of representing the world which benefits some while harming others (Giroux, 1991, pp. 19-21).

If definitions of knowledge, truth, objectivity, and reason are indeed contingent on power and its construction of the grand narrative, are we not in danger of lapsing into a relativism, a nihilism which chokes our ability to act ethically, to act as human agents? As conservatives have confronted the critique of postmodernism, they have answered the question affirmatively, arguing that postmodernism degenerates into a call for anarchy and a destruction of all that is sacred. But grounded upon a democratic system of meaning, the postmodernist critique can help formulate new ways of seeing ourselves, the world, and education—new ways which are more honest and just than the less reflective, more certain traditions.

Our system of meaning makes no pretense about neutrality; it identifies with the subjugated stories, the perspectives of the excluded and the dominated. Thus, one of the main concerns of our postmodern system of meaning is its attempt to uncover the ways that dominant schooling serves to perpetuate the hopelessness of the oppressed. A concurrent concern involves the attempt to gain insight into how our own assumptions are constructed. In the process we begin to disengage ourselves from ideological expectations and socially-driven norms of interpersonal behavior. As a result of our engagement with the subjugated perspectives, we find ourselves in a running meta-dialogue, a constant conversation with self, a perpetual recon-ceptualization of our ways of seeing, our system of meaning. Our view from below, i.e., our understanding of excluded voices, grants us a "double consciousness." This heightened awareness grants new access to the ways oppression works, as we understand the ways of the oppressors and the lived realities of the oppressed. Such double perception allows us to see more clearly what we know and how we come to know it, and in the process, formulate grounded strategies to make the process of learning a democratic act—an act which refuses to be satisfied with dominant definitions of knowledge, intelligence, and school success (Kincheloe, 1991, pp. 28-47).

bell hooks and Henry Giroux clarify and extend our system of meaning with their dramatic fusion of postmodern critique, women's ways of seeing, subjugated knowledge, and critical theory. Salvaging the most progressive features of the modernist story (e.g., social justice, solidarity, and equality), hooks and Giroux assert an educational politics that: 1) recog-nizes the power of racial, gender, and economic difference to shape consciousness and school outcome; 2) expose the way power covertly works to structure inequality; 3) promotes an optimistic narrative which recognizes the complexity of the relationship between humanity's attempt to achieve self-direction and social structures which impede the effort; and 4) conceptualizes new and more self-conscious ways of approaching parenting, work, schooling, play, citizenship, and happiness. Hope exists in the formulation of the postmodern stories. We turn now to an examination of the struggle to make it a part of North American consciousness and schooling (hooks, 1989, pp. 22-25; Giroux, 1991, p. 44).

If the postmodern democratic system of meaning is to play a role in the reform of education, its proponents must hold a clear picture of the forces which exclude it from the public conversation about education. Advocates must understand competing social movements of the contemporary era and their educational stories. During the late 1970s and early 1980s the New Right captured the social and educational imagination with its portrayal of an American decline initiated by the liberalism of the 1960s. The right-wing made the traditional Puritan dream fashionable again, and education was viewed as an avenue to individual fortune. The conservatives told a story of a permissive liberal ethic which precipitated a breakdown of authority, patriotism, and discipline.

Framing the story as "the crisis of schooling," the New Right, since the late 1970s, has forced democratic progressives of any stripe into the position of having to defend failed or unpopular policies of the 1960s. Even though some of these policies were never given a chance to achieve their promise and despite the fact that many of the progressives forced to defend such programs have little or no historical or theoretical connection with 60s reforms, the Right has won hearts and minds with such a tact. While it is accurate to argue that the educational reformers of the 1960s often produced a theoretically immature vision of school reform based on a romantic celebration of student culture and an insensitivity to the economic concerns of minority and working-class parents, it is not fair to argue that they produced a crisis in education (Giroux and McLaren, 1989, pp. xiii-xv). The inaccuracy of the story revolves around the fact

that most schools were unaffected by such reforms (Cuban, 1984, p. 171). Even more ridiculous was the attribution of economic decline to the progressive reformers. Nevertheless, it worked, and during the 1980s and early 1990s voices of democracy and egalitarianism were heard less and less in the public conversation about education.

Even though conservatives gained the power to tell the educational story in the late 1980s, they did not represent a cohesive, monolithic ideological force. The alliance forged in the late 1970s was an unholy pact between business leaders, conservative academicians, and fundamentalist Protestants newly awakened to their own political power. Ronald Reagan was perfectly suited to tie the coalition together. Part right-wing ideologue, part defender of big business, and part purveyor of fundamentalist pieties, Reagan appealed to all fringes of the alliance with a naivete that on TV played as an Ozzie Nelson honesty. Taking his cue from the clippings he collected from *Reader's Digest* and *Guideposts*, Reagan told the story of an America providentially guided to greatness. School's role in the story was to make sure that all understood America's favored standing in the eyes of God (Kincheloe, 1985, pp. 4-17).

But even the popularity of Ronald Reagan could not quell the tensions in the alliance. Business advocates pushing for a back-to-basics education designed to enhance worker productivity vied with both fundamentalists supporting a prayer-based, Christian-oriented curriculum, and academic "guardians of tradition" advocating an old time, humanities-based retelling of the superiority of the Western tradition. Though common ground for the three positions was found, emphases have changed during this conservative era. After 1984, the fundamentalists exerted less power and schooling as cultural uniformity based on a narrow reading of the Western tradition was added to the business-oriented schooling as job training. Consequently, by the late 1980s the Right argued that not only had the schools put the American economy at risk, but Western civilization as well (Aronowitz, 1989, pp. 203-205). Fundamentalists initially supported the Western-civilization-at-risk argument, but by the end of the 1980s many of them were cautioning one another to re-evaluate calls for a curricular

reassertion of Western tradition. Just because traditionalists like Allan Bloom and William Bennett share enemies with us, fundamentalists maintained, this does not mean they share our theocratic view of education. (Nash, 1990, p. 25).

Despite the waxing and waning of the influence of particular perspectives within the right-wing phlanges, common ground in conservative education has revolved around the role of the teacher. The notion of teacher-as-intellectual does not fit in this context, as right-wing groups tend to see the teacher as a technician who passes along the information and belief structures of the standardized test makers and the state curriculum guides. Under the banner of teaching as the transmission of the best of our cultural heritage, teachers are deskilled and deprofessionalized.

Through these lenses teachers do not need to help students interpret, question, relate or apply the information they transmit. What need is there for scholars in the teaching profession? Indeed, the tendency to be scholarly may get in the way, impending the orderly transmission of the facts. Here the accountability-based, standardized orientation of the excellence movement dovetails with the concerns of the advocates of Western tradition. The politically "inoffensive" story of the West can be transmitted and then scientifically assessed to make sure that teachers are performing their jobs properly (Ryan, 1989, p. 159; Giroux and McLaren, 1989, p. xix).

Indeed, teachers must "get the story right." Attacked by so many and in such an "unfair" way, the American Pageant began to disappear from the schools, the right-wing story proclaimed. American virtue was doubted, charges of racism, sexism, class bias and imperialism entered the conversation (Reitz, 1988, p.3). Schools set out to reclaim the legacy of American greatness and to quell the doubts. Turning to the authority of tradition, the right-wing leaders re-told the story of Manifest Destiny only in late twentieth century garb. Basking in the "great victory" in the Persian Gulf, George Bush heralded the story to the world, proclaiming that America had quieted her detractors. "Who can doubt us now?" he rhetorically asked.

Where is the opposition? Liberalism has offered little competition. For example, the liberal presidential candidates of the

1980s, Walter Mondale and Michael Dukakis, denied their own liberalism, devoting much campaign time to an attempt to distance themselves from the position. Liberal opposition to Reagan, Bush, and Bennett's initiatives was minimal, as liberal politicians and educational theorists often in the name of progressivism simply echoed the right-wing concerns. Liberal academicians many times addressed questions of educational opportunity but couched them within the ideological frames of worker productivity, GNP, and economic competitiveness. The public perceived the bankruptcy of liberalism—it no longer had the ability to tell cultural stories. Though he viewed it from the limited perspective of the guardians of Tradition, Allan Bloom sensed liberalism's forfeiture of its claim to the moral plain (Bloom, 1987, p. 30). Unable to take a moral stand liberalism lapsed into an *ethical* relativism which sometimes reflected a positivistic separation of fact from value.

Liberalism's inability to critique the educational perspectives of the conservative theorists involved its failure to develop a sense of its location in history and place. Such an ability would have allowed liberalism to understand the socio-cultural forces which have spawned and shaped the forms that domination and consciousness construction take. Without such contextual grounding liberalism became impotent, unable to formulate educational alternatives which find their strength in an awareness of the process by which questions of justice are repressed by schools. Without such an awareness liberalism became an "unindicted co-conspirator" in the preservation of contemporary social malformations of race, class, and gender.

At their worst, modern liberals reject conservative educational policies without a clear understanding of just what it is they seek to substitute in their stead. Liberals speak of victimization but lack the theoretical frames to connect the process to larger political struggles (McLaren, forthcoming, pp. 32-33; Giroux, 1991, p. 55). Pluralism does not substitute for a deep recognition of the forces of difference, i.e., the deep social structures which isolate individuals and groups and pit them against one another. While we study liberal notions of toleration, multi-culturalism, and acceptance, these tacit forces which pull us apart perform their insidious work. Liberalism can be

an ally of the forces of critical democracy when liberals begin to
gain a self-awareness of their own limitations emerging from
their failure to recognize the deep structures which work to pit
human actors against one another. The liberal desire for us all
to "connect to one another," does not have to fail—it does not
have to be dismissed as just another naive effort of do-gooders.
A post-liberal movement for human interconnection which is
grounded in an understanding of difference and refuses to
ground the connection in the confines of dominant culture's
ideological and discursive practices, can extend human solidarity and the struggle for freedom, justice, and happiness.

In a liberal vein Marilyn Ferguson writes that we have learned
that Western culture does not have all the answers. Beginning
with this recognition, liberals examined their consciousness
construction seeking a "higher consciousness." For all this
concern with self-understanding/knowledge, however, liberalism has often remained quite naive to the *socio-ideological*
construction of consciousness, the production of self. Here
rests liberalism's opportunity to crawl through the crack in the
wall that limits perception. Outside the confines they will find a
new place where there is a recognition of their location in the
web of reality, their historical moment. Such a new perspective
will allow liberals to understand the naivete which results from
an unawareness of how the lived world precludes escape from
the Enlightenment narrative and their own complicity in the
unexamined use of patriarchal and Eurocentric ways of framing
educational experiences. Referring to our democratic system of
meaning, liberals may gain a historical, theoretical grounding
which empowers them to move beyond their present position
and effectively confront the repressiveness of conservative
education. Indeed, the power of the Right to dictate educational policy reflects a failure among democratic progressives to
initiate a public conversation about education (Ferguson, 1980,
pp. 68-69, 306).

Drawing on our system of meaning, our view from the
bottom, democratic educators can cultivate a public educational
conversation which takes seriously the notion of citizenship and
social justice. Such a conversation can lead to an empowerment
which is predicated on the identification of oppressive school

and social practices which place unnecessary limitations on human actions, emotions, and cognition. Such educational oppression impedes citizens and students from egalitarian participation in social and educational institutions alongside those who possess the status of "competence" (Simon, 1989, p. 138). Emerging from this public conversation about justice and schooling will be a recognition of the shackles of the right-wing educational policies on the human mind and spirit. Democratic educators will encourage students to draw upon their own cultural heritages or subjugated knowledges in order to develop academic abilities which empower them to deconstruct existing school knowledge. Extending their analysis students will question the uses of their empowerment. Thus, they will be forced to confront the task of developing progressive social visions, new stories of what could be. Such new stories allow teachers to engage students in the analysis of how experience is named and rewarded in schools and how such naming affects different students in different ways. Such analysis leads to a higher level of thinking which moves teachers beyond the unexamined cultural transmission model of their task and students beyond the nervous test taking role with which they have grown so familiar.

Thus, as an act of educating students for the moral and ideological imperatives of an authentic democratic society, students transcend the repressive right-wing notion of Tradition. The questioning of the educational canon becomes an act of democracy, a manifestation of higher order thinking— knowledge is engaged in tandem with ethics and cognition. Contrary to Bloom, Bennett, and the others, *critical* engagement with the wisdom of the past is not a mark of closed minds and distorted personalities (Bloom, 1987, p. 61; Giroux and McLaren, 1989, p. xx). Where would we be if many of our intellectual ancestors had failed to question tradition, racism, sexism, class bias, and religious intolerance? An education which is uninterested in justice and an engagement with everyday life is not compatible with a democratic society. It is in its own way nihilistic, devoid of hope in the sense that it assumes that all the great ideas have been thought, that the jury is in on the great questions of humanity, that community is lost and cannot be regained, that history has ended (Nussbaum, 1987, p. 20).

This progressive attempt to subject the curriculum, and subsequently, the Western tradition to a reexamination in light of democratic precepts is not a legitimate act in the eyes of the Right. While proclaiming their own ideological innocence, advocates of unquestioned Tradition have not been hesitant to hurl charges of educational politicization at their democratic progressive adversaries. Listening to the conservative story one gets the impression that schools are about ready to wave the scholarly white flag and surrender educational institutions to the radical left. Portraying themselves as beseiged underdogs, conservatives write of school leaders running from the advancing enemy leaving their intellectual principles and moral grounding behind (Weisberg, 1987, p. 52; Kimball, 1990, p. 33). Evoking memories of Richard Hofstadter's description of "the paranoid style of American politics," right-wing proponents write of a grand leftist educational conspiracy. Interest groups pressure schools to revamp their curricula, conservative Roger Kimball writes, in a way that only ten or twenty years ago would have been disregarded because of its flagrant political bias (Kimball, 1990, pp. 3, 34). Questions such as—"Where are women in the curriculum?" or "Where are Blacks in the curriculum?" represent a blatant politicization of the curriculum; but a conservative curriculum which continues to exclude them is framed as politically objective. Are there not political assumptions underlying both positions? Is education not an inherently political act, as it inevitably confronts questions of power and power distribution (Kincheloe, 1991, pp. 23, 170)?

The conservatives have trouble understanding that reading, whether it be of the traditional canon or of student and teacher lives, is a socio-political act—our interpretations cannot be separated from where we are standing when we read, i.e., our location in the web of reality. The simplistic right-wing notion of objectivity will continue to impede a serious analysis of the way modern schools and the modern reform movements of the Reagan-Bush era exclude the socially marginalized. In this context teachers are often asked to parrot pre-arranged and isolated fact bits without attending to their underlying assumptions. Right-wing reform leaders cannot encourage teachers to reflect on the political presuppositions of their lessons (e.g., who is excluded, who is included) because they themselves are blind to the presuppositions of their school reforms in general. This blindness results from their denial of the very existence of political presuppositions. Critical democratic educators must help teachers develop strategies to analyze how knowledge and policy are produced. At this level of deconstruction, teachers will begin to comprehend the "logic" behind the facts, their context and significance, and the difference competing assumptions about knowledge and policy make on the way teachers teach and students live their lives (Kincheloe, 1991, p. 171).

This is the point where our postmodern critique and its concomitant vision of what can be comes back into our discussion. The paradigm shift, the reconceptualization of our way of seeing the educational world, allows us the insight to understand our role in a historical moment where cultural and educational boundaries are disappearing. This disappearance of boundaries involves a panoply of conflicting social changes including, but not limited to, the influence of mass media through its power of representation (i.e., the way our view of the world is constructed) on the restructuring of our self-identity, our political orientation, our relationship to social and educational institutions. The Right reacts to the breakdown by retreating into a nostalgic hiding place, a social amnesia which blinds us to the forces which shape our consciousness. Drawing upon the breakdown of these boundaries we begin as educators to formulate new questions of knowledge, pedagogy, and cognition. We transcend the questions dictated by the narrative of the Right: How do we raise test scores? How do we produce workers who are better suited to work in degrading, deskilled jobs? How do we better control teachers so they teach the standardized materials their superiors deem appropriate? Making use of the postmodern sense of possibility, of freedom from the old stories and questions, we begin to reconceptualize the purposes of schools.

A postmodern reconceptualization of schooling assaults the foundational metaphors and assumptions of the right-wing educational story. Take, for example, the assumption concerning what constitutes successful student and teacher performance, i.e., the nature of what type of thinking is deemed desirable on the part of students and teachers. Our democratic postmodern way of seeing seeks to expand the limits on human thinking imposed by evaluation procedures. When we apply our critical system of meaning and our postmodern deconstruction of the dominant stories, we begin to anticipate new ways of seeing and knowing—levels of cognition that move beyond the type of thinking demanded by standardized measurements of aptitude/ability/intelligence and even beyond Jean Piaget's notion of formal thinking. Men and women do not reach a final cognitive equilibrium beyond which no new levels of thinking can emerge. Indeed, there have to be modes of cognition which transcend the formal operational ability to formulate abstract conclusions, understand cause-effect relationships, and employ the traditional scientific method to explain reality.

Piagetian formalism implies a comfort with a Cartesian-Newtonian mechanistic view of the world that is unable to escape the confines of a cause-effect, hypothetico-deductive system of reasoning. Trapped within the language of certainty and prediction, formal operational thinking organizes verified facts into a theory. Those pesky facts which do not fit into the theory are discarded. The theory which emerges is the one best suited to eliminate contradictions in knowledge. Thus, formal thinking proceeds on the assumption that the resolution of contradiction is a central objective of cognition. Modern schools of excellence in the conservative mode and the omnipotent standardized test makers, assuming that formal operational thought represents the zenith of human potential, focus their labor on its cultivation and measurement. Indeed, this assessment may be too generous, for many times schools of this type fail to transcend low-level concrete forms of thinking. Students who move beyond formality are often not rewarded and sometimes even punished for excessive independence.

Post-formal thinkers are not uncomfortable with the ambiguous, contingent nature of knowledge. They are tolerant of contradiction  and value the attempt to integrate divergent phenomena into new, revealing syntheses. In other words, they are pioneers of the mind attempting to expand the cognitive envelope, to escape the limitations of Cartesian-Newtonian modernity and venture into the realm of the postmodern. Post-formalism can be viewed as a form of cognition which suits an uncertain postmodern world.  Where formality functions on the basis of the Cartesian paradigm's asumptions of linear causality and reductionism, post-formality assumes reciprocity and holism (the ambiguous, non-linear interconnection of phenomena).  No simple, privileged vantage point exists for post-formal thinkers—no perspective which grants them the "truth."  Drawing upon women's ways of knowing, subjugated knowledges, the insight of indigenous peoples, post-formal thinkers rediscover the synergism between logic and emotion and the benefits of disengagement from the socially-acceptable, the expected.

Such speculations about the reconceptualization of cognition necessitate a critical confrontation with the old story of education as simple cultural transmission.  We cannot escape a self-dialogue (and hopefully a larger cultural conversation as well) concerning educational purpose.  Post-formality opens a dialogue with the past which holds dramatic implications for that which is not yet.  Thinking about the purposes of education in ancient Greece, stoic philosopher Musonius Rufus offered a proto-critical perspective which contended that a philosophical education is practical in its attempt to improve the student's own life and the life of the surrounding community.  In this sense, it is action-oriented, eschewing the assumption that students are passive recipients of timeless truths.  From Musonius Rufus' ancient perspective, education works to invigorate the student's ability to think and act ethically in specific situations.  Thus, it follows that like the prescriptions of a wise doctor, education must be tailored to the particular strengths and weaknesses of each student as well as the contextual setting (the place) in which he or she emerges (Nussbaum, 1987, p. 20; Kincheloe and Pinar, 1991, pp. 1-23; Pinar, 1991, pp. 165-186).

Such thoughts are not unlike those of Nietzsche who also advocated the abandonment of education as unexamined cultural transmission in favor of developing the capacity for interpretation.  To Nietzsche interpretation involved acquiring the ability to see, think, speak, and write.  When viewed as inseparable processes, Nietzsche theorized that this interpretative facility allowed learners to sneak through the morass of conventional perception and to view individual cases from a variety of angles (Greene, 1987, pp. 9-10). Such notions not only conceptually anticipate our admittedly unoriginal notion of post-formal thinking but also challenge the right-wing's reading of just what constitutes Tradition. Tradition, even Western Tradition, is a cacaphony of conflicting voices of which the Right has chosen only a few to build its standardized, Eurocentric, androcentric curriculum. Thus, the post-formal challenge refuses to allow Allan Bloom to dictate the official story of how our students came to be so shallow, William Bennett to define educational excellence, E.D. Hirsch to proclaim what constitutes cultural literacy, or Madeleine Hunter to determine the correct strategies by which the official knowledge is to be transmitted to students.

Reading right-wing educational literature one is often struck by the omnipresent assumption that only the conservative guardians of Tradition care about the past. A central tenet of a critical pedagogy that values a post-formal cognitive orientation is the notion of etymology—an awareness of the genesis of knowledge, of self-production, of institutional form. Indeed, it is possible to draw upon the past while avoiding a Bloomian worship of Tradition. One of the outcomes of a postmodern reconceptualization of education involves a reworking of Tradition in light of current concerns. Such a reworking initiates a more general consideration of how post-formalism confronts texts and how this relates to educational purpose. Education as simple cultural transmission fails to confront the complexity of the contemporary significance of what have been deemed the classic texts. Stanley Aronowitz argues that classic texts in a democratic educational context are appropriated not revered— and in this appropriation, transformed (Aronowitz, 1989, p. 215). Post-formal thinkers recognize this and in their understanding unveil contemporary meanings without ignoring the text's historical significance (Weisberg, 1987, p. 50). Thus, in a semiotic mode post-formal teachers ask new questions of the cultural heritage in the process revealing themselves and the forces which have shaped our institutions. Such teachers may study the traditional Western canon (and certainly the nontraditional Western canon and non-Western canons) as a form of social knowledge. But it is more than just that—it is us. It holds buried within it revelations about the tacit dimensions of our consciousness construction.

The knowledge revealed by such study is ever-suprising and unpredictable. Because post-formal educators refuse to simply revere the traditions, the analysis which results creates a question about our frame of reference: how and from where do we see school knowledge? When conservatives fail to question their frame of reference a tyrannical certainty emerges which perpetuates privilege for the privileged and oppression for the oppressed. This allows, for example, what the school defines as the classics to include mainly male Europeans, while denying contributions, and in many instances, the exclusion, of Third World, non-white, or female innovators. To avoid such outcomes Tradition must be subjected to a democratic analysis which explores tacit assumptions, underlying sources of authority used to ground judgments, and unexamined ideological assumptions which shape the questions we ask about the canon. Thus, what the Right has defined as a crippling relativism, emerges as a liberating sense of the inconstancy of meaning—an uncertainty which allows us to see what before was hidden from view.

Our liberatory uncertainty here avoids nihilism and relativism via its grounding in our democratic system of meaning. Contrary to the pronouncements of Bloom and Bennett, the Western heritage does not represent the unfolding of the *absolute spirit* (Aronowitz, 1989, p. 215). As John Dewey argued decades ago (though it was misunderstood by the public), education should avoid the cultural transmission model of preserving "the standard," of perpetuating the myth of the West as the benchmark of civilization. In this context the notion of Human Nature is identified with *our* heritage and, Dewey maintained, education was reduced to a cowardly quest for certainty (Rorty, 1988, p. 30). Humans, thus, relinquished their gift of self-creation and constant redefinition; instead, education as cultural transmission assumed that men and women were already finished, completed projects, unchangeable entities. The possibility of the enlargement of our moral imaginations

offered by the uncertainty which came out of an engagement
with other cultures with their different frames of reference was
lost.

What do we mean by the expansion of our moral imagination?    Our notion of post-formal thinking is intimately
connected to such an expansion of consciousness, as it forces us
to confront the concept of mind.  In contrast to modern right-
wing assumptions, Dewey conceived mind as the variety of ways
that we consciously engage the events that confront us.  Thus,
mind is a verb.  This means that it is never self-contained,
separate from the world, but contingent, ever interacting with
situations and other minds.  Mind is never complete, for it
never stops assimilating, restructuring itself as a result of its
contact with new stimulation (Greene, 1987, p. 10).  Thus, our
moral imagination emphasizes relationships and meaning, not
mastery or simple "being."  For example, we sometimes humili-
ate students who may have grown up around, played and fished
in a river when we demand that they define the word, river,
employing the dictionary definition "water flowing within a
channel."  What about their experience with rivers, the effects
of rivers on their lives and the lives of other people who live
around it, the floods, the politics of water rights, irrigation,
recreation, pollution, etc...?  These questions of meaning make
the study of rivers important—not the dictionary definition.

These questions of significance (which are always questions of
relationships) form the basis of post-formal thinking, of the
expansion of our moral imaginations.  Neither E.D. Hirsch's
"List," Allan Bloom's "Great Tradition," nor Mortimer Adler's
Paideia Proposal deal with Dewey's concept of mind.  The crisis
of modern education revolves no more around our failure to
teach Tradition or to prepare our students for the workplace
than the solution to the crisis revolves around improving
standardized test scores and teaching rote memorized facts
about our civilization.  Post-formal thinking and the expansion
of our moral imagination demand an educational reform
grounded on a reconceptualized function of reason and a
search for meaning in the relationship between self and world
(Silliman, 1990, p. 149).  Stated another way, schools should
help students develop wisdom—i.e., the cognitive ability and the

contextual grounding to make intelligent choices and commitments in the way they shape their lives.

Part of this life-shaping process involves the role of students as members of a larger political community. (Feinberg, 1989, p. 71). In this context the expansion of the moral imagination involves the development of what Henry Giroux often refers to as the development of civic courage. Caught in a media-dominated world of manipulative consumerist images, of covert and morally indefensible governmental activities, of limited access to diverse information sources, students unacquainted with the post-formal exposé of the tacit dimension will have limited ability to make informed civic choices (Greene, 1987, p. 14). The educational vision sold to the public by conservative theorists does not address such concerns. Civic courage, the ability to see beyond the overt propaganda and the covert control of imagery, the grappling with the meaning of democracy and the responsibilities it demands, are not a part of the conservative educational story. There are alternatives. There are more thoughtful answers to the questions we ask about education than the ones provided over the last fifteen years. There are other stories to be told.

# References

Aronowitz, S. (1989) "The new conservative discourse." In Holtz, et. al, *Education and the American dream.* Granby, Massachusetts, Bergin and Garvey.

Bloom, A. (1987) *The closing of the American mind.* New York, Simon and Schuster.

Cuban, L. (1984) *How teachers taught.* New York, Longman.

Feinberg, W. (1989) "Fixing the schools: the ideological turn." In H. Giroux and P. McLaren, *Critical pedagogy, the state, and cultural struggle.* Albany, New York, State University of New York Press.

Ferguson, M. (1980) *The Aquarian Conspiracy: personal and social transformation in our time.* Los Angeles, J.P. Tarcher.

Giroux, H. (1991) "Introduction: modernism, postmodernism, and feminism: rethinking the boundaries of educational discourse." In H. Giroux, *Postmodernism, feminism, and cultural politics: redrawing educational boundaries.* Albany, New York, State University of New York Press.

Giroux, H. and P. McLaren (1989) "Introduction: schooling, cultural politics, and the struggle for democracy." In H. Giroux and P. McLaren, *Critical pedagogy, the state, and cultural struggle.* Albany, New York, State University of New York Press.

Greene, M. (1987) "Some notes on Bloom: toward a new Bloomsalem," Paper presented to a colloquium sponsored by the Institute on Education and the Economy, Teachers College, Columbia University, New York.

hooks, b. (1989) *Talking back.* Boston: South End Press.

Kimball, R. (1990) *Tenured radicals: how politics has corrupted our higher education.* New York, Harper and Row.

Kincheloe, J. (1985) 'Preparing a place for the righteous: Reagan, education, and the New Right' *Journal of Thought,* *20,* 4, pp. 3-17.

Kincheloe, J. (1991) *Teachers as researchers: qualitative paths to empowerment.* London, Falmer Press.

Kincheloe, J. and W. Pinar (1991) "Introduction." In J. Kincheloe and W. Pinar, *Curriculum as social psychoanalysis: essays on the significance of place.* Albany, New York, State University of New York Press.

McLaren, P. (forthcoming) "Postmodernism/post-colonialism/pedagogy." *Education and Society.*

Nash, R. (1990) *The closing of the American heart: what's really wrong with America's schools.* Dallas, Texas, Probe Books.

Nussbaum, M. (1987) "Undemocratic vistas." *New York Review of Books, 34*, pp. 20-26.

Pinar, W. (1991) "Curriculum as social psychoanalysis: on the significance of place." In J. Kincheloe and W. Pinar, *Curriculum as social psychoanalysis: essays on the significance of place.* Albany, New York, State University of New York Press.

Postman, N. (1989) "Learning by story." *The Atlantic, 264*, 6, pp. 119-124.

Retiz, C. (1988) "Bennett, Bloom, and Boyer: toward a critical discussion." Paper presented at a conference of the Southwest Community Colleges Humanities Association, Kansas City, Missouri.

Rorty, R. (1988) "That old-time philosophy." *The New Republic, 198*, pp. 28-33.

Ryan, K. (1989) "Confessions of a teacher educator." In H. Holtz, et.al., *Education and the American dream.* Granby, Massachusetts, Bergin and Garvey.

Silliman, M. (1990) "The closing of the professorial mind: a meditation on Plato and Allan Bloom." *Educational Theory, 40*, 1, pp. 147-151.

Simon, R. (1989) "Empowerment as a pedagogy of possibility." In H. Holtz, et.al., *Education and the American dream.* Granby, Massachusetts, Bergin and Garvey.

Weisberg, J. (1987) "Sex and drugs and Heidegger." *Washington Monthly, 19*, pp. 49-53.

# Chapter I

# The Curriculum:
# What are the basics and
# are we teaching them?

**Madeleine R. Grumet**

**William F. Pinar**

# Madeleine R. Grumet

Often we imagine that in other times this question—"The Curriculum: What are the basics and are we teaching them?" - would never have to be asked. If the basics were basic, we imagine, they would be felt in the pulse of the community. They would be measured in the gait of its people and weighed in the lightness of sorrow. The basics are drawn from a fantasy of communion, and we project this wish onto history, mistaking the rounded edges of the past for a perfect circle of consensus. When the fantasy shifts location from historical sentimentality to a current curriculum, it becomes an agenda of control imposed on a community whose diversity splinters the steady rhythms of shared lives. Rather than describing an existing consensus, the basics are deployed to create an arbitrary compact. They function as forms of control.

The very word, BASIC, compels selection. It demands the discrimination that ranks some issues as essential and others as not. Here's the BASIC thing to remember, we say, wielding the giant spotlight of our attention, and suddenly all else falls into darkness. I, myself, have always been pretty suspicious of that spotlight, always straining to see what lives in its shadow, always hoping that whoever directs its beam will be distracted and turn too quickly, letting the light pour into the world we weren't supposed to see.

As I struggle to write about "the basics", I, too, try to evade the spotlight of selection. I dip and weave and dart into the shadow whenever I can. I am both proud of and a little embarrassed by this fancy choreography of mine. Elder statesmen have taken me aside to caution me that such an elliptical style will never sell in Peoria. Metaphor muddies the waters they say. Actually, they don't say it that way, that's the way I would say what they say when they say, "Madeleine, why can't you just say it simply?" Well, it's just that simply always seems like such a lie.

I am not the only one to be so suspicious. During the last few decades scholars have adopted a structuralist perspective to avoid the lie of simplicity. Rather than reducing the essential to a few items, points, methods, structuralism asserts that all thought and culture is part of a system which incorporates many elements linked in complex relationships to each other. While any particular idea in the structure is not considered essential, the design or relationships that characterize the system is.

Contemporary literary and social criticism, sometimes called postmodernism, disdain structuralism's assertions of systemic coherence. Postmodern criticism distrusts attributions to a single system or to a single author, or a main idea, portraying this focus as arbitrary and discriminatory as it directs our attention toward some values and away from others. Postmodern criticism peers over the spotlight of consensus and certainty to catch glimpses of dispute and doubt; beyond an identifiable origin for thought it discerns a diffuse history of half truths, borrowed phrases and collective fantasies.

I was uncomfortable with structuralism's overarching systems, but I am also uncomfortable with post-structuralism's contempt for identity. Identity is lived before it is thought, and even though thought may help us to press against the borders of our habits and personalities, it is out of these lived and situated intuitions that we make love, war and all decisions that are later described as our values.

We don't need to go to school to learn these basics. They are threaded through body-knowledge, and no amount of resolve can make them disappear. What is basic to education is neither the system that surrounds us nor the situation of each individual's lived experience. What is basic to education is the relation between the two.

THE BASICS in all their generic and reductive splendor are meaningless to me when promulgated without reference to persons, places or times. Basic to whom? For what? When?

Relation is basic to education. But ironically, it is relation that is most often elided when we are asked to list the basics. In its place we get the poles that relation has failed to connect: either literacy, or numeracy; either critical thinking or values; either the great books or multicultural tolerance. These pairs join others that have bifurcated thought about education for centuries: the individual vs. the community; mind vs. body; cognition vs. affect; pure science vs. applied science; public vs. private.

When we say that we are educating someone, we are introducing that person, young or old, to ways of being and acting in the world that are new to his or her experience. And it is the relation between that person's experience in the world and the new material that differentiates education from training, indoctrination, or a mere display of whatever is new or exotic.

This relation of what we know to what we don't know is lodged in the etymology of the word basic, which brings us back to its base, literally a stepping stone. But in our current usage of the word, we have kept the stone and lost the step. Sadly, the history of language is too often a collapse of words for action into words for things. The base of basic is a springboard for action. It is the provision that supports the flexed ankle, the bent knee. It is the necessary condition for movement. Think about your body as you move from one step to another. The steps are static. The movement is in you as you shift your weight between them. What is basic is what goes on in the middle.

We live in the middle. When education forsakes the middle for the ends, or the beginnings it is deadly. Fascinated with the ends, we have celebrated ancestor worship, proclaiming the texts of dead men to be our standards for human experience. Drawn to the beginnings, we have denied the capacity of people to be active agents in the development of their own character, reducing them to biological, genetic, or social determinants. One can talk about the basics of developmental psychology or great literature, because they are, after all, things: collections of words, repeated, cited and entombed in the Library of Congress. But education is about a human being making sense of her life in the world, and when we confuse her movement with the stops on her itinerary, or worse with someone else's travel memoirs, we obstruct it.

Because we have been fascinated with the ends of education and not the middle we have not been teaching the basics. We have reduced the elementary school curriculum to a developmental mythology, draining the texture and wonder of the world from the books we give young children to read and from the school day stuffed with deadly age-appropriate routines. We have compensated for the emptiness of the elementary school curriculum by dedicating secondary and higher education to ancestor worship, oblivious to the world that students actually live in and care about.

In our anxiety to protect, promote and produce our children, we regularly leave out the second step. We wedge them into the base, calling it a firm foundation, and sink them into the cement of its assumptions. We prohibit their movement by providing no other stepping stones. They will move anyway. They will zone out, tune out, freak out, drop out.

Take black holes, for instance. I have sat in the back of classrooms where students read aloud from science textbooks describing black holes as if they were pot holes. Only someone steeped in the theory of eternal return could pay attention to that text without terror. Neither text nor teacher acknowledged or questioned the horror of the relentless destruction, the great cavernous suction that the text described. I looked around the classroom. The only terrified person in it was me. The seventh graders, even those taking notes, seemed isolated from the text, from the world and from the universe that it described. Black holes were in the assigned chapter with five questions at the end of it to be done for homework. The questions merely mimicked the chapter prose, so they could be answered without having to even imagine a black hole, let alone worry about one. All the kids had to do was scan the pages to find the black hole paragraph and copy out the appropriate sentences for answers. The really savvy kids had learned to scan the questions before reading the chapter, marking the answer paragraphs as they found them, thus making a reading that dipped below the surface of letter recognition unnecessary.

Like Jack Webb, this lesson sought "the facts ma'am, just the facts." All the details, associations, asides that complicate the testimony are scoured from this curriculum as they were from *Dragnet*'s macho inquiry. And in the name of the basics, relation, feeling, fantasy, anxiety, aggression, association, memory, irony are all banished. Now the problem is that there is little that we can truly think about that is not hooked to us by these and other thoughts and feelings. When we bypass these routes to knowledge, we bypass the knowing, the thing to be known, the world.

Our relationships to the world are rooted in our relationships to the people who care for us. Their interest in us is necessary to our capacity to be interested in the world that interests them. All of our cognitive manipulations, phonics or miscue analysis, schema presentation or hands-on mathematics and science are irrelevant unless we surround children with adults who care about them. What is basic to the elementary school curriculum is the space and time and presence that make these relation-ships possible. Small classes. Family groupings. Duration, stay-ing with a group of teachers for a few years, being known, recognized, loved.

In later years what is basic can not be reduced to the Great Books or American History, to world geography or geology. It is the relation of these histories of human action and interpreta-tion to the lives of the children studying them that is essential. Those connections are not merely motivators, clever intros to trick a group of students into interest. Those connections are the source of the questions that support research, of the desires that seek expression, of the choices that constitute values. What is basic is not a certain set of texts, or principles or algorithms, but the conversation that makes sense of these things. Curricu-lum is that conversation. It is the process of making sense with a group of people of the systems that shape and organize the world that we can think about together.

The spotlight of the curriculum is necessarily arbitrary or, at least, conventional. The expectation that everyone will turn to page 87, work on question 4 or go to the library to research a social studies project serves to remind us that knowledge is a social project, something we do in common with other people. Even if the text we find on page 87 is the Ten Commandments, or the task posed in question 4 reveals the law of conservation, what is basic to curriculum is the opportunity to consider the opposites and alternatives to these theses. Each proposition about the world that constitutes the body of knowledge is asserted by suppressing its opposite. The function of curricu-lum is to nest that propostion in the network of its alternatives and opposites; that is why curriculum is never the text, or the topic, never the method or the syllabus. Curriculum is the act of making sense of these things and that requires understanding the ways that they do and do not stand for our experience.

Well, for someone hesitant to expound on the basics, I do seem to have found my footing. The base of these assertions is located in the hundreds of narratives written by people in answer to the question: What is educational experience? The stories written in response to that question are always about connection. They are stories about the separation from loved ones, or about being recognized by a teacher or by other students. They are stories of travel, when lonely presence in a new place reveals the law of relation that supports human identity and community.

This short story was written by a woman who came to William Smith College as an adult student. Her answer to the question, What is educational experience? is this account of the connection she made between learning letters and understanding the relation of intellectual and lived experience.

> I remember sitting in Sr. Marie Therese's kindergarten class sometime in November when I was five years old. I was sitting at a brand new blonde wood table with shiny formica top, cold to the touch. The table was near the window, the glare of which reflected all around my work book. My book was open and the assignment was to do rows and rows of letters. This day was for the letter V.
>
> I was about halfway down the page of V's when something reflecting on the table caught my eye. It looked like lots of flying V's. I looked around and saw in the sky migrating geese, and they did look like V's. They even flew together forming one big V. I was amazed. I never say anything like this before. Those geese flew away and as I looked around for more I saw the upside down skinny V the church steeple made against the sky, and the fatter also inverted V's of every roof of every house. Every branch of every tree seemed to make V's. The street corner where Mr. Strang, the crossing guard, stood was the bottom point of the biggest V in the whole world.
>
> I laughed out loud to think what Mr. Strang would say if I told him he worked on the world's biggest V. Sister heard me laughing and called me up to her desk. She wanted to know what was funny. I told her, everything. About my page of V's, the geese, Mr. Strang; and how everything seemed to have a V in it. She smiled, said I was being silly, patted my head and told me to go sit back down and finish my work.
>
> I was feeling so happy, so accomplished, that her disinterest didn't faze me. I was boldly confident in my discovery, and actually felt she was missing out on a biggy. For my last row of V's on the page I made them flying away geese with little feet hanging down. This was my first recol-

lection of drawing from real life.   It, drawing, was and still is an
important part of my life.

The junctions crossed in this narrative link text, community,
nature and school.   What is formal and abstract, the letter V,
becomes intertwined with a system of meanings tied to this
child's world.   Like the migrating geese, that understanding will
carry her to distant places without undermining her ability to
come home again.   With little feet hanging down, these birds
have landing gear intact.   Sister Marie Therese smiles, and pats
Mary's head but she doesn't celebrate her discovery of relation,
expressed in her insight and drawing.   I don't know if Mary ever
told Mr. Strang, the crossing guard, but I do know that after
twenty years, Mary told the story again, this time to me, when
she was studying to be a teacher.   That was years ago, and I am
still celebrating.

# William F. Pinar

Such a question is inextricably linked with questions of national and private identity, themselves intersecting issues. The conservatives of the 1980's have insisted that **their** identities are basic. Predictably they have listed what they were taught and what they have learned as what everybody must be taught, what everybody must learn. We Americans are not—historically, the contemporary period, or in the future—fundamentally European-American men. Important as European-American men have been to the development of the American character, they represent a fragment of that character. To characterize their achievements, which to an immeasurable extent **are** also the achievements of those who have historically served them—women, homosexuals, African-Americans, Asian-Americans, Hispanic-Americans (and those whose land they occupied, Native-American), as "basic" to knowledge, to what we shall attempt to pass to the generations who will outlive us, is mistaken. A Eurocentric and patriarchal curriculum is not basic; historically and in the present period, not to say the future, it is marginal. In what follows I focus upon African-Americans to illustrate the more general relationship between identity and curriculum.

## Curriculum and Identity

"We are what we know." We are, however, also what we do not know. If what we know about ourselves—history, our culture, our national identity—is deformed by absences, denials, and incompleteness, then our identity—both as individuals and as Americans—is fractured. This fractured self is a repressed self. Such a self lacks access both to itself and to the world. Repressed, the self's capacity for intelligence, for informed action, even for simple functional competence, is impaired. Its sense of history, gender, and politics is incomplete and distorted.

Public debate over a "common" or core curriculum reveals an explicit racial aspect. The exchange at a 1989 conference, sponsored by the conservative research and education policy center founded by former Education Secretary William Bennett

and *The Closing of the American Mind* author Allan Bloom, at the
Madison Center, is illustrative.   The Center's president, John
Agresto, characterized the conference as "response to the
academy's current trivialization of liberal education and the
continuing attacks on the canons of traditional collegiate instruction.  "Under the cover of pluralism is," criticizes Agresto,
"the dismissal of the past" (O'Brien, 1989).   In opposition,
Houston Baker, noted literary critic and professor of English at
the University of Pennsylvania, charged that the continued
curricular emphasis upon western civilization constitutes "A
willfull ignorance and aggression toward Blacks" (O'Brien,
1989).  Regarding the so-called "great books" curriculum of St.
John's College (Maryland), Baker commented:   "The Great
Books won't save us but rap may because it might finally allow
us to recognize that the world is no longer white and one might
even say no longer bookish." Jonathon Culler, the famous post-
structuralist literary critic and professor of English at Cornell
University, cited a 1988 study of that literature taught in high
schools conducted by the center for the Teaching and Learning
of Literature at the State University of New York at Albany.
Albany researchers found that 27 books were required in more
than 30 percent of the schools surveyed.  Culler commented: "I
find it scandalous that long after the civil rights movement,
there are no books by Black authors in the top 27, and books by
and about women are so poorly represented" (O'Brien, 1989).
    Current debates regarding the "canon"—about what is basic
to the curriculum—can be linked with questions of self and identity.  Such an understanding shifts the curricular debate from
preoccupations with equity or with multiculturalism to debates
regarding the relationship between knowledge and ourselves.
The Eurocentric and patriarchal character of school curriculum
functions not only to deny "role models" to non-European-
American male students, it denies self-understanding to "white
boys" as well.   The American self is not exclusively or even
primarily an European-American male self.  Fundamentally, it is
African-American, Asian American, Hispanic American, Native
American, female, homosexual self.  To a still unacknowledged
extent, the American nation was built and is occupied culturally
by African-Americans, Asian-Americans, Hispanic-Americans, by

woman, and by homosexuals. The presence of these persons and the cultural traditions they represent and embody informs every element of American life. For European-American male students to understand who they are, they must understand that their existence (and identity) is predicted upon, inter-related to, and constituted in fundamental ways by African-Americans, Asian-Americans, Hispanic-Americans, Native Americans, by women, and by homosexuals.

The American self-denied and repressed "acts out" repression via imperialism in foreign policy and political and economic repression domestically as it attempts to maintain the denial. The refusal—sometimes unconscious, sometimes not—to incorporate, for instance, African-American knowledge into the mainstream curriculum can be understood as a psychoanalytic as well as political process of repression. Understanding curriculum as the revelation and construction of identity implies understanding education as a form of social psychoanalysis. The American identity is constructed partly by denial, by maintaining fictions. It is not exclusively or even primarily European or male. That delusion represents a fantasy, a flight from truth.

The absence of African-American knowledge (again the argument applies to the other traditions and knowledges) in many American schools' curriculum is not simple oversight. Its absence represents an academic instance of racism, or in Baker's apt phrase, "willful ignorance and aggresion toward Blacks." Just as African-Americans have been denied their civil rights in society generally, they have been denied access to their history and culture in school. Not only African-Americans have been denied, however. Institutional racism deforms white students as well. By refusing to understand curriculum as a racial text, students misunderstand who they are as racialized, gendered, historical, political creatures. Such deformity occurs—for most "whites"—almost "unconsciously". Many European-American students and their parents—and many curriculum specialists—would deny that curriculum is about identity. Such denial is done "innocently;" it represents an instance of repression in its psychoanalytic sense. Socially, psychological repression expresses itself as political repression.

Repression impairs intelligence, as it siphons off energy from, for instance, problem-solving to maintain the repression. Further, repression implies that information is limited, as well as distorting that information which is available. The contemporary crisis of American education is complex in its nature and causes; it is not reducible to one factor or one set of factors, such as poorly prepared teachers, out-of-date curriculum, malnourished students, developmentally and/or culturally inappropriate examinations and other school practices. One overlooked factor is repression, the repression of African-Americans in American society, the repression of women, the repression of other marginalized groups, and the repression of non-European knowledge. Such repression is evident in the schools in several ways, including funding inequities, tracking, teaching practices, and curriculum that is Eurocentric and unrelated to the lived experience of students.

Freudian imagery of the self is provocative here. During the decades of the 1980's the businessman represented the American prototype. Lee Iaccoca, Donald Trump, Michael Milken: white, male, savvy, shrewd, calculating, devoted to the bottom line. If this prototype represented the American ego: realistic, adaptive, adjusting in self-profiting ways to "reality" then African-Americans represented the "id pleasure seeking, unpredictable, accomplished in athletics and the arts. American culture projected African-Americans as the "id," and in classical Freudian style, maintained relative repression of the "pleasure principle" so that—presumably—ego stability and hegemony could be maintained. Those elements of American life could be said to represent the "superego", fundamentalist religious groups, were permitted by the "business" ego to grow in size and influence. Those groups marginal to this version of the "ego"—African-American, other marginalized ethnic groups, women, children, gays—were undermined, via public policy and in political practice.

Christopher Lasch has argued that the conservative political prescription for schools and society during the 1980's can be characterized as superego in nature. Illustrative of this "superego" voice are slogans such as "more homework," "just say no," "work harder." Conservatives insisted that the problem with American society was simple laziness (not their own of course), and in this simpleminded analysis African-Americans were assigned a major blameworthy role. True enough, liberals continue to call for rational deliberation, incorporating aspects of the unconscious (African Americans in the parallel) into the conscious ego (mainstream society), but in controlled and planned ways (cf. the liberal conceptualization of an orderly, incremental civil rights movement. My point is that the question of school curriculum is also a question about the self, the American self. Understanding curriculum as a racial text means understanding America as fundamentally a racialized and gendered place, as fundamentally an African-American place, and the American identity as inescapably African-Americans as well as European, Hispanic/Latino, Native American, Asian-American, female and homosexual. African-Americans are ego and super-ego as well as id. Debates over the debates over the constitution of the American self.

European-Americans and African-Americans are two-sided of the same cultural coin, two interrelated narratives in the American story. The former cannot hope to understand themselves unless they are knowledgeable and knowing of the latter, and vice-versa. The sequestered suburban white student is uninformed unless he or she comes to understand how, culturally, he or she is also African-American. As Baldwin has pointed out, "white" does not exist apart from "black." The two co-exist, intermingle, and the repression of this knowledge deforms us all, especially those who are white and male. All Americans are racialized, gendered beings; knowledge of who we have been, who we are, and who we will become is a text; curriculum—our construction and reconstruction of this knowledge—is indeed a racialized, gendered text.

During the past decade much has been made of the failure of public-school students to learn even the most elementary and necessary facts regarding their history, geography, and culture. Cultural literacy is a non-controversial requirement for any citizenry. What becomes controversial is the composition of such literacy. In the popular press voices express views of cultural literacy that are informed by, primarily, Eurocentric and patriarchal knowledge systems. Without question Ameri-

can students must know and understand the European
antecedents of contemporary American culture. However, this
knowledge ought not to be used as a defense against
"otherness," a denial of our cultural unconscious.

Understanding curriculum as a text of identity is especially
urgent in the present period of neo-conservatism during which
racial and gender attacks and racial and gender antagonism
have increased (Omni and Winant, 1986; *Chronicle of Higher
Education*, 1990). In the November, 1990 election, David Duke's
white supremacy candidacy for the U.S. Senate brought him
60% of the white vote in Louisiana. The military adventure in
the Persian Gulf masks the continued deterioration of the
American cultural "infrastructure." The hour is late; Baldwin
knew it is "the fire next time."

**Conclusion**

Curriculum is "cultural capital," and under current—politically
conservative—conditions, African-American culture is "black-
market currency." Because knowledge of American culture is
characterized by distortions, repressions, and silences—what
holds true for the South holds true in regional different ways
for the nation—American identity is deformed. Estranged from
African-Americans, European American men are estranged
from themselves. Being repressed unfortunately, also means
being stupid, and in order to realize our national intelligence
we need to remember—in social psychoanalytic fashion—those
denied and repressed elements of who we are. This means, in
part, incorporating African-American experience in the school
curriculum, not marginalized as "black studies" (although also
institutionalized in that form as space for separatist, intellectually autonomous research and action) but integrated throughout the curriculum.

Organizationally a next step might include the establishment
of an American cultures requirement in the general education
of elementary, secondary as well as university students. The
University of California's Center for the Teaching and Study of
American Cultures (opened May 11, 1990) will create courses
that will fulfill the American Cultures requirement at the

University of California, a requirement approved by Berkeley faculty in April 1989. The requirements must explore at least three of five ethnic groups: African Americans. American Indians, Asian Americans, Chicanos/Latinos and European Americans (*San Francisco Chronicle* May 11, 1990, p. A6). Every university ought to enact such a requirement, as one initiative to challenge intellectual repression. However, this information must not await the college experience. Beginning in elementary school and continuing throughout secondary school courses in American cultures ought to be required. Such courses will hardly guarantee the end of racism; indeed what we know about repression suggests that 'backlash' will occur periodically.

Curricular integration in the public schools is underway, of course. For instance, reports of the "infusion of African and African American knowledge in the school curriculum will be made, among other places at the second national conference on this topic. Among the sponsors if this meeting are American Airlines and a Georgia utilities company, surely a sign that the effort has begun to enter the rhetorical mainstream. Entering the curricular mainstream on a mass scale will prove to be, I suspect, another matter.

Obviously, these are complicated issues. Debates over what is basic to the curriculum are also debates over identity. Construed as questions concerning who we are, history and culture make it clear that we are—in a fundamental sense— African American, Asian American, Hispanic American, Native American, female and homosexuals. It is not only African American who are deprived when their history is underemphasized, it is European—and other American as well. It is in our own self interest—read European American self interest—to incorporate an expanded and more accurate concept of who we are as individuals and as civic creatures. Educationally, this requires understanding curriculum as a text of identity, and in so doing, we begin to understand ourselves.

[A version of this paper appears as the introduction to *Understanding Curriculum as a Racial Text*, edited by Louis A. Castenell, Jr., and William F. Pinar, State University of New York Press, in press.]

# References

Lasch, Christopher (1984). *The minimal self.* New York: Norton.

O'Brien, E.    (1989).    "Debates over curriculum expansion continues." *Black Issues in Higher Education*, 6-18 (November 23, 1989), 1-26.

# Chapter II

# Power and Education: Who decides the forms schools have taken, and who should decide?

**Magda Lewis**

**Rodman B. Webb**

# Magda Lewis

When first asked to write a paper on the topic of power and education I wasn't sure where to begin. For those of us teaching and writing from the perspective of critical/feminist pedagogy the answer to the question of who decides educational forms seems obvious. It suggests the promise of a short discussion. *If we are not men, if we are not white, if we are not economically advantaged, if we survive by the labour of our hands, if we are not heterosexual, and if we do not embody and display the valued assets of the privilege of Euro-American culture,* the school curriculum and schooling experience fling us to the margins. Nowhere in the curriculum do we see even a vague glimpse of a reflection of ourselves, of our present realities or of our future dreams. "Typically," says Alison Dewar (1987), "the stories we tell in schools, colleges and universities are ones that reflect the past, present, and future of powerful groups in society. The knowledge we teach in our educational system has a white, middle class, androcentric bias. More importantly, this bias is not presented as one possible version of reality, but more often is taught as the only legitimate and therefore, representative version of reality" (p. 265).

While any number of studies might show this to be the case my knowledge of it comes more directly through the body—my body—overtly contained within the academy by the ideological frames of allowable knowledge. The body of knowledge that is the curriculum and the body experience of being schooled—learning to be still and quiet—are not separable from each other in the process of education. However else we understand the world; indeed however we might wish to intellectualize and thereby hide the lived effect of the realities we know we have lived, the concrete experiences of inclusion or of marginalization are the negotiated memories which we carry and which become the educational moments through which we come to explain the world to ourselves.

As form, education through schooling both offers and requires the consent to a contained agenda. For students marginalized through their gender, class, race, ethnicity, culture and sexuality, questions of the relationship between education

and power have substantively to do with how they are encouraged to embrace forms of schooling that systematically require
them to deny who they are; that measure their performance in
school by how well they succeed in negating themselves; that
leave those parts of their lives that do not fit inside the
dominant molding forms to pour and splash over the edges of
what's acceptable and allowable.

In this paper I shall draw on my own history in order to tell
this side of the schooling experience. This is not an easy thing
to do. To begin I need to say that for me this telling of my own
educational experiences presents itself as a paradox. The social
and cultural implications associated with being a female university professor implores me to keep silent by making unspeak-
able the realities I know I have lived. Yet who I am is not only
constructed by who I have become but as well by the memories
of those parts of my life that I have been asked to leave as
unformed/unframed pools both uncontained as well as unac-
counted for inside the forms that articulate education and
schooling. I use my experiences not as a form of catharsis but
as a series of metaphors that reveals for me in graphic and lived
ways the relationship between education, form and power.

In the context of education the question of how ideas, knowledge and conceptualizations arise brings to the fore exactly the
problems to which critical/feminist critique has pointed.
Schooling practices support a particular set of ideological beliefs
surrounding the work of intellectual production: that as intellectuals we do our work apart from how, where and with whom
we live our personal and intellectual lives; that in order to this
work in its most pure and therefore desirable form we need to
disassociate ourselves from the lived "trivialities" of our everyday lives; that the best text is that which silences what Susan
Sontag (1987), referencing Roland Barthes, calls "the most delicate mechanisms of social exchange" (p. 459).

Yet at the level of everyday life where is that moment when a
seemingly insignificant individual event becomes a moment of
possibility, a speakable/revolutionary moment, or conversely a
moment of closure and loss? What is the measure of significance of these everyday relationships and events? It seems to
me, that valorized academic practices steeped, as they are, in

notions of "objectivity" and independent" work, guarantee that what ought to be considered most important is trivialized into insignificance and what is elevated to truth is generated mostly out of irrelevance. It also mystifies the reality of how knowledge is produced, by whom and under what conditions.

By definition social life is collective and interdependent. Historically we enter and live out social relations unequally. Whether or not we choose to acknowledge it, the knowledge we derive from our experiences is a consequence of these social/ historical realities lived in minute detail. That dominant social, cultural groups claim the privilege of being able to renege ownership of the knowledge they derive from their experience and call it universal, speaks more about their power than about the "truths" they claim to have uncovered.

The stories I learned in school had a remarkable singularity about them—a single voicedness where debates, if they took place at all, questioned only the details without remotely touching the foundations of the basic paradigms upon which the stories were premised.  Throughout the seventeen years of formal education that preceded my graduate studies I had not studied the history, culture and political realities of women, of the labouring classes, of racial and ethnic minorities, of gays and lesbians.  This is all the more remarkable when I consider that my area of study was the great thinkers of Western intellectual tradition.  A couple of years ago I revisited my undergraduate philosophy texts still sitting—now somewhat sundrained— on my book shelves, only to discover to my dismay that there was not a single volume among them written by a woman.  Nor had any of them been written by anyone who could be identified as an author of colour.  To my recollection issues of ethnic and cultural difference were never discussed.  There were no voices from the labour movement.  Nor indeed was it made remotely possible for me to learn from those texts a discourse beyond the massive assumptions and prescriptions of heterosexuality.

All of this might be astonishing enough.  Given the language of educational rhetoric that claims for itself ideologies and practices that embrace notions of freedom, democracy and equality, the distinctly one sidedness of the story I learned in school seems a curious oversight—even more so since I earned my pre-graduate education in the heady reformist days of the sixties and early seventies. However, on looking back, what seems even more astounding than that these should have been the books from which I was asked to absorb the knowledge of the culture which promised me equality of possibility, was that at the time I read these books I had not even registered the deeply exclusionary practices that they both created and made to seem natural. Not to have noticed my own violation speaks of a process more deeply violating that I could have imagined at the time. This experience is what I have since come to call the double-cross-reversal: the privilege of the dominant to talk at great length about that which is not and to stay silent about and ignore that which is. In this reversal, for socially subordinate groups, possibility is defined through denial, freedom is reinterpreted through constraint, violence is justified as protection, and in schools, contrary to the belief that it is a place where knowledge is shared, knowledge withheld articulates the curriculum. More recently this awareness has brought me to rethink my own educational experiences and to use them as the ground from which to explore the question of 'education and power'.

Over sixty years ago Virginia Woolf (1929) pointed out that in education we do not come together equally. She was neither the first nor the last to make this point. However, she makes it exquisitely. The stories I carry with me about my own educational experiences arise from my own locus of desire—to sing, to dance—to speak—simple acts of possibility. Yet history has shown us that such possibilities are never simple. We carry the baggage of our history and it makes us *shy*:

> and the shyness of the poor is another mystery. I myself in the midst of it can't explain it. Perhaps it is neither a form of cowardice nor of heroism. It may be lack of arrogance (The School Boys of Barbiana, 1971, p. 4).

At one level we are made shy by our collective history and experience of marginalization. But at another level—at a level that is lived more closely—at a level that is less easy to distance—we are made shy by our personal histories; those strands of experience that weave the patterns of our lives. Our social identities are cross cut not only by who we are but, as well, by the ceaseless reinforcement of who we are not. And in this schools play a major part.

I remember some considerable years ago arriving as a grade nine student in a new high school. As for many students, for me, the transition between elementary and high school signalled the possibility for new beginnings. I was excited at the idea of what I thought I was about to learn. And I was excited about where I believed this learning was going to take me. In looking ahead I was determined to leave behind what as a child I had learned to live as the silencing vestiges of my ethnic/immigrant background often experienced as a deeply carried "shyness"—an unwillingness to demand that I be noticed.

As a child and then as a young adult I had learned early that the self embraced project of my education required the abandonment of the cultural/social practices I had carried with me across two continents to this new place I was to call home. Along with a new language, I had learned to pack a lunch I no longer needed to sneak unseen out of a brown paper bag for fear of being associated with the cultural oddities of taste and cuisine that it carried. One of the legacies of my education is, for the most part, the loss of this culture that is no longer an identifiable aspect of who I am. Except for a slight 'lilt' in my enunciation, noticed only by those with a 'good ear' and often mistaken for regional exoticism, there is nothing about me that would signal the cultural shifts of perspective I was required to accomplish as a child of nine. Lost in this imposed yet self embraced transition from Other to Acceptable were the familial practices wrapped inside the external specificity of the culture of my childhood that embraced it and were embraced by it—there are still words of endearment I can speak only in the language of my childhood for them to have any significance deeper than the dictionary meanings they carry.

Never acknowledged as a loss, the shedding of the skin of my ethnicity was supposed to be painless—and I told myself that it was. It was only much later that I understood that even the possibility of this self imposed pain was made available to me only because I was white in a deeply racist culture. It was a privilege I could not have appropriated had I been a black child or a child whose visible ethnicity makes them even more invisible in the curriculum and schooling experience that I was made. My brother and I learned to mimic and then laugh at the culture of the children we both struggled not to be. We internalized the violation of our negation to ease the pain of our loss. I still take delight in the richness of the nuances of a language I now speak, read and write with hesitation and uncertainty. Yet, as a child in a school system obsessed with the devaluation and marginalization of multiple language speakers/multiple culture carriers—where the ability to speak more than one language was seen to be an intellectual liability rather than a richly useful asset—my struggle to leave behind the culture/language of my childhood created in me an equal and opposite obsession to get the new language right as it simultaneously and, I believe deliberately, alienated me from those, like my parents, who could not. Gradually my syntax and accent gave me away less and less.

Questions of ethnicity long since suppressed I was ready to create new possibilities for myself. Yet, on the particular day which I remember so vividly, my experience of Other was rearticulated across what I eventually came to learn were a new set of parameters, that of gender. Having been cajoled out of the stuffiness of the library into the warm sunshine of that bright September day I set about to find a quiet place in which to spin my dreams about my future. My arms loaded with books and my mind preoccupied I proceeded to cross what appeared to me to be a large lovely green space. Suddenly I saw a cluster of young men charging toward me. In panic and with knees weak with terror I realized I was standing in the middle of the football field. Not knowing which way I should go—and in reality having nowhere to go—I stood transfixed and bewildered. In retrospect I should have known:  in most high schools (certainly and of those I went to) the only available green space was, by priority, given over to the playing of football, an activity that not only eliminated many of the young men but all of the young women. As they mowed me down I realized I had trespassed into a space not intended for me. My presence in that space, not unnoticed by this advancing steam roller, had no effect on their will, desire or inclination to stop short of what to me was a potential disaster. The game was all.

It is because of the way this story has stayed with me for well over twenty years, that I now choose to read it as a metaphor not only for the experience of girls in school, not only for all marginal cultural/social groups in a society that is marked so massively and unmistakably by the privilege of domination but for the condition of the world itself scored profoundly by the horrors of unprecedented military weaponry, constant political tensions and a global awareness of pain, cruelty and injustice that tries our sanity daily. As I write these words following the war in the Persian Gulf, the world is caught in the aftermath, yet still ongoing brutality, of the evil phallic posturing of insane men who have learned the lessons of their unexamined privilege well: the ritualized game of exclusion, violation and obliteration of the many for the narcissistic pleasure of their own power to destroy.

With this experience lodged firmly in my subconscious, because it is only recently that I have been able to understand the psychological/emotional import that the incident had on how I formulated the possibilities of my own schooling and future, I proceeded through the various levels of credentialization in the increasingly marginalizing world of academia. That this world is also increasingly masculinized and male centered is not beside the point. And while I found myself again and again back in the middle of that metaphorical football field, picking myself up, looking still and again for that quiet place where I could spin my dreams, I found that increasingly the mowing down was less arbitrary and while more subtle and sophisticated certainly more profound.

Proceeding through high school, then university and finally graduate school, as a woman in the academy I found myself repeatedly faced with the production of the demonstration of my knowledgability and skill with words in an environment where both what I knew and the words through which I understood this knowledge hovered on the margins outside the pale of masculine homosociality catching only partial and momentary glances, as bodies shift, of the fire that burns at the centre of male academic practices and camaraderie. Mary Daly's

(1978) remarkable exposition of social practices that rivet patriarchal power into place (witchburnings, suttees, footbinding,
genital mutilation, modern gynecological practices, and the
socially sanctioned and institutionalized violence against women
world wide) would suggest that the fuel for this fire is to be
found in the bodies of women.

Like a seductive lover, my education both offered and simultaneously withheld the promise of a future I could embrace.
Moving closer the tips of my fingers warmed. Simultaneously I
caught the sideways glances that were sometimes bewildered by,
sometimes hostile to, yet sometimes grateful for my presence.
No longer marginalized through my ethnicity it was now as a
woman that I became aware of my signification as the Other—a
body that did not conform to the straight lines of the masculine
body of knowledge that makes acceptable discourse and self
presentation.   Bewildered by the ambiguities of my place
around the warming fire, bruised by my inability to decode
these contradictory discourses my immediate inclination, almost
intuitive. . . (and what is intuition beyond a profound sensitivity
to lived realities?). . .my intuition was to pull back into a terrain
that I knew. As my eyes began to focus and adjust to what the
light at the centre had made to appear as a black void, I caught
the movement of the other bodies in the shadows. Having
stayed focused in this direction long enough, what had been
made to appear as darkness and formlessness has begun to
present itself with the clarity of a moonlit winter night.

Transforming experience into metaphor has enabled me to
"render visible the visible" (Bersianik, 1986, p. 48). It has
allowed me to break the code of silence enforced by the
mandates of objectivity and finally speak what through my
experience I had always known: *if we are not men, if we are not
white, if we are not economically advantaged, if we survive by the
labour of our hands, if we are not heterosexual, and if we do not
embody and display the valued assets of the privilege of Euro-American
culture,* schools are not the sites of possibility which the rhetoric
of educational discourse wishes to portray. What I learned in
school was that successful forms of self violation are rewarded
with credentials; that the study of the accomplishments of great
men simultaneously hides the life realities of those whose

labour—often gratuitous—were/are required to reproduce the world in which some men (very specific men) could become great; and finally that educational rhetoric conforms to the mandates of the double-cross-reversal, offering a great deal of information about that which is not, and withholding information about that which is.

Now I sit on the other side of the classroom divide. The stories my students tell me about their educational experiences are not unlike those I already know all too well. Women speak of unconscionable sexism while those in power co-opt the language of the powerless. Women's struggle for equality and inclusion, and our attempts to gain public acknowledgement of our violation and marginalization are countered by claims of reverse sexism, preferential treatment of women and the silencing and intimidation of those who have never known what it means to be truly without voice, as women are, not because we cannot speak but because we are not heard and not being heard we cease to speak. Women repeatedly tell me of their conscious decision to stop speaking in classrooms where sexism is a non-negotiable dynamic of the curriculum and classroom practice. Some women tell me of not having spoken in class for years. Economic marginality continues to limit students' access to education. The division between mental and manual labour continues to suppress what counts as acceptable knowledge. Many students who carry the weighted baggage of their racial/ethnic identity slow and eventually step to the sidelines in the race for academic success. And questions of sexual identity never enter the classroom even as we turn a blind eye to the violations of homophobia that hold many students physically, emotionally and psychologically hostage to their peers.

This is not to say that there are not courageous teachers who struggle to maintain programmes and create curriculum against the will of those whose interests are not served by students who know too much. These teachers know all too well that the question posed in the title of this article can only be rhetorical. We know who should decide the forms schools should take: those for whom schools are ostensibly intended inclusive of all of the multiple identities of individuals and social groups. Yet we also know who does articulate educational forms and re/forms. In this context, the challenge of critical/feminist pedagogy is to find that vacuous space between rhetoric and practice; between the language of democracy, freedom, possibility and justice and the actuality of constraint, denial of voice and containment of possibility, and claim that space—like a crack in the pavement where a flower might grow—as a place from which to listen and speakin order to enact with our students transformative practices in the classroom.

# References

Bersianik, L. (1986). "Aristotle's lantern: an essay on criticism." In S. Neuman and S. Kamboureli (eds.). *Amazing Space: Writing Canadian Women Writing.* Edmonton: Lonspoon Press.

Daly, M. (1978). *Gyn/Ecology: The metaethics of Radical Feminism.* Boston: The Beacon Press.

Dewar, A. (1987). "Knowledge and gender in physical education." In J. Gaskel land A. McLaren (eds.). *Women and Education: A Canadian Perspective.* Calgary: Detselig Enterprises Limited.

Sontag, S. (Ed.). (1987). *A Barthes Reader.* New York: Hill and Wang.

The School Boys of Barbiana. (1971). *Letter to a Teacher.* Trans. by N. Rossi and T. Cole. New York: Vintage Books.

Woolf, V. (1929). *A Room of One's Own.* London: The Hogarth Press.

# Rodman B. Webb

Philosophical questions about power (What is it? Who deserves it? What legal and moral limits should we put on its use?) have interested political theorists since antiquity, but empirical studies of power (Who has it? How did they get it? What do they do with it?) are rather new in American social science. Until about the 1950s there were few useful studies of power, perhaps because so much about the topic was distasteful. Power, after all, is the ability to get your way, to make things happen as you intend them to happen, to get others to do things they may not want to do. Such a definition flies in the face of the democratic credo that political power ultimately resides in the people and nearly is always an expression of democratic consensus. For that reason, there was little tolerance for the suggestion that political power may reside, not with the people, but with small groups who worked behind the political scenes to get their way. In the 1950s, however, social scientists began to question whether conventional descriptions of power spelled in our civics textbooks were accurate. To find out, they designed community studies to see who had power, how they got it, how they maintained it, and what they did with it.

This essay explores the question of power in education. To achieve that goal we need not review the voluminous literature on power that social scientists have produced over the last 40 years. It will help, however, if we examine a few representative studies of power. Such an examination will show how our understanding of political power has evolved and tell us something about power and public education.

We will begin by looking at the work of Floyd Hunter, who contended that power in American communities is concentrated in the hands of a small, somewhat secretive, power elite. We will contrast that view with the conclusions of Robert Dahl. Dahl, like Hunter, found that power structures existed somewhat independent of government, but that those structures were more differentiated, complex, and pluralistic that Hunter had suggested. We will call Hunter's view the *power elite hypothe-*

*sis* and Dahl's view the *pluralistic hypothesis*. These two perspectives still inform current studies of power.

## Two Early Community Studies of Power

### Hunter and the Power Elite Hypothesis

Studies of power can be done at the micro level (within organizations and communities) or at the macro level (within a nation or across national boundaries). The advantage of micro-studies is that they allow social scientists to get close to power holders and see how and when they wield their power. A good example of a community micro-study is Hunter's *Community Power Structure*. Hunter became interested in the realities of political power while doing social work in Atlanta, Georgia. He suspected that many important decisions—decisions that affected the lives and well being of Atlanta's citizens—were not made by elected officials but rather by a small group of powerful men who worked outside government.

Interviews with the city's most influential people told Hunter a lot about unofficial power and how it is used. A few quotes from one of his interviews provides a reasonable summation of his findings. One respondent discussed a project idea that Charles Homer, "the biggest man in our crowd," wanted to get underway. "When he gets an idea," the respondent explained, "others will get the idea. Don't ask me how he gets the idea or where. But recently he got the idea that [Atlanta] should be the national headquarters for an International Trade Council" (Hunter, p. 173). The project needed financing and the support and approval of various civic and governmental groups. In a paragraph that Sinclair Lewis might have written for Babbitt, Hunter's respondent explained how Mr. Homer got what he wanted:

> He called in some of us [those in the inner circle], and he talked to us about the idea. He did not talk much. We do not engage in loose talk about the "ideals" of the situation and all that other stuff. We get right down to the problem, that is, how do we get the council. We all think it is a good idea. . . . (Hunter, 1953, p. 173)

The group made plans, divided the work to be done, and secured the support of others in the power structure. Later, they called a meeting at an exclusive men's club because "eventually this [project] is going to be a community proposition." The purpose of the meeting was to raise money and drum up support among less powerful members of the community. Many people were invited into the project, but control remained with the inner circle. Hunter's informant explained, "We went into that meeting with a board of directors already picked. The constitution was already written, and the man who was to head the council as executive was named. . . a third-string man, a fellow who would take advice" (Hunter, p. 174).

Hunter's study received much attention among social scientists and in the popular press. If he was right (and that was a matter of debate), American democracy was not as open and egalitarian as was commonly assumed. Hunter was one of many researchers to concluded that everyday citizens have little or no say in important government and community decisions, that a power elite has a tight grip on the strings of power, and that information and public opinion are manipulated so that the power elite can get its way (Domhoff, 1978, 1983; Dye, 1976; Mills, 1956).

Hunter had his critics. Some contended that his method mistook the image for the reality of power. The fact that people identified a power elite and that members of that circle claimed they ran things in Atlanta did not prove that insiders were as powerful as they claimed. Hunter also was criticized for assuming that the power elite was a cohesive group, that it agreed on most matters, and that its power stretched into every domain of public life. Other critics contended that Hunter had not paid enought attention to the actual workings of political institutions. These criticisms notwithstanding, Hunter had raised important questions about power that scholars rushed to study. For example, Robert Dahl, a Yale political scientist, studied power in New Haven, and published his finding in the still influential book, *Who Governs?* (Dahl, 1961).

**Dahl and the Pluralist Hypothesis**
Robert Dahl offered a pluralistic refutation of Hunter's work. He studied New Haven's history to see if the city's power arrangements had changed over the years. Dahl found that New Haven once had been ruled by a small group of powerful

people, but that the power structure had grown increasingly pluralistic since the turn of the century.  Interest groups of ethnic voters, middle-class merchants, professionals, religious groups, neighborhood groups, and union members organized themselves around common interests and completed for power with other groups in the decision-making process.  Business interests were powerful, but their power was significantly curtailed by other groups that had their own resources and voter support.  Sometimes one group would get its way, sometimes another, but most contests ended in compromise.  Dahl's pluralistic description of power does not square exactly with the textbook version of democracy, but it does not contradict the American credo as severely as does Hunter's power elite hypothesis.

Dahl's work also had critics.  The decisional method that Dahl used attributed power to those elected officials assigned to deal with issues in the  areas he was studying.  Dahl's method was unlikely to uncover the kinds of back-room power that Hunter had tracked down.  Also, by focusing on actual decisions, Dahl could not study the processes by which certain issues, such as the rights of minorities, were kept out of political discussions (Dumhoff, 1978).

**Community Studies and Power in Education**
Community studies usually include some information on public education decisions and who made them.  For example, Dahl found that the power to influence educational decisions was contested among several groups in New Haven and that no particular power elite consistently won the day.  Robert and Helen Lynd, who studied Muncie, Indiana, came to a similar conclusion.  Businessmen, professionals, patriotic groups, and parents all vied for power to influence what was taught in schools.  These groups did not always agree, but they shared an opposition to curricular or other changes that challenged the core values of the middle-class.  Nowhere was this unity more apparent than in battles over the ideological content of the curriculum.  As the Lynds explained,

> In [Muncie] the community pressure forces are mobilized against
> dissent.  Business knows what it wants.  The patriotic groups know what

they want. The D.A.R. [Daughters of the American Revolution], always
on a hair-trigger of watchfulness for "disloyalty," is reported to feel that
both the high school and the college have "some pretty pink teachers"'
and it is reported as characteristic of its activites that sons and daughters
in the classrooms of suspected teachers have been enlisted to check up
on the latter's teaching.
(Lynd & Lynd, 1937, p. 235)

The point we can draw from most community studies is that
public education does not appear to be controlled by a single
power elite and that power in this domain of public life is
contested among several interest groups. However, pluralism
does not often extend to the lower strata of society. Maybe the
strongest proof of middle-class power in education is to be
found in studies of school board membership.

George Counts did the earliest studies of the social and
economic standing of school board members. He studied 1,654
school boards in the 1920s and found that almost no board
members were African-American, only a few belonged to labor
unions, and only 8% worked as manual laborers (Counts, 1927,
p. 79). Board members typically were businessmen, professional men (primarily doctors and lawyers), bankers, and, in
smaller number, housewives.

The characteristics of school board members have not
changed significantly in the past half century. Today, school
board members tend to be white males earning about $45,000 a
year and working as professionals, managers, or business
owners. Women are better represented now than in the past
(40% of today's board member are female), but African-Americans only make up 3.6% of school board members and Hispanics only 1.5% (Cameron, Underwood, & Fortune, 1988).

It is fair to say that in school-related matters, middle-class
interests generally dominate lower-class interests. However, the
interests of less powerful groups occasionally are heard and
sometimes carry the debate. For example, Gans documents
how working-class groups managed to change a Levittown
school budget that reflected the college hopes of middle-class
students. The debate, which was over a proposal to increase the
school budget and raise taxes, was, as Gans pointed out,
"Clearly between the haves and the have-nots." (Gans, 1967,
p. 98).

We need not look to community studies, however, to find instances where working-class or minority interests have challenged the hold that middle-class groups have on public education. The struggle to integrate the public schools, the effort to remove sexist language from textbooks and to include the contributions of women and people of color in the curriculum, even the battles over school prayer and the teaching of creationism are examples of how various out-of-power groups occasionally organize to challenge the status quo. They do not always win, but on certain issues they manage to be heard in debates over educational aims.

The weight of community study evidence tends to support the pluralistic hypothesis over the power-elite hypothesis, at least in the area of public education. However, public education may be an atypical area of political life in America. After all, power-elite families have only a limited interest in public schooling. The rich and prominent usually send their children to private day schools and elite boarding schools (Baltzell, 1958). Those who do send their children through the public system tend to live in homogeneous suburban communities where schools are sensitive to the interests of the power elite. School systems in other communities tend to reflect the interests of middle-class groups. Those groups do not always agree but, as stated above, they generally unite around core values and in opposition to change and dissent. They are guardians of tradition, suspicious of dissent, and quick to mobilize when their interests are threatened.

### Critical Theory and Power in Education

Dahl and other pluralists found that power was a contested commodity in the communities they studied. However, they did not pay close attention to the nature of power contests or the experiences of individuals who are excluded from the political debate. Such questions are now being raised in education by critical theorists who often use life history and ethnographic methodologies in their work. Critical theory, which embraces ideology as an instrument of (rather than an impediment to) inquiry, contends that society's power arrangements are reflected in all arena's of public and private life; school curricula, law, gender relations, and so on. The biographical study by Magda Lewis is an example of critical research. Her biographical approach exposes some limits of community power studies, at least as they have been done in the past.

A community study in the Canadian town where Lewis grew up might have examined debates over public education and probably would have found evidence to support the pluralistic hypothesis. Researchers might have found that the debates over education were public and boisterous, that many voices were heard, that several groups vied for power, and that, in the end, democratic compromises were struck. Yet, such conclusions seem trivial from the perspective of one child struggling to find her identity. The schools Lewis attended reflected the interests of a narrow cliental and, by her telling, did not serve the interests of students who were out of the mainstream.

As we read her account, we come to see that for Lewis, and the silent millions like her, the Hunter-Dahl debate is of limited relevance. From her present perspective, nearly everything about school denied the legitimacy of her being and adumbrated the most pressing and personal questions in her life. Her education did not call and clarify those questions and, therefore, left her without a social and intellectual location from which she might build an authentic identity.

The life history Lewis offers is a tale of homelessness, solitude, and silence. As she worked to find location and connection within the categories offered by the school, she was encouraged to blend in and become like her classmates. *To be was to be like* those around her. Note the sad ironies alive in the story. The more successful Lewis became at imitating her peers, the more she distanced herself from her family and heritage. The more she identified with others, the more she silenced her deepest questions about herself. The more she denied her origins and ignored the questions within her, the more isolated she became and, one suspects, the more the school rewarded her for her academic and social success.

Sometime in her life, Lewis doesn't tell us when or how, she revisited the questions that schooling had silenced and the categories of selfhood her education had denied. It was then that she broke the silent circle of oppression she now believes char-

acterized her youth.   But what of students whose life stories
include no such insights and no happy endings?

A growing number of researchers have done critical ethno-
graphies investigating the lives of students who live at the
bottom of the economic heap.   Paul Willis (1977) chronicles the
lives of some British working-class students whose only source
of identity and social location in school was found in rebellion.
Jay MacLeod (1987), who studied young men living in Boston's
public housing projects, offered similar findings.   Michelle Fine
(1991) studied dropouts in New York City and asked why and
how city schools silence and discharge a shockingly large
percentage of their pupils.   These ethnographic studies revealed
that students from poor families had some critical, if confused,
insight into how schools excluded them and silenced their
questions about where they fit in society.   Denied self respect by
the school, many of these students forged identities by
embracing the very things the institution required they disclaim.
In this anti-world, what officially is *bad* is redefined as *good* and
*vise versa.*   For example, when MacLeod asked two white
teenagers what they had to do to be "bad," Slick and Frankie
answered:

Slick:      You hafta make a name for yourself, to be bad, tough, what-
            ever. You hafta be, y'know, be with the "in" crowd. . . . Once
            in awhile you hafta, if you haven't gotten into a fight, if you
            have a fight up the school, you're considered bad.  Y'know
            what I mean?  If you beat someone up up there, especially if
            he's black [you're bad].  If you're to be bad, you hafta be
            arrested.  You haft at least know what bein' in a cell is like.

MacLeod:    So how is it that to be what's good down here, to be
            respected. . . .

Slick:      You gotta be bad.

Frankie:    Yeah, if you're a straight A student, you get razzed.

Slick:      Then you're a fucking weirdo, and you shouldn't be living
            here in the first place. (MacLeod, p. 26)

Comments such as these terrify middle-class sensibilities,
which is exactly what Slick and Frankie intend to do.  They have
some insight into their situation and believe they know what

their life-chances really are. They ridicule the school's achievement ideology because they believe there are insurmountable
barriers separating them from success. Many expect that they
will die young or will spend most of their adult life in jail. Few,
however, translate their insights into the type of exploration of
self that Lewis accomplished. Their youthful rebellions eventually take them out of school, and their lack of education
excludes them from work that promises upward mobility. In
the end they blame themselves and not the system for their
situation. What began as a crude social critique ends as deep
self criticism. As Fine suggests,

> Younger dropouts carried a powerful critical voice while older ones, who
> had been out for sometime and had tried what was available, lost their
> critical edge. Except to turn on themselves. In a society with a few
> mechanisms for mobilizing, sustaining, and sharpening social critique,
> especially among low-income young adults, critique eventually reverses
> and self-impels. And the dropout is ultimately alone, and silenced.
> (Fine, 1991, p. 126)

Critical theorists have expanded the debate over power in
education. Community studies examined who had power and
how they used it. Critical theorists show that the power of priv-
iledge extends far beyond the back-room decisions of a power
elite or out-front victories of one or another interest group
during a pluralistic contest for power. The very structures of
public schools and the knowledge it transmits serve to advance
the interests of some groups and retard the interests of others.

**The Present Situation**
The debate between the power elite and pluralist positions
continues today. That debate has been extended and deepened
by recent life-history and ethnographic research conducted by
critical theorists. I have stressed the differences that separate
these three positions, but a few commonalities are worth noting.
Together they show the complexities of power issues in education. All suggest that the realitites of power politics have little
in common with idealized versions of democracy. All throw
into question the assumption that public schooling serves to
eradicate the arbitrary disadvantages of birth and provides an
equal educational opportunity for all students. Proponents of

all positions contend that the nation will become more perfectly democratic if public education prepares individuals to take part in the political debate.  All agree with Jefferson's contention that no people can be ignorant and free.

Power studies have made some teachers more conscious of class, race, and gender issues.  Faculties on college campuses and in some public schools have widened their curricula to reflect the backgrounds and perspectives of groups that long have been ignored.  Some teachers now are asking what kind of knowledge and educational experiences will empower students who are disempowered in the culture and the classroom.  New ways of organizing schools and classrooms have been suggested so that students from different backgrounds will be able to find a voice and place within the educational conversation.

Such suggestions have worried those who believe that students are best served when they are invited to study classical knowledge in schools that promote middle-class values.  E.D. Hirsch (1987), for example, bemoans the fragmentation of the curriculum and warns educators that the very knowledge that Lewis found so inhibiting "constitutes the only sure avenue of opportunity for disadvantaged children, the only reliable way of combating the social determinism that now condemns them to remain in the same social and educational condition as their parents" (p. xiii).

Allan Bloom (1987), in a book that flew to the top of the *New York Times* bestseller list and came to rest on the coffee tables of many upper-middle-class homes, bemoaned the removal of core requirements from the curriculum.  According to Bloom, democratization of the curriculum and the ethos of openness that goes with it, discourages the very inquiry it claims to promote.  When we see all knowledge as a simple expression of cultural location, there is no way for us to determine truth and, thus, no reason for us to argue about things of ultimate value. The political debate that the pluralists celebrate and that critical theorists want to widen is closed down, Bloom contends, when students are offered relativistic notions of truth in schools and colleges.  In the end, Bloom concludes, an expanded curriculum fails democracy and impoverishes the souls of students.

What is the difference between the Hirsch-Bloom position and that implied by the studies by critical theorists? Both groups contend that knowledge can empower or disempower students. Knowledge is the way we come in touch with the world and with ourselves. It also is the instrument by which we free ourselves from the iron cage of culture. On the surface, the argument is over what knowledge is most liberating. Bloom and Hirsch argue for the classical knowledge of the Western tradition, or what some critics call the knowledge of dead, white men. Critical theorists argue for a wider knowledge that allows students to see the power relationships in their world, see how they are privileged or deprived because of those power relationships, and find ways to spread power more evenly. As Giroux argues, "This means providing students with the opportunity to develop the critical capacity to challenge and transform existing social and political forms, rather than simply adapt to them" (1991, p. 47).

On a deeper level, however, the argument is about knowledge itself. Bloom finds authority in the wisdom of "the ancients" and discusses their writing as though there is no question about what the authors meant or how we might apply their knowledge in our time. Many critical theorists (and other groups not reviewed here) do not see knowledge as something fixed and separate from us, but as a human construction. Knowledge is always and inalterably socially located and contestable. Knowledge can only be known and its warrant can only be established in terms of the response it elicits and the uses to which it is put. Bloom asks us, among other things, to have faith in the knowledge of the ancients and tells us to struggle to understand their wisdom. Bloom's critics ask us, among other things, to investigate all curricular suggestions in terms of their power relations. A beginning question for such an enquiry is, "Who created this knowledge and whose interests are served when it is taught?"

# References

Baltzell, E.B. (1958). *Philadelphia gentlemen.* New York: Free Press.

Bloom, A. (1987). *The closing of the American Mind: How higher education has failed democracy and impoverished the souls of today's students.* New York: Simon and Schuster.

Cameron, B.H.; Underwood, K.E.; & Fortune, J.C. (1988). "It's ten years later and you've hardly changed at all." *American School Board Journal* 175, 20.

Counts, G.S. (1927). *The social composition of school boards.* Chicago: University of Chicago Press.

Dahl, R. (1961). *Who governs?* New Haven: Yale University Press.

Domhoff, G.W. (1978) *Who really rules? New Haven and community power reexamined.* New Brunswick, NJ: Transaction books.

Domhoff, G.W. (1983). *Who rules America now?* Englewood Cliffs, NJ: Prentice Hall.

Dye, T.R. (1976). *Who's running America? The Carter years.* Englewood Cliffs, NJ: Prentice Hall.

Fine, M. (1991). *Framing dropouts: Notes on the politics of an urban high school.* Albany: State University of New York Press.

Giroux, H. (Ed.). (1991). *Postmodernism, feminism, and cultural politics: Redrawing educational boundaries.* Albany: State University of New York Press.

Hirsch, E.D. (1987). *Cultural literacy: What every American needs to know.* Boston: Houghton Mifflin.

Hunter, F. (1953). *Community power structure.* Chapel Hill: University of North Carolina Press.

Lynd, R.S., & Lynd, H.M. (1937). *Middletown in transition: A study in cultural conflicts.* New York: Harcourt, Brace.

MacLeod, J. (1987). *Ain't no makin' it: Leveled aspirations in a low-income neighborhood.* Boulder, CO: Westview Press.

Willis, P.E. (1977). *Learning to labor.* Aldershot: Grower.

# Chapter III

# Teachers Under Suspicion: Is it true that teachers aren't as good as they used to be?

Shirley R. Steinberg

Deborah P. Britzman

# Shirley R. Steinberg

I remember myself as a skinny, freckled, unpopular freshman at West High. My hair was curly in an age where straight hair was essential. I asked too many questions, interrupted in class. My friends were equally awkward and I knew early that my looks and aggressive manner would be my badge of inadmission to the "cool" group. Teachers didn't like me much, I asked the wrong questions, argued and made asides to no one in particular. By the ninth grade, the citizenship spaces on my report cards had been filled with: "behavior problem", "Shirley has potential but refuses to use it," "egocentric," "interrupts in class," "talkative," "a disturbance," . . . ad nauseum.

Martha Gatsinaris was my ninth grade English teacher. Young, vibrant, an excellent dresser, Mrs. "G" knew *everything*, especially about books. I was a closet reader and felt most of my school-mandated reading was a real drag. My previous teachers had used anthologies or condensed books and Mrs. G taught from the *real* novels.

Our first book was *Nigger of the Narcissus* by Joseph Conrad. In 1965 the risk of teaching a book with that title was not lost on our class. Parents complained, yet we combed through that novel for months. Mrs. G facilitated us to reveal literary symbols and sociological concepts throughout the novel. (In those days, however I just thought she was an "out-of-sight" teacher). Our lives were filled with the dangers and dreams of James Waite and other characters—our vocabulary was from the book, our in-class journals integrated our lives with those of the characters and when we approached Mrs. G to write and produce a play in lieu of a final exam, our theatrics melded our world with Conrad's masterpiece.

Mrs. G was the teacher who we stopped by to see in the morning, her room was our lunchroom, we erased boards after school and collected books. She invited our class to her home to have a "real" Greek dinner and her husband taught us Greek dancing.

Mrs. G had a way of tolerating my interruptions, accomodating and answering my questions to the point that by mid-year, someone noticed that I wasn't interrupting anymore, that the whole class listened to my comments—they didn't laugh and I no longer heard them whisper or saw them roll their eyes when I spoke.

The year I finished ninth grade, I was established as an important part of the speech and drama club,; people actually were interested in my opinion (without my forcing them), and I looked forward to my final three years of high school. My physical appearance hadn't changed much (in a year of bra-burning, I still wasn't wearing one), but I felt good about who I was.

Two years later, I left West High, and one summer day, Mrs. G drove three hours with my best friend to spend the day. As she left, she handed me a copy of *Tristan und Isolde*, and told me to never stop asking questions, to read everything, to be critical and never stop being myself.

Twenty-six years later, I tried to find Mrs. G, to tell her that I too, was an English teacher . . . to thank her for teaching me—I left a message at West High, and they phoned back to tell me that sometime in the early 70s, Mrs. G had killed herself. I guess the only way to remember her and to thank her is by writing about her— and by trying to be a good teacher.

What is a good teacher? good teaching? what does it mean to be a good teacher? are teachers as good as they used to be? do we have reason to think teachers are not as good? what made them good? how do we define good? is there a model for good teaching? a system of meaning that we can attach to good teaching? are there different types of good teachers? what stories do we hear from teachers about good teaching? what stories from students? is good teaching intuitive? is it learned? how symbiotic should schooling and teaching be? What does learning have to do with teaching? can one really *teach* anything? what is the responsibility of the learner? what is the text of teaching? of good teaching? can we define good teaching?

In investigating a student's death, Sargent Joe Friday suggested "if you really want to know something about a kid, ask his coach". Embedded in Friday's observation is that the people who know children best are neither parents or academic teachers, but those that spend extra-curricular time, less structured time with children—fun time.

While describing a "good" teacher, a ninth grader told me that the teacher would have to be fun, even while teaching serious subjects; to allow humor in the class and to be able to make students feel loose, natural. . . comfortable. . . and above all, not to be on a "power trip."

Why isn't teaching fun time?  Schools seem determined to impress upon children and parents that "being a good citizen" entails not having fun, and that good teaching consists of rule-making, structured lessons, stringent curriculum and right or wrong answers to formula questions.  Our childrens' junior high handbook describes good teachers as those that are "competent". . . "all teachers must meet minimum qualifications. . . students and parents will find the faculty willing to go beyond normal duty to assist them in any way."  What qualifications are met?  are these purely academic, or do these qualifications include certain attitudes towards children?  what is a faculty member's "duty"?  is teaching a duty?  Many schools isolate learning time and fun time.  The New Right's thrust to the "good ole days" of schooling have reinforced the lack of humor and diversity in teaching.

When asked what the purpose of schooling was, the student I spoke to divided schooling into three stages:  the first stage of schooling is to keep one occupied until reaching the second stage, in which workbook-type teaching occurs; after students are taught, the final stage, from ninth grade to graduation is developed in order to keep students in, off the streets and out of society until they are old enough to know how to be responsible—to stay "out of trouble."

Teaching is considered a profession, yet when considering this young man's  terrifying opinion of schooling, there is the undeniable evidence of the deskilling of a profession into a job . . . something to be filled competently and to be evaluated quantitatively:  Lesson plans, time on task behavior—these reflect good teaching—high evaluations, high exam scores, good public relations images. . .all leading to a New Right definition of good teaching, which advocates a return to an unthoughtful respect for authority.  "Back to basics" means far more than simple concern with the course of study.  A meta-narrative works behind the concept, a story marked by a protection of patriarchy, Eurocentrism, and "family" values.

Teacher talk about surprise school visits, target evaluations, achievement test scores and complete lesson plans define a collective consciousness of what makes good teaching.  Student talk about how easy he or she is, or how one can really "goof" off in class, or never has homework defines good teaching. Parent talk about Jennifer really "straightening up" or Nathan finally "settling down" or "Meghann actually doing homework", defines good teaching.  Talk about teaching provides a tacit meaning about the importance of control, of conformist thinking, of good image, and of perpetuating my ninth grade friend's image of schooling: *Stage 1:* to be occupied, *Stage 2:* to be taught through prescribed workbook curriculum, *Stage 3:* to be held down.

Many who answer "no" to the question, "are teachers as good as they used to be?", blame the breakdown of family structure, drugs, lack of discipline and good parenting skills, and a failure of community will.  In actuality, they are framing the teachers "good-ness" as dependent on their ability to cope with the problems of our age.  The right-wing attributes bad teaching to "innovative" methods. . . schools that don't teach the basics produce teachers who don't know the basics.  Innovative methods pose a threat to the Fundamentalist Right, many stories and myths are viewed as LIBERAL. . . exciting new facilitation of creativity is called NEW AGE and these labels translate to Satanic.

The success of Ronald Reagan and George Bush rests on their ability to portray attempts to foster egalitarian educational policies and thoughtful graduates as misguided—indeed, as catalysts for a decline in teacher quality. If teachers are not as good as they used to be, then simple-minded tests of teacher aptitude, teacher-proof materials, deskilled job descriptions are justifiable.  Such policies are necessary measures in the fight against the legacy of the "permissive, equality-obsessed" 1960s.

Do we find ourselves in the middle of the proverbial vicious circle? When the Right convinces the public that teachers are not as good as they used to be, and offers its shallow "quick-fixes" in the form of constraining teacher self-determination, then teachers really don't have the freedom, the professional perogative to be as good as they used to be.    Frustration abounds.  Students insist that schooling is designed to not let them learn to think, teachers complain that creativity and critical thinking is impossible to facilitate due to the structure imposed by administrative and governmental pronouncements. Civic courage, self-actualization are irrelevant, "learning" is public relations, a shallow attempt to present a positive image to the community—"putting our best foot forward".

No, teaching can't be as good as it used to be under the definitions set forth by education's right-wing critics, Bloom, Hirsch, Bennett, Reagan, and the "Education President", George Bush.  Rather, teaching is relegated to a model of efficiency, quantitative evaluation, curriculum that defies social imagination  and student handbooks that espouse rules that deskill teachers and oppress students.  Images of the "good" student in the form of *Family Ties'* Alex Keaton haunt creative thinkers and students who insist on individuality through expression and/or appearance are quickly suppressed and taught to "love it or leave it."

But, possibility lives, images of alternatives flicker at the level of the popular.  Fox television's Lisa Simpson was given a reprieve from her dreary teacher in the form of a substitute teacher who spent two weeks with her class.  Lisa's world became a kalideoscope of investigation, open-ended questions and intrigue in the form of alternative methods of teaching the curriculum.  Mr. Bergstrom was interested in who each child was and what they had to contribute to the class in the form of their own stories and knowledge.  Dimensions of gender and class were acknowledged, not suppressed as Lisa was urged to see herself within the context of the forces which shaped her. The children were appreciated and in turn, appreciated the authenticity of the teacher and his desire to teach them.  Teaching and learning became symbiotic and school was thought-provoking, fun.  When Mr. Bergstrom left, a tearful Lisa was admonished to be herself and to follow her own vision, not the standardized, packaged vision promoted by "competent" teachers in National Schools of Excellence.

Martha Gatsinaris was a good teacher. How she taught, the effect she had on her students, the change she facilitated in me would never show up on a teacher evaluation form. Forms don't measure empathy, humor, driving three hours to visit a former student, or ability to connect students' lives with schooling and curriculum. The qualities that Mrs. G had as a good teacher could have easily been considered liabilities in many schools. As a result of being a student of Mrs. Gatsinaris, I was changed. I gained confidence, learned to channel my "enthusiasm", understood my place in the scheme of school and realized my potential as a student and finally as a teacher. No student should leave any classroom unchanged; without the empowerment to rewrite his or her own life in even a subtlely different way.

If teaching is going to be good work, we have to be able to get beyond the simplistic, teacher-proof curriculums, standardization of evaluation, and an excellence read as conventionality. Making use of our critical system of meaning, our social imagination, while renewing our commitment to democracy, we can honor "good" teachers of the past by redefining the role of teacher of the future.

# Deborah P. Britzman

The slippery thing about history is that it must always be arranged. Some arrangements are more comforting than others and at times, the arrangement of the story hides its interestedness and thus the politics of selection. Milan Kundera's novel, *The Book of Laughter and Forgetting*, begins with the dangers of arranging history. He describes the evolution of one photograph: the original people who posed, and how years later, the empty spaces left because some individuals were suddenly erased, airbrushed from historical consciousness, because they fell from official grace. History is overpopulated with such stories and the familiar question, are teachers as good as they used to be?, seems to provoke the impulse to airbrush and thus sanitize our memories of schools.

Thus some stories about the educational past are more comforting than others. And some questions invoke the stories we wish we could tell. Are teachers as good as they used to be? is one of those oddly familiar questions that bestow cultural authority onto everyone. Teachers were an important presence in our past lives and, at times, they may even seem to haunt our present. We have all played a role opposite to teachers and because significant parts of our lives unfold in schools, we implicitly fashion some particular understandings of what a teacher is and does. Most of our childhoods were devoted to observing them, trying to anticipate their moods, and imagining their hidden lives. It seems almost secondhand nature to leave school believing we understand how teachers are made and what work they must do.

This cumulative knowledge of teachers is no such a part of us that it is taken for granted. Indeed, the mass experience of public education has made teaching one of the most familiar professions in this culture. Implicitly, schooling fashions the meanings, realities, and lived experience of our childhood: residing in our heads and hearts are contesting views of good and bad teachers. The question, are teachers as good as they used to be, may even seem pleasurable because it invites us to return to our own educational biographies. It is a question that is as much about who we are as it is about who they are. That is, one cannot tell stories about teachers without telling stories about students, schools, and the communities where we live. And yet this question is as slippery and as elusive as the histories it attempts to stabilize. The hidden dilemma is that the question of whether teacher are as good as they used to be traps us in an impossible chronology.

The particular phrasing of whether teachers are as good as they used to be couples our stories with the fictions of nostalgia. It would be nice to think there once was a time when schooling worked, teachers taught, and students learned. That once upon a time, schools were protected from contesting demands, incredibly complicated social strife, and were populated with smiling, satisfied subjects who did what they were supposed to do. In a story fused with nostalgia, things become simple: textbooks tell the truth, everyone listens quietly and waits their turn and when children are asked to line up, it really only expedites the smooth movements of large groups of children. The conjuring of this idyllic past depends upon an order of things somehow better than the disorder of the present It is a version of the past that implicitly says that somewhere along the road, the dream of education-for-all-involved became lived as a nightmare on Elm Street.

Embedded in this nostalgic narrative is a disturbing version of the present: the idyllic has its messy counterpart. This is the nightmare that rehearses what used to be good because of what we take to be bad. Its logic collapses multiple contexts and poses effects as causes because it offers reasons in the guise of motives. The question, whether teachers are as good as they used to be, requires no contextual distinctions and so the answers become so many ranting slogans. The next few paragraphs will suggest some of the anxieties conjured by this question.

The first anxiety concerns questions of preparation. This anxiety says that at some point, teachers stopped being as prepared as they used to be. Teacher education accepted anyone into their programs, and besides, only the worst students apply. Those who study teaching are required to take too many education courses and not enough courses in academic knowledge. They then graduate from college without the proper skills. They even have trouble reading and speaking, and this makes necessary the mandatory literacy testing of teachers. Newly arrived teachers are too idealistic and lack the discipline techniques to control the students in the ways they used to control students.

A different anxiety addresses the conditions of teachers. Somewhere along the way, teachers became involved with things like teacher's unions and began to view their profession as labor. They became far too involved with negotiating the conditions of their work and thus are not concerned with their students. In this confused version, unions are viewed as constraining and manipulating teachers' actions. Teachers aren't as good as they used to be because nasty unions force them to limit their work. But with or without unions, this version also asserts that teachers became disenchanted with teaching because they are now required to do things that should have been done elsewhere: like teaching values, offering medical advice, counseling students, and even washing students' clothes. In this conflated story, teachers could be as good as they used to be if families, communities, and cultures did what they were supposed to do and if unions would leave them alone. Students and their parents are also blamed in this version: teachers are not as good as they used to be because students no longer enter school with the proper respect for education and for teachers.

Yet another kind of anxious nostalgia, gathering different threads of history, becomes woven into this fictive sense of time and of identity. Teachers are not as good as they used to be because of the women's liberation movement. Today's women have more career choices than ever. Their choice of career is no longer determined by maintaining traditional gendered family roles and no longer tied to being the sole person to care for their children. In this story of gender tyranny, while their choice of career is no longer being determined by conventional imperatives, the actions of women are ruining both the sanctity of the family and the schools. So teachers are not as good as they used to be because women have abandoned the field and those male teachers left behind, as well as those male teachers just entering, are not as good as the female teacher.

The above versions of history are not comforting to those who work in schools. Not can they make sense of the fact that teaching and learning are overburdened with conflicting meanings. These meanings shift with our lived lives, with the common sense invoked to render our stories generalizable, with the deep convictions and desires brought to and created in education, with the practices we negotiate, and with the kinds of identities we try on as desirable, or shed as undesirable. The contradictory myths working through such nostalgia are that teachers should be both selfless and self-made, that everything depends upon them, and that teachers are always certain in their knowledge. The discomfort suggests that teachers are people who experience deep doubt about what schools actually do, that their understanding of competence and success are more vulnerable than imagined, and that the conditions of their work and daily lives are more complicated that our educational biographies are capable of imagining.

It is difficult to unravel all of the myths mobilized by the question of whether teachers are as good as they used to be because so many different voices speak and because this is a question that answers itself. The past it conjures is too selective, and the present is too close to sort out. This is a question where the present can never be addressed on its own terms and where the future is overburdened with what is taken as the past. This implicit value on time hides the very process of selection and valuation. The question never requires us to define our criteria of the past or trace what it is that structures our sense of the good, the bad, and the ugly. When time supplants humanity, ethical responsibilities are abandoned. To ask the familiar question, are teachers as good as they used to be, is to reject the myriad relations that make education possible.

Are teachers as good as they used to be unleashes such dissonance because the question conjures an impossible time and this doubly shuts out thoughtful understandings of what good teaching means and critical considerations that are necessary for good teaching. As originally posed, this question can only invoke common sense. The problem is that what seems most obvious, most common is that which is never explained. Like the myths and the fictive chronologies that support them, common sense makes the world appear as natural, and as never in need of change. Common sense covers its own narrative tracks. And so, as posed, the question is overpopulated with assumptions that leave no trace.

But there is an additional explanation for why the question— are teachers as good as they used to be—seems to resonate with the familiar. And this has to do with the fact that this question has always echoed throughout the history of schooling. It hides the difficult reality that there has never been agreement as to what good teaching means and that what once seemed good twenty-five years ago may now be viewed as harmful. History does not stand still and neither do the meanings we make of it. One need only consider the history of corporal punishment in schools where beating the "good" into children, "for their own good" is now understood as child abuse. Caught within the question of whether teachers are as good as they used to be are contesting histories of what education might mean and of which version of the good holds currency. Caught as well in such a question are the insistencies of race, class, gender, ethnicity, and generation, and how these social differences contest or affirm dominant versions of "the good." The point is that this question about the past is only capable of invoking empty promises.

We are capable of raising intelligent questions about good teaching and still consider our deep investments in schools. Relevant questions can provoke us to refashion and articulate our educational, historical, political, and emotional imaginations. What kinds of teaching contribute to the building of democracy in the present as well as in the future? What might encourage students and teachers to imagine, in deep and compassionate terms, the possibilities offered by their own identities and the identities of others? How might teaching engage everyone involved in social justice and in the attainments of civil rights? What kinds of values allow students and teachers to work together in dignified ways? What conditions allow teaching and learning to be meaningful, creative, and pleasurable? If we can imagine schooling as a wonderful place, what kinds of identities would be available to teachers, students, and the larger communities? If education could live as a utopia, what kinds of practices, values, beliefs, and relationships would sustain it? What if teachers and students could shed the stereotypes that trap them? How would their work and their lives be different?

These new questions suggest teaching as a social process of negotiation rather than an individual problem of behavior. This dynamic is essential to any humanizing explanation of the work of teachers. Teaching concerns coming to terms with one's intentions and values, as well as one's views of knowing, being, and acting in a setting characterized by contradictory realities, negotiation, and dependency and struggle. Engagement with these complications requires that we acknowledge that there is something quite vulnerable about teaching and learning. Teaching means coming to terms with the power to shape young identities and their views of the world. And given this encounter, the teacher is also in the process of becoming. This view of teaching admits an unknowable chronology because neither students nor teachers stand still. Teaching suggests an unsettling moment when new ideas disorganize what one thought was long settled. And so teaching means taking and inviting interpretive risks as part of the process of coming to know. Most unsettling, teaching means being intellectually and emotionally open to that which one cannot foresee, predict, or control. In other words, teaching means acknowledging and working with all of the uncertainties that are the sum of our lived lives.

Given such complexities, what kinds of conditions provoke good teaching? First, teachers need opportunities to move beyond their isolation from one another and their isolation from the community. As it is presently lived, teachers are expected to single-handedly work in crowded classrooms. Because teachers are expected to control the class alone, they implicitly understand this to mean that asking for help or support is viewed as a source of weakness. Moreover, rarely do students observe teachers interacting with other adults and thus cannot imagine teachers as people who also work with others, seek advice, and need support. To move beyond the terrible isolation teachers daily experience, teachers must have oppor-tunities to shape their work collectively and to organize their time in ways that can allow thoughtful dialogue with their colleagues, creative interactions with students, and meaningful time in the communities in which they work.

A second condition is that teachers have the time and space to continue their education in ways they determine. Presently, in-service education is typically designed by administrators who rarely work in classrooms and whose imperatives are shaped by needs that are not pedagogical. Teachers are rarely given the time to determine programs that may be helpful, or even research what might be illuminating. Yet schools could be organized to facilitate the education of teachers and students. For example, part of the teacher's work should be devoted to teacher study groups that collaboratively research their teaching and learning needs. Such a direction necessitates a significant restructuring of schools where classrooms are not the only context for teaching and learning and where teachers have the opportunities to think through their practices.

A third direction for good teaching concerns carefully linking those just entering the profession to those already there in ways that value the contributions of the newly arrived and the experienced teachers. Everyone involved needs opportunities to experiment with new methodology, familiarize themselves with the most recent arguments in the research literature in order to construct their own views, and talk though their practices. As presently lived, however, those entering the profession are as isolated as those already there and far too often, learning to teach dissipates into the narrow terms of taking up existing practices without opportunities to practice in meaningful ways. Providing the time, space, and guidance for experienced teachers to work with the newly arrived would mean rethinking the work of teaching to include leadership in the revitalization of the profession.

A fourth direction involves extending the present boundaries of learning and teaching. The curriculum of school need not be confined to classroom settings and to the pages of textbooks. Communities have much to offer students and teachers when they become another context for education and the historic tension between the schools and the communities must be addressed in pedagogical terms. Like the isolation of teachers, the segregation of youth from their community context works to fragment education and the complexities of life. Community oriented schooling would mean involving new identities in the education of youth, extending the meaning of teaching and learning beyond the confines of classroom walls, and repairing the distance between school and life.

The question, what makes for good teaching, then, requires everyone to become more curious about the present structure of education and about the future possibilities opened when this structure is rearranged. Imaginative thinking can move us beyond the constraints of nostalgia and the anxious impulse to arrange history without an awareness of what it is that structures our destinations or how the inherited contexts and practices constrain our possibilities. Because we have all spent significant time in schools, we are obligated to shape its possibilities in ways that advance what we inherit. Imagining good teaching then, should invite us to move beyond the dreary cycle of self blame or blaming others and onto future visions of that which is not yet.

# Chapter IV

# Students Under Suspicion: Do students misbehave more than they used to?

Clinton B. Allison

Kathleen Berry

# Clinton B. Allison

## The Myth

Our mailbox in rural East Tennessee collects some of the darndest things. Among other unsolicited periodicals, we received the tabloid of a fundamentalist Bible college, located just a few miles down the road. Except for locality, we have little in common with the members of that community, nevertheless, I always dutifully read the Johnson Bible College *Blue and White.* In the April 1987 issue, there was an astonishing article, written by the president of the college, David L. Eubanks. "It sounds like to scenario of a horror story," he begins, and adds, "the problem is, it's true!" According to the article, "researchers" in 1948 surveyed teachers to find the "top" discipline problems in the public school. They found:

> Talking. Chewing gum. making noise. Running in the halls. Wearing improper clothing. Not putting waste paper in the waste paper basket.

Teachers in the 1980s were asked the "same question," with frightening results; "the degeneration in the span of only one generation is shocking." The current "top" discipline problems, according to the article, were:

> Rape...! Robbery...! Assault...! Burglary...! Arson...! Bombing...! Murder...

"The truth is that in one generation," the article continues, "our nation has been brought to the brink of moral and spiritual disaster." The surveys were found, according to Eubanks, in an article by Dr. James Dobson (the child-rearing expert of the religious right) in the March 1987 issue of his magazine, *Focus on the Family,* (Eubanks, 1987).

As an aging educational historian with a longtime interest in the history of childhood, I was bemused by the article. Surely, no rational person could believe that such a degeneration of discipline in the schools had taken place since 1948; researchers could not possibly have asked the same questions of a similar cross section of American public school teachers with that result. If the surveys existed at all, I suspected that the problem was in the ambiguous word, "top," which could mean either most common or most severe. Teachers across the generations have spent their lives warning children that they have about reached the end of their patience with whispering and admonishing students not to run in the hallways, and so it continues today. And serious crimes have always been committed by the schoolchildren; but rape, murder, assault (unless you count one ten-year-old bloodying the nose of another) and the other "top disciplinary problems" are not part of the daily life of most teachers, except in the most difficult of schools where they have always been problems. Surely, I comforted myself, only a minority that use such "evidence" of moral decay to spread their salvation message would accept such degeneration as fact.

However, the *Knoxville News-Sentinel* immediately reprinted the surveys on the editorial page of the Sunday newspaper, and on November 26, 1989, the newspaper, as part of article, concerning discipline problems in the Knox County Schools, included the following:

"Problems in School"
According to Knox County
Schools teacher surveys

1948
Loud talking
Throwing paper
Gum chewing
Disruptive Behavior

1988
Teacher assault
Student assault
Drugs
Weapons
Gang activity
Vandalism
Thefts

These surveys, of course, looked remarkably like the ones in the *Blue and White*. Were they really Knox County teacher surveys?" I called the feature writer of the story. He said that he had gotten the results of the surveys from security investigators with the Knox County School system. I telephoned them. One said, "I have no idea where it [the surveys] came from . . . The reporter must have found it in a newspaper somewhere." The other indicated that they were national surveys rather than Knox County surveys, but he could not remember their source. He graciously called back a few days later, telling me that he had gotten the results of the surveys from the Director of the National School Safety Center in a seminar at Pepperdine University.

On December 3, 1990, I saw the now famous survey without attribution, on the Donahue show. Deciding that I really needed to see the original article in *Focus on the Family*, I called the Johnson Bible College library; they did not keep issues of the magazine that far back. I called President Eubanks' office; he did not have that issue. I called *Focus on the Family*. The people in their correspondence department were helpful. They too, had read the surveys but they were not in the April 1987 issue (or any issue, they thought) of the magazine. One remembered a book in which the surveys had been reprinted and suggested that they might have come originally from Mel and Norma Gabler, the rightist watchdogs of school textbooks. Since thereafter, I received a notice that I would start receiving *Focus on the Family* in the mail.

The original source of the "research" is not particularly important; the surveys have become a part of our educational folklore. They only reinforce an already widespread, existing belief that children in the past were more innocent, better behaved, and less troubled than they are today. In the rest of this essay, I will first review some of the historical literature on student behavior and childhood delinquency, and then indicate some of the policy problems with believing in the myth of a lost world of good children.

**The Myth Explored**
Did children engage in violently disruptive behavior in public schools in previous generations? Of course. Unruly children is a problem as old as schooling. Horace Mann, often called the "father of the public schools," in his *Annual Reports* of the Massachusetts Board of Education during the 1830s and 1840s, kept a running account of schools closed because of student unruliness and rebellion. He publicized excerpts from the

reports of local school committees which would be seized upon
today as certain evidence that our nation has, in President
Eubanks' phrase, "been brought to the brink of moral and spiritual disaster."     "School broken up by the disorderly and
insolent conduct of the scholars," read a typical excerpt (Mann,
1841, p. 87).   He reported that, in the 1830s in Massachusetts,
300 to 400 public schools "were annually brought to a violent
termination, either by the triumph of a rebellious spirit on the
part of the scholars, or by . . . gross incompetency on the part of
teachers" (Mann, 1843, p. 38).

In seeking a perspective on youth in contemporary society,
historians of childhood and of education often look to the mid
and late nineteenth century.   Precursors of social changes which
characterize our world were taking place:  urbanization, industrialization, secularization, and immigration of diverse people.
Ministers, educators, and other social commentators of the time
were warning that families seemed to be losing their moral bear-
ings, that there was a social and moral breakdown.   There were
already cries, as an example, that fathers were too often absent
from the home, away on business, or too permissive.   The failures of parents to discipline children properly were widely
condemned.    A mid-nineteenth century textbook in teacher
training warned teachers that "good government in the family is
the exception and not the rule.   Parents indulge their children
at home nay, indirectly train them to utter lawlessness" (Kaestle,
1978, p. 9).

For those who perceive an epidemic of immorality in America
today, perhaps even evidence of "end times," no better evidence
exists than the sexual abuse of children.   Mothers and fathers
simply didn't   do that sort of unconscionable thing in their
fantasy America of the past.   But, unfortunately, some children
have always had to suffer the anguish and shame of sexual
abuse.   In her history of the first reform school for girls in
America, Barbara M. Benzel, tells us that one type of inmate
was there for protection against parental abuse, including
forced incest:

> One 1863 entrant whose "mother says the girl is beyond control," was
> the victim of incest by her stepfather . . . Another entrant, a thirteen-
> year-old who arrived in 1875, was undoubtedly also a victim of sexual

abuse . . . Susan K. [a twelve-year-old] another example from 1885, . . .
had "been terribly abused by her mother and compelled to submit to
lewd men on numerous occasions." (Benzel, 1983, p. 129)

Accompanying a perception of a moral breakdown in the
nineteenth century was a widespread belief in an epidemic of
youthful crime and violence that rivals the worst fears of doom-
sayers today. In 1849, New York Police Chief George W.
Matsell warned of "the constantly increasing number of vagrant,
idle and vicious children. Their numbers were almost incredi-
ble," he reported, and he feared that the situation was to
worsen: "each year makes fearful additions to the ranks of
these prospective recruits of infamy and sin, and from this
corrupt and festering fountain flows a ceaseless stream to our
lowest brothel—to the Penitentiary and to the State Prison!"
(Hawes, 1971, p.91).

Historian of childhood Joseph M. Hawes found an epidemic
of juvenile crime in the nineteenth century *New York Times*:
"Nearly every day small boys commit highway robbery—usually
by snatching the purses of ladies—in the streets of New York
and Brooklyn." In 1890, the *Times* reported a case in which two
boys, one seven and one ten, were charged with stealing horses;
for the ten-year-old, it was a second offense for the same crime.
The *Times* also complained about juvenile gangs, "half-drunken,
lazy, worthless vagabonds," shooting guns and sometimes
terrorizing people in their homes (Hawes, 1971, pp. 130-31).

Children were, of course, not just committing crimes in sin-
ridden New York. Hawes begins his book on juvenile delinquency in nineteenth century America with a chapter on Jesse
Pomeroy, the notorious "Boy Fiend" of Boston, who tortured
and murdered young children in the 1870s (Hawes, 1971).
Down in mid-century Houston, a ten-year-old boy drew a pistol
from his pocket and shot his younger protagonist, fortunately,
in this case, without killing him(Mennel, 1973, p. 73). And at
the turn of the century, the president of the University of
Tennessee despaired that more than half of the persons
indicted for crimes in Knox County, the home of the University,
were children (Dabney, 1901, p.46). If readers think that these
examples of youthful crimes and violence are exceptions cited
simply to support the thesis this essay, I challenge them to

spend a few hours reading a daily newspaper of any previous period. Every generation has a youth crisis.

In the minds of many social reformers, the solution to the crisis of youth and the moral degeneration of society in the nineteenth century was public schools. They were established not just to foster literacy, but to teach proper values to the young; not only to save the individual from crime, poverty, sin, and aimlessness, but to save the society from social degeneration as well. Those who perceive a moral breakdown today because of court decisions on school prayer or "secular humanism" in textbooks would find comfort in the persistent evangelical Protestant messages in nineteenth-century school textbooks; moral relativity was not a theme. In the omnipresent moral lessons in textbooks, good boys and girls obeyed their parents and teachers or suffered dire consequences, and good deeds were rewarded, often immediately and materially. Ruth Miller Elson's *Guardians of Tradition* provides an analysis of the themes of nineteenth century schoolbooks (Elson, 1964). Those who hope for a moral regeneration by returning to the unambiguous teaching of virtue in school might also ponder Horace Mann's outrage about students' drawings in such books and their carvings on school desks: "with such ribald inscriptions, and with the carvings of such obscene emblems, as would make a heathen blush" (Mann, 1841, p. 59).

Faith in character education as the panacea for a perceived epidemic of societal "immorality" may have exacerbated the problems of school discipline. As state-wide systems of public schools were established and then made compulsory, schools enrolled a larger proportion of unruly children. In 1889, Illinois passed a new and tougher compulsory education law. The Chicago Public Schools attempted to enforce the law, and "a number of "incorrigible" children came into the schools," but they were soon dismissed because their behavior could not be controlled (Hawes, 1971, p. 164).

But the point should not be missed: incorrigible, even violent, behavior by some schoolchildren has been a continuing problem in American society. The growing size of the list of references collected for a projected study of discipline problems in the first half of the twentieth century is making me ponder early retirement. And severe discipline problems preceded compulsory education in urban schools. In my study of schools on the frontier, for example, I found numerous cases of flagrant misbehavior and sometimes outright rebellion. In a log school in Michigan, as a teacher (who from accounts of his cruelty got what he deserved) prepared to whip one of the students, the others "piled onto him like an enraged swarm of bees, with fistcuffs, kicks, pinching, biting, sticking pins and awls into him." Other students held the door closed, but some carpenters who had been working nearby forced themselves into the room and saved him from the enraged students (Williams, 1882, p. 547).

Ancedotal evidence may be interesting, but it can also bias our images of an era. The key question in this essay remains unanswered. Do a higher ratio of children and youth seriously misbehave than they used to? I don't know and, in a quantified sense, there is no accurate way to find out. As historians often point out, nineteenth and early twentieth century social statistics are notoriously unreliable. And misbehavior is contextual; perceptions of the seriousness of youthful behavior change over time. Masturbation and idleness (the latter especially by lower-class youth) were viewed as especially serious in mid and late nineteenth century. Gender, class, and racial bias were even more pronounced than they are today. Lower class girls were frequently punished or even committed to reform schools for alleged promiscuity or "sluttish" behavior. Behavior that might have caused working class or black youth to be expelled from school or sent to reform schools was often overlooked or tolerated when committed by middle-class children, especially by white children in the South (Schlossman and Wallach, 1978; Sutton, 1988). What is clear, however, is the constancy of a perception by each generation of American that it is in the midst of an epidemic of juvenile delinquency, resulting from a moral breakdown.

## The Problem with the Myth
What is wrong with the myth of a more innocent time when children actually behaved as they do on reruns of *Little House on the Prairie* or *The Waltons*? When we live in a resented present,

we like to "remember" a lovelier past, even if it is more fantasy than real. Such a past is akin to those idealized paintings of rural scenes that Southerners, and I suppose others, call barn art. They may not realistically depict the past, but so what? We can't hurt the past by distorting it. What harm does it do to idealize it?, lovers of such art might ask. Art critics may look down their noses at the picture of the Model T Ford, rusting in front of the abandoned old home place. But their views can easily be dismissed by those who admire such pictures; are the critics not merely effete snobs anyway?

Isn't the same true with idealized history? The answer, of course, is no. History is a policy study—we justify particular policies rather than others on the basis of what we believe our experiences to have been. The way we remember our past will have much to do with our perceptions of our present and its problems. It is not enough to show that children were not the way they are depicted by the traditional minded, we must understand why they are depicted that way. And we must be aware of the dangers of believing the myth: it causes us to look in the wrong places for answers to real problems.

Historians understand that even personal memories do not represent objective reality; rather memories are constructed in particularly ways to meet present needs.* Conservative-minded people in particular, are likely to recollect a past that is warmer, more harmonious, and more virtuous than a present in which their values may no longer dominate. In turn, their solutions to contemporary problems are likely to involve attempts to recreate conditions that resemble an idealized past. If they believe that the "surveys" cited in the *Blue and White* are just another piece of evidence for a loss of goodness in social changes such as insidious growth of "secular humanism". They may argue for solutions such as returning group prayer to classrooms, more corporal punishment, returning group prayer to classrooms, more corporal punishment, textbooks that reflect "traditional" values, and educational choice, including the right to attend private schools at public expense.

---

* The March 1989 issue of the *Journal of American History* was devoted to an exploration of this phenomenon.

If, on the other hand, we understand that discipline problems are as old as schools and that some school children have always engaged in destructive, violent behavior, we may look to more realistic ways of reducing the need for children to behave in ways that are costly to them and to society. Nostrums based on distorted perceptions of the way it was only exacerbate the plight of troubled children.

# References

Brenzel, B. (1983) *Daughters of the State: A Social Portrait of the First Reform School for Girls in North America, 1865-1905,* Cambridge, Massachusetts, The MIT Press.

Dabney, C. (1901) "The Public School Problem in the South." *Proceedings of the Fourth Conference for Education in the South.*

Elson, R. (1964) *Guardians of Tradition: American Schoolbooks of the Nineteenth Century,* Lincoln, University of Nebraska Press.

Eubanks, D. (1987) "Only God and His Word Can Save Our Nation", *The Blue and White, 59.*

Hawes, J. (1971) *Children in Urban Society: Juvenile Delinquency in Nineteenth-Century America,* New York, Oxford University Press.

Kaestle, C. (1978) "Social Change, Discipline, and the Common School in Early Nineteenth-Century America," *Journal of Interdisciplinary History,* 9, pp. 1-17.

Mann, H. (1841) *Fourth Annual Report of the Board of Education,* Boston, Dutton and Wentworth, State Printers.

Mann, H. (1843) *Sixth Annual Report of the Board of Education,* Boston, Dutton and Wentworth, State Printers.

Mennel, R. (1973) *Thorns and Thistles: Juvenile Delinquents in the United States, 1825-1940*, Hanover, New Hampshire, The University Press of New England.

Schlossman, S. and Wallach, S. (1978) "The Crime of Precocious Sexuality: Female Juvenile Delinquency in the Progressive Era," *Harvard Educational Review*, 48 pp. 65-94.

Sutton, J. (1988) *Stubborn Children: Controlling Delinquency in the United State, 1640-1981*, Berkeley, University of California Press.

Williams, B. (1882) "My Recollections of the Early School of Detroit that I attended from the Years 1816 to 1819," *Michigan Pioneer and Historical Collection*, 5, pp. 547-550.

# Kathleen Berry

**What does it mean to misbehave?**
In Anthony Burgess' book, *Clockwork Orange*, the youths of the community garnish their lives with incomprehensible language and acts of violence. Written in the 1960's, the images and actions of this fictional work have became a reality in the minds of the general public; an image that suggests the youths misbehave more than they used to. Before we survey the conditions that give predominance to the notion of students as misbehaving, the organic meanings of the word misbehave will be presented.

The Latin meaning of misbehavior return us to the original experience in which the word emerged. For misbehave, the Latin root is *male se gerere* which means: *male* - badly, wrongly, unfortunately, not; *se* - himself/herself; while *gerere* means to carry about, to wear, to display an appearance, to act a part, to conduct oneself or to entertain a feeling. Which now leaves us with the sense of a person who misbehaves as someone who badly or wrongly conducts himself/herself, does NOT act a part and so on. Now we cannot, as concerned readers, take the word misbehave for granted. Given different situational contexts in which the word misbehavior is used can actually create a fuller understanding to the question of whether students do in fact misbehave more than they used to.

**Student behavior is situationally judged:**
When others consider the way students behave, a judgment is being made; a judgment based on the assumption that there is a proper, correct, standard, or agreed manner of carrying oneself. In other words, to behave means to conduct oneself in accordance with recognized and approved criteria. Which criteria is used depends on many different situational contexts; historical, social, political, economic, religious and many more.

Popular books, such as those by Bloom (1987) and Hirsh (1987), are examples, which abuse the situational context in order to present the view that today's students are culturally illiterate and closed-minded. Authors, such as previously mentioned, use the propaganda techniques of degrading present day students by glorifying the past; a view which distorts the true conditions and attitudes of today's students. If students are being educated in an atmosphere of neo-conservatism and fundamentalism—the outcome of the dominant cry of "back to the basics"—authors like Bloom and Hirsch, politicians like those of the Bush administration, and religious leaders reduced to fundamentalism are only a few of the many who capitialize on the situational context to portray students as lacking many qualities of the students of the past. So what were the qualities of students in the past? Whose past?

For example, let me reminisce about student life in the fifties and early sixties. Students from that generation can share stories of conformity, complacency, and silenced voices. Stories about regulations that forced us to wear middle class clothes in spite of our parents blue collar incomes; incidents of writing lines and hours of detentions if we dared to question the information transmitted. And to be seen as different meant isolation. To be heard, for example, as a physical handicapped female with a voice and a curious mind was impossible. In fact, it seems students of the past, except for the select few, very few, were less interested, less exposed, and less able to participate in what Hirsh and Bloom romantize as cultural literacy and rigourous intellectual pursuits.

However, neither an attack on right wing education nor advocacy for left wing policies is what is ultimately in question here. The problem lies with understanding student misbehavior as a necessary means of questioning not only the allegedly required cultural content which "every American should know", but also seeing misbehavior as a means to challenge the status quo and cultural bias of the content. Another crucial aspect to consider about student misbehavior asks what it is about the students' life which evokes particular misbehavior; from that of "horsing around" in class to that of extreme physical and mental violence, to all the types of misbehavior in between. Deliberation on the contexts in which student misbehavior reveals itself leads us to ponder the value of their misbehavior as an indication about how we are as human beings and, more importantly, how we want the quality of our future life to be. The quality of life question requires critical thoughts and actions.

**Misbehavior as critical thought and action:**
When a student is labeled as misbehaving, two elements are in play. First, according to the previous definition, a student who misbehaves does not conduct himself/herself or play a part in the standard, expected behaviors. Secondly, to misbehave means to fracture the ordinary; to break from the conventional structures that are already in place. It is in the misbehavior of the latter type that we can find the seeds of critical thought and actions.

I intend, in the context of this discussion, for critical to be used in the metaphorical sense of a "critical care" unit of a hospital. A person in charge of a critical care patient is sensitive to every vital sign of existence, every minute detail, every fine discrimination. A time where every judgment and every action determines whether a person lives or dies. Thus critical, in the educational context, means to have teachers and students living together with a attitude of caring for every detail of life, to be aware of the dangerous and vital quality of our existence. Misbehavior is necessary to keep us alert and conditioned for critical thought and action. So what does this unconventional view of misbehavior evoke?

Misbehavior arises out of some sense of dissatisfaction with the structures of the human condition; out of boredom, mean-inglessness, frustration, or curiousity about the way life is. In this manner of not behaving as expected there is an attentive-ness to the details of life; an attentiveness that does not neces-sarily occur in the passive thoughts and conforming actions of standard behavior. As creatures of habit we can pass over or take for granted the critical details of life. Perhaps we have experienced separation, divorce, illness, death, or some other fracture in the structure of our daily lives. Whether by natural events or through misbehavior, it is in the collapse of ordinary, everyday structures where illumination and attentiveness to details receive critical thought and action. We no longer take life's moments for granted when structures which govern our lives are in jeopardy.

Once the structures that governed behavior are changed, eliminated, modified, clarified, or questioned by misbehavior, a student lives in that flux. On the one hand, the gaps left by a break down or elimination of familiar structures can be filled by exploiters ready to blame student behaviors or colonizers ready to fill the gaps with great promises of solutions and return to "the good old days." On the other hand, adults involved with students begin to accept the ideas of the exploiters and coloniz-ers without noticing that students are usually caught in the middle, wanting only to make sense of their lives and trusting education to prepare them to create and live in future struc-tures.

What emerges in all the chaos of break-down is what, as Foucault (1977) claims, are educational structures based on bourgeois ideology which exercises functions that traditionally belonged to the police and also reinforces all the structures of confinement. Students who, living within these institutional organizations, attempt to find adequate forms of struggle against the confines of imposed powers, are labeled as misbe-havior problems. In turn, to avoid confrontation, they fall prey to various forms of verbal battering and disenfranchised partic-ipation in their own education. A return to the old structures, such as the so-called basics (which really have come to mean the familiar structures of the past to those who use this term), only serve to confine students further and eliminate them from the initiatives needed for participation in the different struggles of their future.

No matter what the organizational structures, elements or idealogical bent is, a student in times of liberalism, learns in the liberal way and the liberal content. In the 1960's for example, when the left wing ideology was more influential in determining the view of what and how students should learn, the atmosphere of radicalism was the predominate view of students. If we remember correctly, passivity and conformity in students of the sixties would have been considered by some as misbehavior.

What is needed is an exposure to all the contents and forms of life but always with a critical understanding of what it means for the quality of life. A grandiose statement—the quality of life—but to keep the critical consciousness alive by asking: what it means for our lives? So where does this leave the students at any time in their education?

With a critical consciousness, the student learns the content and the form of all the games played in education. Whatever the political, economic, social, religious or other views of the world, it is the critical consciousness that must remain alive without succumbing to any of the pressures of one view. In this way the student recognizes the existence, not only of the world views available that construct the world but also how the student's knowledge and values are constructed. On the one hand the student recognizes the world as constructed of many views, knowledge, and values. On the other hand, and perhaps more significant, is that the student recognizes his or her place in the world. With these elements in place, the task is no longer just to be or know the world.. The task is to live critically in the world, with as vast and deep understanding as possible but with a constant questioning of the world and self. It is in this constant questioning that teacher and students become sensitive to gaps and shift in their knowledge, values, and actions.

**To question is to open the mind:**
Merleau - Ponty (1962) states: "We don't lose the life of curiosity as long as we keep the question before us, who are we?" (p.81). When five year old Michael asked his mother; "Mom, how did you know I was going to be a Michael when I was born?" is an indication of the priority of the question as an attitude in life. However, research tends to show that by the age of seven or eight, the high-level curiosity questions, similiar to that asked by Michael, are very limited to non-existent in the repertoire of questions. But it is our critical questioning that excites and arouscs us to be responsive to the matters being encountered. The questioning of life's contents, forms of knowledge, beliefs, and actions, is where the logical structure of openness is found. For a question to open the world for the student's exploration and interpretation, one is required to accept that to question means to "not conduct oneself as others." Similiar to the notion of critical thought and action as misbehavior to break, modify, change, or eliminate traditional structures that have no meaning, a question implies misbehavior also; that is, don't go

along with the thoughts and actions of others just to "act the part."

A question refuses to take the world for granted; it becomes a way of being in the world as much as a knowing about the world. The intent of students' questions should remain as a possible means for them, not just to grasp at facts, but to "apprehend a possibility for being" (Ricouer, 1981, p. 56). Openness to experience involves many moments of disappointment, risk-taking, and a terrifying energy of playing in the unknown. What may seem like misbehavior to the concerned adult, may be no more than the student's way of questioning the world. Yes, there are the little questions that create everyday misbehavior and there are the questions that emerge as violent. For our purposes, it is to keep in perspective the intensity of the questions, but also remind ourselves that misbehavior has the structure of a question; not to be spared the students but to emerge as possible insight into world and self.

Insight, a seeing into, a light into, is always an escape from that which was dark or unclear but is no longer just a question that holds the student captive in the behaviors of others or one's own. As students break through the knowledge of the before moments and into self-knowledge they are no longer deceived or captive. It is this break with the old that can be frightening and appear as mindlessness to the adult. The self-knowledge that comes from asking questions is not to be misinterpreted as selfishness (a misbehavior wrongly associated with the "do your own thing era"). Self-knowledge, which requires a question, propels the student from the external descriptions of the outside world to the inner discipline at the personal level of knowledge and being. The strength of self-knowledge empowers a student. The misbehavior of a questioning student is necessary and on-going.

**The need for infinite misbehavior:**
We can view life as the romantic, scientific, analytical, religious and in many other ways. But in all the history of thought, the cliche most appropriate is "the most constant thing about life is change" (taxes and death also but that changes too!). In so noting, we must accept that life is in a constant flux of ways of

being and knowing. Although some people might hold stedfast to life as a form of solidarity while around them, blindly so sometimes, lies, within that pseudo-solidarity, the notion of crisis.

To repeat the line of thought previously developed, crisis means a rupture of traditional thought and action. Within the gap left by the collapse of structure, lies a whole region of possibilities for revised or new thought and actions. It is this region of possibility, created by the critical and questioning "misbehavior" of students, where the original intention of education takes place; *educate* - the power to bring forth, lead forth the potential of students to reach their highest abilities. Until students enter into the region of infinite possibilities for thoughts and action does their real education begin. And that entry process depends on the student ability to question and break with the closed systems of thoughts and behaviors already in place; which leaves students and teachers with, instead of the comfort and enclosure of a finite system of knowledge and behavior, a compulsive power for the development of an infinite consciousness.

Bloom, Hirsch and others may talk about the lack of tradition or structure in today's education. These authors and their proponents forget, conveniently, the flux in exposure to cultural knowledge and actions. In so doing, their ideas if put into action, retard if not eliminate the fundamental promise of education; which is the development of an infinite conscious-ness for creative thought and actions in our students. So what?

Why misbehave is like asking why bother with getting an education or, one step further, why bother with life like it is. Well, a question may evoke the infinite consciousness but it also has limitations. However, to impose limitations to the possibil-ity for infinite thoughts and actions undermines the fundamen-tal notion of democracy: the freedom of thought and action for every individual. Yes, individual thought and freedom has its limit also, given that we are social beings. So our possibility for the development of the infinite consciousness demands that students' "misbehaviors" begin to question and be critical of the way life is. Questioning is not necessarily a debate or argument to win or lose but a way to open the students and teachers up to a conversation; conversations about the world and self.

So in ending this conversation, I hope that students misbehave more than they used to. The complacency and passiveness of "behaving" students frightens me. Is the world really O.K.? Do we really live in Utopia? Why do students have to "know what every American should know;" to be contestants on game shows — or — to put into actions those ideas which will raise the quality of life for every "individual"?

# References

Bloom, A. (1987) *The Closing of the American Mind*, New York, Simon and Schuster.

Foucault, M. (1977) *Language, Counter - Memory, Practice: Selected Essays and Interviews*, Oxford, Basil Blackwell.

Hirsh, E.D. (1987) *Cultural Literacy: What Every American Should Know*, New York, Random House.

Merleau - Ponty, M. (1962) *Phenomenology of Perception*, London, Routledge and Kegan.

Ricouer, P. (1981) *Hermeneutics and the Human Sciences*, Cambridge, Cambridge University Press.

# Chapter V

# Teacher Education: What is good teaching, and how do we teach people to be good teachers?

**Eleanor Blair Hilty**

**Andrew Gitlin**

# Eleanor Blair Hilty

The past decade has produced numerous national reports that have called for the reform of American education. These reports have reflected the depth of public dissatisfaction with the schools. In a recent publication of the Office of Educational Research and Improvement (1990), Assistant Secretary, Christopher T. Cross added his voice to this call for reform:

> Schools have changed less than any other public institution in meeting the requirements of our changing society, even though education is the fundamental tool that enables all other public and private institutions to exist.

The schools are perceived as institutions that no longer "work;" a significant portion of young people fail or dropout of school each year and good teachers either leave the profession or "burnout." Critics of American education argue that the welfare of this nation is in jeopardy if the public schools do not commit to meaningful change in this decade.

The first wave of school reform efforts has focused on the need for good teachers. If we cannot train good teachers and place them in schools where they will be successful, then the future of American education is tenuous indeed. The focus of these reform efforts has been a reconsideration of teacher training and entry into the profession. This focus, while useful, may be premature. Attempts to restructure or "re-form" the schools in a new image lack an ideology that informs or shapes the direction of these efforts. While questions about good teaching and the training of good teachers are central to any serious effort to make the public schools more amenable to the needs of society, even these questions require a set of beliefs about the aims and purposes of the educational process. The calls for action, however, are general and provide little direction for the restructuring of teacher education. Recommendations for reform address selected problems, but a vision of the public schools that considers the social, political and institutional influences on the educational process is not evident in these reports.

A discussion of good teaching and the training of good teachers must consider the context of teachers' work, the schools. What good is served by restructuring teacher training in the absence of a consideration of how good teaching functions within the institutional constraints of most schools? Teachers operate in an environment that is structured in such a way that good teaching becomes the exception, rather than the norm. Jackson (1986) argues that a consideration of good teaching must include reference to the "cultural context" of teaching. Under this rubric he includes "the awarenesses, presuppositions, expectations, and everything else that impinges upon the action or that contributes to its interpretation by the actors themselves and by outsiders as well" (p. 96). The social milieu of schools perpetuate stereotypical gender roles. Bennett and LeCompte (1990) describe schools as "pedagogical harems" where the activities of female teachers are governed and directed by male administrators (p. 258). Most of the decisions that guide the daily lives of teachers are made by individuals removed from the daily tasks and responsibilities that characterize teaching. A lack of control over their work environment diminishes the attempts of teachers to practice as autonomous professionals. As a group, teachers are powerless to implement meaningful change in their own classrooms. The talents of individual teachers are "chained" to "teacher-proof" curriculums that limit independent and creative action (Giroux, 1988). This orientation has contributed to the deskilling of teachers; a process where there is a reduction in the level of skill required to teach (Pinar, 1989). Teacher education does little to prepare teachers to become leaders in institutions where they have little power, status or decision-making ability. A failure to recognize the lack of congruity between teacher training and practice means that potential teachers receive training that provides little preparation for placement in teaching assignments where the "realities" of teaching force new teachers to exchange their ideals for educational practices that do not meet the educational challenges of a new decade. Teachers are the key to good teaching, yet we won't see good teachers emerge in an environment that is authoritarian and does little to liberate the talents of individual teachers.

### What is Good Teaching?

Good teachers *do* exist despite a preponderance of evidence to contrary. Efforts to define and identify good teaching have been plagued by attempts to standardize the form and function of good teaching. The language of "effective" teaching research denotes a focus on efficiency and outcome, rather than process. An Office of Educational Research and Improvement publication (1990), *Issues in Education,* included among its recommendations for middle school improvement the following proposal: "Education must be rigorous and interesting. The people who work in it must be accountable." The implication, of course, is that teachers are simply workers who must demonstrate their worth through productivity. Good teaching, thus defined, translates into good test scores. Recommendations like these reflect a view of teaching that is unacceptable.

In a recent essay, Erickson (1984) recounts the story of a young Eskimo who learned to hunt seal from his father. The young man was advised that "if you want to hunt seal you have to learn to think like a seal" (p. 527). Likewise, if you want to understand, identify, or even teach good teachers you have to learn to think like a good teacher. This analogy is intended to convey two thoughts:

1) Good teaching is a cognitive process that cannot be understood in the absence of a consideration of "teacher thinking," and

2) Teaching is a personal experience. The voices of good teachers must be included in discussions of teaching. These propositions seem obvious, however this kind of thinking is not reflected in the literature on teaching.

Good teaching must be defined as an intellectual process. The process must be emphasized, not the outcomes. A focus on outcomes obstructs a consideration of the proper role of the classroom teacher as an intellectual (Giroux, 1988). Resnick (1987) recommends that "models of shared intellectual functioning" must shape our views of classroom practice (p. 19). Contemporary research on teaching directs our attention to teacher thinking and the construction of meaning between students and teachers (Cochran-Smith & Lytle, 1990). There is an absence of research on the ways in which teachers understand and think about their teaching or even the manner in which students experience good teaching. Good teaching can never be a set of skills in isolation of a capacity to think about one's actions or reflect critically on the process or product of a teaching effort. Giroux (1989) admonishes recent efforts to define teachers "as clerks or technicians." Good teachers are intellectuals first and critical decision-makers second. It is the ability of teachers to be constantly reviewing their actions and evaluating outcomes that sets them apart from machines. At a minimum, teachers must constantly question the unstated or "taken-for-granted" assumptions and beliefs that guide classroom practice (Bennett & LeCompte, 1990, p. 257). Good teaching defies simple explanation and requires a vision of teaching that encompasses the creative and intellectual components of the process.

Seeing teachers in this manner requires that we have multiple models of "good" teaching. Teachers, good and bad, bring to teaching a culmination of experiences both personal and professional. It is imperative that the voices of teachers be integrated into any discussion of good teaching. McLaren (1989) discusses "voice" as a significant "pedagogical concept" because it acknowledges the interaction of cultural and historical variables in the dialogue that occurs between teachers and students (p. 229). Teachers come to teaching with a set of beliefs about the world generally, and about teaching and learning specifically. Good teaching is idiosyncratic and takes different forms. It is a process that is defined and mediated by the experiences of a particular teacher and a group of students. It is paradoxical that efforts to improve the schools have excluded teachers from the dialogue when ultimately they are the individuals who will fail or succeed at reforming American education. Discussions of good teaching that ignore the voices of teachers are incomplete and produce the lists of measurable skills and behaviors that characterize attempts to make teachers accountable.

Good teaching cannot be measured, but the process can be described. Good teachers view the teaching process as a creative endeavor. They establish learning communities that produce students who are independent, self-motivated learners. Good teaching is often exciting and seldom boring. The classrooms of these teachers are characterized by mutual respect, collaboration and connection. Good teachers recognize and support cultural diversity. A good teacher helps students to understand the democratic principles that shape our society while questioning practices that lead to the inequitable distribution of knowledge, power and resources (Greene, 1985; Giroux, 1989). Good teachers create a positive atmosphere for dialogue, reflection and debate. Good teachers encourage the development of intellectual skills that lead to critical, reflective thinking. An emphasis on basic skills, minimal literacy, and standardized tests are the antithesis of good teaching. Critics will, nevertheless, charge that classrooms should be well-managed and academically rigorous. Good teachers do share the responsibility for learning and behavior with students, however, I will argue that students taught in this manner are more successful on tests, in schools, in the workplace, and in social relationships. Good teaching produces good students.

Not surprisingly, good teachers are also good learners. They are exemplary models of a lifetime commitment to thinking, questioning, and learning. An appreciation of the many forms of good teaching would liberate teachers by giving them the freedom to develop a style of pedagogy that reflects their understanding of teaching and learning. No one would ever request, or even desire, that all doctors or lawyers practice according to *one* model. Does it not seem equally unreasonable to assume that all teachers must teach the same way?

Good teaching requires a restructuring of the school environment. Proposals for reform have emphasized "top-down" control of the profession (Hill, 1989; Bennett & LeCompte, 1990). This will *not* produce good teachers. Good teachers must have control over the instructional process in their classrooms (Giroux, 1988). Good teachers are pedagogical leaders who are attempting to transform and empower students through learning experiences that foster critical and reflective inquiry. Teachers must work in environments that allow them to model these same skills. Administrators should work for teachers, or at the very least, they must be colleagues who share equally the responsibility for designing successful schools. Many people would find this latter proposition laughable, since it is a radical departure from the situation in most schools. However, it is the unequal distribution of power in most schools that has consistently led to the mediocre performance of both teachers and students. I argue that we will *not* see good teaching become the norm in our schools until new teachers enter the schools with the knowledge and skills to confidently demand the right to work in an environment that recognizes them as competent professionals and allows them to freely and optimally do what they have been trained to do, teach.

**The Training of Good Teachers**
The imperative for teacher education is to produce good teachers. Robert Maynard Hutchins stated that "the best education for the best, is the best education for all." Adler (1982) used this quote to support his proposals for educational reform in *The Paideia Proposal.* In discussing the education of teachers, the same principle holds true, "the best education for the best, is the best education for teachers."

Teacher education has historically been a second-class education; a ghetto for students (and teachers) who are perceived as intellectually shallow and lacking the ability to study a "real" discipline. These programs typically reflect a lack of commitment to scholarly ideals. This is not surprising when one considers that research findings consistently show a lack of scholarly activity on the part of teacher educators (Cruickshank, 1990). Correspondingly, the involvement of teacher educators in school reform has been minimal. In reality teacher educators suffer the same lack of status and power as the teachers that they train. It is not likely that teacher educators will ever be totally excluded from the preparation of teachers. However, even if their involvement is limited, the success of teacher preparation will hinge on the commitment of the education professoriate to a new model of teacher training; a model that is scholarly and intellectual. If that commitment is absent, a restructuring of teacher education will have little impact on the public schools.

There is a relationship between good teaching and the quality of the preparation of teachers. Teacher education is a bridge between content and practice through the study of pedagogy. Teacher education becomes the "scaffolding" that negotiates and supports the social and cognitive relationships between the "how" and "what" of good teaching (Wood, Bruner, & Ross, 1976; Erickson, 1984, p. 533). Shor (1987) argues that "all of school is actually 'teacher education,' a paideia socializing teachers in how to teach and what to learn" (p. 18). Thus, every aspect of the education of teachers must embrace the highest academic ideals and clearly reflect a renewed vision of good teaching. Good teachers will only become critical, reflective practitioners if their training encourages the development of those skills. In my syllabus for an undergraduate foundations class, I use the following quote from Paulo Freire (1987):

> This is a great discovery, education is politics: when a teacher discovers that he or she is a politician, too, the teacher has to ask, What kind of politics am I doing in the classroom? That is, in favor of whom am I being a teacher? The teacher works in favor of something and against something. Because of that, he or she will have another great question, How to be consistent in my teaching practice with my political choice? I cannot proclaim my liberating dream and in the next day be authoritarian in my relationship with the students.

Teacher education in a very broad sense is an education that recognizes the social, political and institutional influences that shape personal action. Good teachers understand the relationship of these influences to teaching and learning. Teaching, thus defined becomes an experience that liberates and empowers both practitioner and student.

The reform of American education demands that teacher education be fundamentally restructured and organized to be academically rigorous and interdisciplinary. Teacher education as it is presently conceived emphasizes vocational skills rather than intellectual skills (Pinar, 1989). Teachers spend a significant part of their training studying pedagogy to the exclusion of basic knowledge and concepts in the liberal arts and sciences. Most recommendations for reform in teacher education focus on limiting the professional education requirements for teachers and increasing the teaching field component. These proposals translate into fewer teacher education courses and more content, less of the "how" and more the "what" of teaching. These changes, however, are quantitative rather than qualitative (Shor, 1987). The quality of the educational experience provided in all classes is a concern. Classes throughout the college curriculum are characterized by rote memorization of isolated fragments of knowledge. There are few attempts to situate knowledge within broader themes or concepts. Shor suggests a quality education that is shaped by Freirean principles and encourages active student participation that is "critical, values-oriented, multicultural, student-centered, experiential, research-minded, and interdisciplinary" (p. 22). These are the characteristics of a quality education. The education of teachers must reflect this orientation at every level of their training. Less or more of specific courses will not produce good teachers. Accompanying recommendations for a more rigorous education of teachers must be a commitment by all educators to *quality* educational experiences.

For many teachers, the most meaningful experience in teacher education is student teaching. The influence of this experience on teachers demands that teacher educators consider ways to connect this experience to a new understanding of the educational process. However, even this experience becomes problematic when preservice teachers are inadequately prepared and then placed with teachers who do not model good teaching as I have described it. Under the guise of "reality," these teachers demonstrate "tired" practices that get the job done, but do nothing to fundamentally change the way we "do" school. These experiences obviously leave an impression on new teachers who are frantically trying to cope with the demands of teaching, but these experiences frequently defeat the efforts of teacher educators to proclaim a new vision of teaching and learning. Student teaching, in this manner, indoctrinates and socializes preservice teachers to an unacceptable norm.

Obviously, there needs to be more collaboration between teacher educators and practitioners in the schools. A commitment to a new model of teaching requires that efforts be made to connect training to practice. This requires that *both* teachers and teacher educators combine their knowledge and experience to consider ways to bridge this gap (Cochran-Smith & Lytle, 1990).  Good teachers should be deeply involved with teacher education programs in higher education and in the schools.  A coherency between training and practice is the only way to make good teaching the norm rather than the exception.

The public fascination with school reform will not last.  We must take this moment to seriously embrace meaningful change in the field of education.  A reconceptualization of teacher training is the first step (Pinar, 1989).  The problems that characterize teaching will remain unchanged until the *entire* process of teacher education is reconsidered and a new vision is articulated.  The emphasis in the training of teachers must be on intellectual development.  Within this realm, preservice teachers should have experiences that model and facilitate the development of the capacity to be a critical, reflective thinker.  Remember, this is not just the best education for teachers, it is the best education for all students.

# References

Adler, M. J.  (1982).  *The Paideia Proposal: An educational manifesto.*  New York: MacMillan.

Bennett, K. P. & Lecompte, M. D.  (1990).  *How schools work: A sociological analysis of education.*  White Plains, NY: Longman.

Cochran-Smith, M. & Lytle, S. L.  (1990).  "Research on teaching and teacher research: The issues that divide."  *Educational Researcher, 19,* 3, 2-11.

Cruickshank, D. R.  (1990).  *Research that informs teachers and teacher educators.*  Bloomington, IN: Phi Delta Kappa Educational Foundation.

Erickson, F. E. (1984). "School literacy, reasoning, and civility: An anthropologist's perspective." *Review of Educational Research, 54*, 4, 525-546.

Freire, P. (1987). *A pedagogy for liberation: Dialogues on transforming education.* South Hadley, MA: Bergin & Garvey.

Giroux, H. (1988). *Teachers as intellectuals: Toward a critical pedagogy of learning.* South Hadley, MA: Bergin & Garvey.

Giroux, H. (1989, May). "Rethinking education reform in the age of George Bush." *Phi Delta Kappan,* 728-730.

Greene, M. (1985). "The role of education in democracy." *Educational Horizons, 63*, 3-9.

Hill, D. (1989, September/October). "Fixing the system from the top down." *Teacher Magazine,* 50-55.

Jackson, P. W. (1986). *The Practice of Teaching.* New York: Teachers College Press.

McLaren, P. (1989). *Life in Schools.* New York: Longman.

Office of Educational Research. (1990, August). *Issues in Education.* Washington, DC: U. S. Department of Education.

Pinar, W. F. (1989, January-February). "A reconceptualization of teacher education." *Journal of Teacher Education,* 9-12.

Resnick, L. B. (1987). "Learning in school and out." *Educational Researcher, 16*, 10, 13-20.

Shor, I. (1987). "Educating the educators: A Freirean approach to the crisis in teacher education." In Shor, I. (ed.), *Freire for the classroom: A sourcebook for liberatory teaching.*

Wood, B., Bruner, J. S., & Ross, G. (1976). "The role of tutoring in problem solving." *Journal of Child Psychology and Psychiatry, 17*, 89-100.

# Andrew Gitlin

Considering what is good teaching requires an analysis of the question itself and a response. To analyze the question, I will focus primarily on the issues of authorship—who is responding to the question—and purpose—what I hope this essay will accomplish. After doing so, I will then respond to the question as I conceive it. Included in this response will be a discussion of the tension between ambiguity and certainty, the politics of education and the school context.

## The Question

Who is responding to a particular question or concern, the author, is not usually viewed as an important piece of information in examining the nature of the argument. As a consequence, the issue of who gets to speak and who is silenced is rarely considered. For example, without considering the question of authorship, the way this essay supports a historical trend where academics have been given the opportunity to speak about teaching while teachers have for the most part been denied such an opportunity, would not be apparent. By pointing to this trend, I don't want to suggest that only teachers should comment on teaching. Rather, my point is that one of the more hidden aspects of this essay is the way it strengthens a hierarchical relationship between teachers and outsiders that leaves those most intimately involved with students without much opportunity to speak out about teaching. While the intent of this essay is to raise some issues typically not discussed in debates about good teaching, when viewed from the point of view of who is speaking and who is silenced this essay is quite typical.

Besides clarifying the issue of authorship, it is also important to consider how my understanding of the question influences my response. Of particular note is the question of context. Is good teaching something that can only determined by knowing contextual factors such as the type of students found in the school, the mandated district policies, and the class size? Or, are schools so alike that one can make some generalizations about good teaching without explicitly considering context?

Because good teaching takes place in a context that makes certain types of activities possible and likely , and others less likely, my position is that good teaching is enhanced by stripping away contextual constraints, thereby allowing the abilities and insights of teachers to emerge.

Another important issue that must be addressed before I launch into a response is what I hope this essay will accomplish. Is the purpose to lay out a singular notion of good teaching that others should adopt as their own? Is the purpose to provide several views of good teaching and let the reader choose? Or is the purpose to encourage debate, and through debate, assist others in clarifying their own positions about good teaching? Because I do not believe there is one model of good teaching, it would be inappropriate to outline a conception of good teaching to convince others to adopt some part of what is said. On the other hand, I do have opinions about what good teaching is and so to suggest that it really doesn't matter which version a reader chooses is not quite honest. In contrast to these two approaches, I have decided to outline my position about good teaching in the hope that the reader will use it as a text to consider the question for themselves.

### The Response

**Ambiguity:** As one of my closest colleagues has often noted, teaching is a messy business. In fact, there are few questions about teaching that can be answered with a simple yes or a no. Instead, the response to any significant question concerning teaching is typically "maybe" or "under these circumstances" or "with these resources." Although outsiders, most notable the psychologically oriented researchers from the university, continue to assert that there are a set of laws or rules that characterize good teaching, at the level of practice the situation is always more complex, more conflictual, and less straightforward. While teachers clearly see this complexity, many strive to remove ambiguity and find certainty in what they do, no matter how fragile.

There are many good reasons for seeking out certainty in teaching, not the least of which is that teachers are rarely viewed as experts by other members of the educational community.

Coupled with the never ending stream of criticisms directed at teachers and schools, this assault puts teachers in a defensive position, where acknowledging that ambiguity is a part of teaching only furthers the suspicions and doubts about their expertise and the educational experiences offered students. Striving for certainty has advantages, in that it promises a small amount of relief from the relentless criticisms voiced about teachers, teaching, and schooling. It also, however, can act to constrain a teacher's relationships with students and their development over time.

Teachers that have a strong sense of certainty about teaching often respond to teaching situations based on a set of informal rules that are the result of numerous experiences. Don't smile until Christmas, you're the teacher not the students' friend, high expectations achieve high results, are typical of the types of informal rules teachers develop over time. These rules may be valid in a number of ways, but they also make it less likely that teachers will see the need to find out who their students are, what their background is, and what they know. In essence, the informal rules become a substitute for the time consuming process of basing teaching practice on an in depth study of students. Teaching, as a consequence, becomes a one way process where the unique and complex characteristics of students are often obscured.

Teachers with a strong sense of certainty about teaching also don't have much of a need to involve themselves in a continuing educational process that investigates issues of schooling. Because they have worked hard to be seen as expert, to be certain about what they know and how they go about teaching, education is for those who are novice, who haven't taken teaching seriously, and who are not cut out to be teachers. Being certain is part of a rite of passage from those who need to those who know. One teacher I have worked with summarized this position by saying, "I don't have any problems, why should I raise concerns about my work?"

In contrast, other teachers try to deal with ambiguity, by accepting it, by seeing it as an integral part of teaching. The quest is not to remove ambiguity from the process of teaching but to find a balance between certainty and ambiguity. These teachers do not try to remove certainty completely from teaching, because to do so is to foster frustration and chaos.  They do, however, allow ambiguity to play an important part in the teaching process by posing questions about their students, the curriculum, and the school context and base their practice on this understanding.

In my view, good teaching involves finding a point along the continuum between certainty and ambiguity that allows one to function while acknowledging the inherent messiness of the process.  This point between certainty and ambiguity encourages teachers to view teaching as a process involving continuous inquiry as opposed to a product governed by rules, both formal and informal, that can "pre-scribe" how they are to act in the classroom.  In this regard, thinking deeply about the culture, class and gender of the student before practices are outlined for what is to be done in the classroom, is part of accepting ambiguity as an inherent part of teaching.  And finally, while good teachers are confident about their knowledge and abilities, they have enough uncertainty to want to rethink what they know and to know more.  Within this view the expert is no longer someone who has arrived, who already knows, but one who is continuously engaged in educative experiences. Good teaching, in this sense, involves education for both student and teacher.

**Potitics:**  Schools are political places and teaching a political act. One of the most obvious ways schools are political is that they serve a gate keeping function which helps determine job opportunities and career paths.  Schools determine to a large degree who goes onto higher education, what types of institutions one can enter and the kinds of jobs that an individual is likely to get. Who goes through the gate, however, is not based on a set of objective criteria, but rather is closely tied to a number political decisions the school has to make about curricular form and content and the assessment of student performance . Whether a social studies text includes information on Blacks and women and how they portray these groups, for example, is inherently a political question because it influences what knowledge is seen as legitimate and attitudes about the group.

Teaching is also political because it helps shape relationships between groups and individuals. While relationships may not seem political at first glance, almost all relationships reflect power and power is political. Because the teacher/student relationship, for example, often reflects a power struggle, political questions such as is the relationship *just* are part of understanding teaching. The teacher/student relationship, therefore, should be understood not only in terms of its effectiveness but also in terms of the relations of power that are constructed. Much the same argument can be made about teachers' relationships with other teachers, administrators, and parents.

Unfortunately, the structure of schooling is set up to hide the political nature of teaching. Given that many teachers' curriculum choices are constrained by mandated textbooks and that required assessment devices make seemingly objective judgments, issues of what is legitimate knowledge and questions about the gatekeeping function of schools seem to reside outside the teacher role. In much the same way, the popularity of standardized tests reinforces the notion that relationships of all kinds are to be assessed in terms of what they produce not the relationship itself.

In spite of these structural constraints, good teachers find ways to reflect on the political side of teaching. They find ways to examine the implications of selecting particular curricular content over other content, they think through what perspectives are included and left out and importantly they adjust their practice based on this understanding. In addition, they critically consider the implications of assessment approaches and use this understanding to develop or find new approaches that reflect the diversity of their students. Finally, good teachers pay close attention to their relationships with others. They don't simply accept the typical competitive and/or isolated teacher relationship or the dominant teacher/student relationship as the way it is, as natural. Instead, they work to develop relationships among teachers and students that are based on a set of articulated and examined political ideals. In summary, they understand that questions of learning cannot be separated from questions of equity, justice and even oppression, because what is learned by students is informed by the particular teacher/student relationship as much as the material covered. In this sense, the political is not something added on to concerns of effectiveness and efficiency but are integral to those concerns.

**Context:** As I have argued earlier, good teaching cannot be understood outside of the teaching context. Unfortunately, when one steps back and looks at the types of typical school structures found in schools, it is hard to deny that they are based on the assumption that teachers are the major source of educational failure, and in need of guidance and strict control. Put simply, given the view of good teaching espoused in this essay, structures for the most part act to limit good teaching. Good teachers must find ways around these structures to practice good teaching.

There is not room in this essay to illuminate all the common school structures, so I will choose a few that appear to significantly constrain good teaching. Over the last 20 years what is called a rationalized curriculum form has gained in popularity, especially at the elementary school level. This form divides curriculum into discrete units or objectives. For each objective there is a pre and post test that determines whether a student to ready to learn the objective and once finished with the material whether she/he has mastered the material. The intent of the curriculum is to help students move along as fast as possible given their abilities.

There are surely some benefits to the rationalized curricular form. However, this form creates a one-way approach to teaching where the teacher doesn't have to know if the student is Chicano, Black or from a working class neighborhood. The teacher also doesn't have to worry about the content of the curriculum, for it is predetermined and sequentially laid out. And finally the teacher doesn't have to be concerned with assessment because these instruments are part of the curriculum package. Put directly, the teacher doesn't have to be concerned about a range of political questions that are an inherent part of teaching.

Some teachers can and do find ways to get around the rationalized curriculum. However, given the small amount of time teachers have to develop curriculum, to consider alternative assessment devices, and, yes, even the small amount of time they have to get to know their students, the rationalized curriculum has the advantage of lessening the strain on their work. Many teachers, therefore, accept this curriculum as a trade-off, a compromise forced on them from the outside. To do otherwise is to further intensify their work.

Another structure that greatly influences teachers' work is teacher evaluation. Among other things, teacher evaluation has traditionally focused on teaching outcomes such as, a quiet classroom, a well organized classroom and the ability of students to proceed through their work in an orderly and efficient manner. There is nothing inherently wrong with classrooms that are quiet, organized and efficient, however, these outcomes ignore the political nature of teaching and importantly impose a product view of teaching that is less likely to acknowledge differences among students. Finally, teachers' ability to question what is legitimate knowledge and to consider issues of opportunity is not valued by traditional teacher assessment approaches. Rather, it is the ability to get students to digest information in an orderly fashion. As is true of the rationalized curriculum, teacher evaluation endorse a narrow view of teaching that challenges the need for continuous inquiry on a wide range of issues including the important political domain.

Finally, at a fundamental level nothing influences teachers more than class size. Although much has been written to show that class size really doesn't make much of a difference, the underlying assumption of this scholarship is that teaching is a one-way process of depositing information into the heads of students. And it could be that given this mode of teaching class size is not all that important. However, if good teaching involves taking account of who the students are, and a concern for the power relations between students and teachers, among others, then class size is an enormously important consideration. This is so for several reasons. First, the larger the class size the more difficult it is to get to know who the students are, what they know, and how they differ from each other. Second, even if a super teacher could gather this sort of information, trying to alter practice based on a study of students becomes nearly impossible with large classes. Finally, as the class size becomes larger so to does the need for the teacher to resort to techniques that will establish control *over* students as opposed to sharing power *with* them. Put simply, as class size increases so too does the need for types of teacher/student relations that are inherently unjust. For all these reasons class size works against the type of good teaching articulated in this essay.

If good teaching is something the public wants to see more of, then this analysis of school structure suggests that the nature of our schools needs to be radically altered. Teachers need to have more say on the form and content of the curriculum. They also need more time to not only get to know their students but time to reflect on a range of political issues that are part and parcel of curriculum making. However, the problem isn't one of simply giving them time, it is also one of changing the reward structure of schools so that reflection on what might broadly be called the politics of teaching is valued. This means that teacher evaluation schemes can no longer be limited to what teachers do but expanded to include consideration of what they think and what they see as problems. This does not mean that an evaluator accepts teachers' views but rather that these views as is true of their behavior is part of the assessment process. Finally, class size needs to come down to the point where teachers can act on their understanding of students, assessment approaches and curricula context and form among other things.

**Conclusion**

Good teaching is not simply a matter of teachers doing this or that. Instead, good teaching as outlined in this essay, is a complex process that results from what teachers do, as well as how they think about education, the relationships formed, and the context in which they work. Fostering good teaching, there-fore, involves both changes in the structure of teaching and the teacher role. Structures need to be developed that encourage teachers to see ambiguity about teaching as a potential strength that enhances question posing. An once this process of question posing is firmly established as a part of the teacher role, further structures need to be put in place that enable teachers to examine and act on the vast array of political concerns that are often neglected. Finally, new structures need to be established that value and reward the types of thinking and activities I have outlined in this essay. Currently good teachers survive by getting around structures, and developing alternatives. While this is hopeful, it also makes more likely that our best teachers leave teaching after only a few years. What we need is not only an expanded teacher role but structures that complement such a role. Under these circumstances good teaching will be supported by our schools and importantly these teachers may just stay in the classroom to continue to provide quality educational experiences for our children.

# Chapter VI

# Education and Democracy: Should the fact that we live in a democratic society make a difference in what our schools are like?

**Harvey J. Kaye**

**Dalton B. Curtis, Jr.**

# Harvey J. Kaye

Through schooling and education a people expresses and cultivates its public values, identities and aspirations, and prepares its newest generations to engage them. Thus, *a democratic society requires a democratic education*. Declaring ourselves a democracy, the proposition that America must provide a democratic education to its children and young people (at the least) is not really at issue. What has been and continues to be contested is the actual meaning of "democracy" and, in those terms, what a "democratic" education ought to entail. To appreciate the challenge we confront, we must see things historically...

Filled with paradox and contradiction, American experience, along with its record of economic growth and development and its chronicle of continental and imperial expansion, has been a long struggle to realize the democratic dream that *the people shall govern themselves*. The American Revolution and war for independence; the populism of Jacksonian politics, the Civil War between North and South and ensuing abolition of slavery; the campaigns for women's suffrage and equality; the many generations of farmer and labor movements and Black struggles for survival, freedom and justice: the first 200 years and more of our history can be read as a narrative of continuous efforts *from the bottom up* to make real the aspirations that "We, the people" shall rule. Comprehending our past in this way, the struggles of the long decade of the sixties for the civil rights of racial and ethnic minorities, the social rights of the poor, and the equal rights of women, along with the movement against an imperial war in Southeast Asia and the less-celebrated but, perhaps, equally significant insurgency of working people, white and black, male and female, in industry and the workplace, not to mention the environmental and consumer movements, are all recognizable as reassertions of the finest traditions of American life and history (Buhle and Dawley, 1985).

Yet, for almost a generation now we have been subject to a persistent and, arguably, concerted "class war from above" resisting, opposing and, even, seeking to reverse the "advances" which had been accomplished in the spirit of liberty, equality and democratic community. Against the achievements and

reforms secured from the New Deal of the 1930s through the
Great Society of the 1960s and, for most immediately, the threat
they perceived of a coalescence of the several struggles of the
day into a broader popular movement seeking ever more extensive radical-democratic changes in the American social order,
the powers-that-be mobilized. And, in the course of the 1970s,
with the encouragement and manifold support of significant
sectors of American business and corporate capital, there was
formed under the banner of the New Right Republicans a political coalition of conservatives and neo-conservatives which
included cold-warriors, free-marketeers, moral-majoritarians,
and a host of other right-wing single-interest groups and organizations variably committed to undermining the post-Second
World War liberal consensus and to halting the democratic
struggles from below of labor and the "new social movements."
The ascendance to power of this diverse coalition was registered
in the 1980 and '84 election victories of Ronald Reagan and,
again, in that of George Bush in 1988 (Blumenthal, 1986;
Himmelstein, 1990).

From the start there was inherent contradictions in this New
Right alliance—for example those existing between the aspira-
tion of the free-marketeers and those of the religious fundamentalists and, in another area, between the foreign-policy
views of conservatives and those of neo-conservatives—and after
a decade and more of Republican Administrations, it is not only
clear that the New Right has failed to accomplish its many
enunciated goals but that the coalition itself is breaking up.
There is, however, little reason to be joyful or optimistic for
there is no denying the consequences of a dozen years of New
Right regimes. They have wrought confusion disarray and
hardship. We have experienced a "decade of greed" and a
"politics of inequality" in which the rich truly have gotten richer
and the poor have been made poorer— a process by no means
limited to the margins, that is, to the Donald Trumps at one
end and the poor and homeless at the other, but, rather, one
conditioning the lives of the vast majority of America's working
people (Phillips, 1990). Moreover, the collapse of the New
Right coalition has been due for less to organized and coherent
opposition from the Left and resurgent movement from below

than to the manifestation of its own contradictions and the difference between the various groups composing it.

In fact, in one major respect the Right has triumphed. That is, it has succeeded, to the decided benefit of the powers-that-be, in further fragmenting if not all but routing the struggles of working people and the oppressed. Evidently, the antagonisms of class, race and gender not only persist but are intensified, and studies reveal that there is continuing popular commitment to the programs and priorities of New Deal and post-war liberalism; never the less, the various movements for freedom and justice appear enervated and enfeedbled, pursuing at best defensive actions. What we find is not merely increasing inequality, but political and cultural freedoms under attack and democratic activity becoming narrower and shallower, subordinated to the "freedom of the market," the imperatives of capital and the manners of the media. In short, public culture and discourse is more and more subject to commercial norms and values and devoid of critical thought and debate about the future of American society. The New Right's legacy, therefore, would seem to be the "depoliticization" of public life and, thereby, the enhancement of the status quo and the position of the powers-that-be, especially the political and economic elites of corporate capital. Philip Mattera has described the current scene:

> These days there is not much collective dreaming in America. The erosion of living standards and the increase in economic insecurity have brought about a climate of quiet frustration and cynicism. People have been caught between official pronouncements that these are the best of times and their personal realization that life is getting tougher every day. The contradictory evidence is having an immobilizing effect: most Americans do not see a way out of this Dilemma and consequently have grown wary of any change at all. While people in other parts of the world, notably Eastern Europe, are boldly confronting their oppression, the U.S. feels like a political backwater (Mattera, 1990: 187)

It is debatable whether or not the politics and ideas of the New Right have been actually *anti*-democratic. However, it is clearly the case both that their conception of democracy, of democratic life and practice, is a limited one and, stated in *historical* terms, that they conceive of it as already having been achieved. In other words, in their view *democracy in America* is accomplished. Indeed, they insist, not only does contemporary American liberal and capitalist democracy represent the high point of democratic development thus far, it represents *the* high point of democratic possibilities, the *culmination* of democracy's historical evolution. As one of their number, Francis Fukuyama, put it in a much-vaunted and widely-discussed article, we have at the "end of history" beyond which the choice is either more of the same or political, economic and cultural retrogression (Fukuyama, 1989; Kaye, 1991). The New Right's program of "democratic education" indicates just such an understanding of history.

Now, at first sight it would seem that there have been actually two different and conflicting campaigns pursued by conservatives and neo-conservatives (not necessarily respectively) for reforming and renewing American education in the 1980s and '90s. Both point to the apparently poor performance by American schoolchildren on standardized objective tests in comparison to their European and Asian counterparts and regularly blame liberal and Left educators for the problem; however; the respective campaigns proclaim different concerns and assert different priorities. On the one hand, there are those who warn of the dangers of American economic and industrial decline and propose that education be reformed to address it. Looking toward the creation (or *re*creation) and provision of a skilled, disciplined and productive workforce for American industries and enterprises in their competition with German and Japanese corporations (or, as is increasingly said, a workforce attractive to investments by the latter in the American economy!), they stress a "back-to-basics, teach the facts and nothing but the facts" approach to schooling generally emphasizing training in math and science. The priorities of this campaign are vocational, industrial and economic. On the other hand, there are those who speak less of economic decline and far more of political and moral crisis, that is, of the fragmentation and disintegration of America's "common culture" and "shared values". They, too, call for a "return to the basics," but, emphasizing schooling in the humanities, especially literature and history, they stress the restoration of a core curriculum of ideas and ideals entailing, at the least, a common body of knowledge and information and, preferably, a canon of Great Books and personages representing "Western Civilization." The priorities enunciated here are civic, political and cultural (Bennett, 1988; Bloom, 1987; Hirsch, 1987).

Yet, however much stressing seemingly different concerns and priorities—respectively, the making of workers and the making of citizens—the two New Right campaigns for American education arise from the same vision and register the same understanding of America's past, present and possible future, that we have arrived at the end of history, *and* express the same political project, that of assuring that we actually have! Both schemes for schooling delimit democratic education to a process of *transmission*, in the former that of skills and competencies and in the latter that of ideas and values. To be sure, schooling to develop skills and capacities for productive and valued employment and to communicate knowledge and ideals for informed and active citizenship are, in principle, essential to any vision of democratic education. However, bound up with a version of history which conceives of contemporary America as the terminus of democratic development, the New Right vision of democratic education aspires (at best) to no more than the *reproduction* of the American economy and polity and culture as they are presently constituted. Bluntly stated, the New Right notion of democratic education reduces schooling to being a support of the world *as it is*.

For those of us who do not believe that we have come to the end of history, who do not believe that the contemporary American social order—however "progressive," relatively speaking—represents the culmination of democratic development, such a state of affairs is obviously unacceptable. But our task is formidable. For a start, in the face of the triumphs of the New Right we need not only to make clear the inadequacies and limitations of their rendition of history and attendant conception of democracy but, also, to cultivate a popular awareness that the contemporary order of things, both the good and the bad, was not inevitable and that it need not remain this way. We must work towards the development of a popular comprehension that the present, too, is history and that nothing is gained without struggle. This entails both recovering and communicating the struggles for liberty, equality and democratic community which have contributed to the making of past and present (both the victories and the defeats) *and* revealing the possibilities which exist today for renewing that history.

Furthermore, along with our efforts to create a more critical and democratic historical memory, consciousness and imagination—indeed, as part of such efforts—it is imperative that we articulate and proffer a conception of democratic education which supports the project of extending further the development of democratic life and practice and, if enacted actually enhances the likelihood of its realization. The political scientist, Benjamin Barber, expressed it well when he wrote that "all education ought to be radical—a reminder of the past, a challenge to the present, and a prod to the future" (Barber, 1988: 173).

Unfortunately, all too often such aspirations have involved both a simplistic opposition to and a too hasty rejection of the educational initiatives enunciated by the New Right. I would argue that in certain crucial instances our response should not be that of opposing and disavowing their proposals but of critically appropriating, rearticulating and turning them in a more truly democratic direction. For example, at the cost of being portrayed as unconcerned about not only "academic standards" but, also, about the needs of working people and the oppressed to become literate and skilled and, moreover the economic future of our country, we have in the past too readily denounced the campaign to reform education in support of economic and technological development. Instead, we should have been taking the lead in this area, seeking to make all the more effective the acquisition of basic skills, literacies, and competencies by America's schoolchildren for the sake both of improving their chances to secure and pursue productive livelihood and of helping to assure continued American economic growth and development. *But that is not enough!* And this is where our conception of democratic life and practice differs from that of the Right. As Antonio Gramsci observed more than half of a century ago: "Democracy, by definition, cannot mean merely that an unskilled worker can become skilled. It must mean that every 'citizen' can 'govern' and that society places him, even if only abstractly, in a general condition to achieve this" (Gramsci, 1971: 40). In essence, we must develop a mode of education which not only does not predetermine or limit the "life  chances" and livelihoods of young people but, beyond that, one which does not accept as natural or inevitable the socially-created division between economy and polity, between our lives as workers and consumers and our lives as citizens. A democratic education must, that is, not only prepare upcoming generations to be both capable and effective workers and capable and effective citizens, but, also, be capable of critically considering and, possibly, effectively challenging the separation between the two experiences, between the dictatorship characteristic of the former and the democracy of the latter, leading, hopefully, to the making of democratic changes and the developments in both.

To accomplish such changes will also necessarily entail a different kind of response to the New Right's educational initiative regarding the crisis of American polity and culture than those usually afforded by radical democrats. *There is a crisis!* And here, again, it is a mistake to simply reject the idea of a common culture, even when defined in terms of the "Western tradition."   Rather, it is a question of critically appropriating—or, better, and more historically accurate, *re*appropriating Western *traditions* and American history and culture "from the bottom up," and of endeavoring to rearticulate them in a democratic and pluralistic fashion for  ourselves and for future generations.  Moreover, a democratic education must involve not just a process of tranmission and inculcation of ideas and ideals but, also, an experience of engaging, working through, and possibly even transforming them (Kaye, 1991). That is, not only the ideas and ideals, but the activity itself must be recognized as contributing (or not) to the making of active and critical democratic citizens.  As Gramsci insisted, a democratic education should be "forming" of a young person as one who is "capable of thinking, studying and ruling - or controlling those who rule" (Gramsci, 1971: 40).

Let us continue to insist that "We, the people" shall rule and, so inspired, create a democratic education whose purpose and promise is that of preparing ourselves and our children to do so.

# References

Barber, B. (1989) "Cultural Conservatism and Democratic Education: Lessons form the Sixties". *Salmagundi*. 81, pp. 159-73.

Bennett, W.J. (1988) *Our Children and Our Country*. New York: Simon & Schuster.

Bloom, A. (1987) *The Closing of the American Mind*. New York: Simon & Schuster.

Blumenthal, S. (1986) *The Rise of the Counter-Establishment*. New York: Times Books.

Buhle, P. and A. Dawley (1985) *Working for Democracy*. Urbana, Ill.: University of Illinois Press.

Fukuyama, F. (1989) "The End of History?" *The National Interest*. 16, pp. 3-18.

Gramsci, A. (1971) *Selection from the Prison Notebooks*. New York: International Publishers.

Himmelstein, J. (1990) *To the Right: The Transformation of American Conservatism*. Berkeley, CA.: University of California Press.

Hirsch, E.D. (1987) *Cultural Literacy*. Boston: Houghton Mifflin.

Kaye, H.J. (1991) *The Powers of the Past*. London: Simon & Schuster International.

Mattera, P. (1990) *Prosperity Lost*. New York: Addison-Wesley.

Philips, K. (1990) *The Politics of Rich and Poor*. New York: Random House.

# Dalton B. Curtis, Jr.

From the early years of the American republic, education has been seen as essential to the success of democracy. That idea certainly was uppermost in the minds of the nation's founders. Thomas Jefferson and Benjamin Rush, for example, believed that democracy needed an enlightened citizenry to ensure the protection of republican institutions and the effective functioning of government. To accomplish these goals, they proposed similar, albeit ill-fated, plans for tax-supported schools in their respective states. By the first half of the nineteenth century, industrialization, urbanization, and immigration as well as the continuing concern for republican institutions led Horace Mann, Henry Barnard, Calvin Wiley, John Pierce, and others into a campaign to establish common schools. The success of that effort in the Northeast and the Midwest, the advent of the corporate industrial state, and the desire to assimilate a second wave of immigrants helped to spread schooling throughout the rest of the country by the early decades of the twentieth century. By that time, schooling and democratic citizenship had become inextricably linked in the minds of Americans.

Today, most Americans say without hesitation that the school is responsible for teaching their children, and to the question, should the fact that we live in a democratic society make a difference in what school are like? They would probably answer, "Yes." Many Americans, however, are likely to be emphatic in answering "Yes!" to the question, Should the fact that we live in a capitalist society make a difference in what schools are like? They are far more concerned about the school preparing their children for the world of work than educating them for participation in public life. This attitude was clearly reflected by the National Commission on Excellence in Education in its 1983 report, *A Nation at Risk*. The commission expressed grave doubts about America's ability to compete with Japan, South Korea, and Germany in the world economy, but said little or nothing about the failure of Americans to be responsible citizens (National Commission on Excellence in Education, 1983). This, the society expects the school to provide it with a trained workforce and only incidentally with enlightened citizens.

This essay is concerned with schooling for citizenship in a democratic social order and the concomitant responsibility of the society at large in the making of citizens. Without question, the fact that we live in a democratic society should make a difference in what our schools are like, but it should also make a difference in the behavior of adult citizens. If a democratic society depends on the rational decisions of its citizens in the practice of politics, then the school must teach the young both what it means to be a citizen and how to act responsibly in that capacity, and the adult citizenry must take seriously its commitment in democracy. This thesis raises several questions: What is meant by democracy, what are some of the ways of teaching the young how to be good citizens, and what must adult citizens do to make democracy work? These are the same questions the community and its educators ought to be trying to answer as they engage in the practice of democratic living.

Modern liberal democracy is a form of government in which power rests with the citizens who conduct the business of the state either directly or indirectly through elected representatives in what is called a republic. Democratic government is intended to serve public ends, to protect the rights of individuals, and to guarantee equality of all citizens before the law. To these responsibilities has been added ensuring material survival, which some see as the chief business of the state. Ultimately, the means of government are to be directed toward the purpose of liberal democracy; to free the individual to seek her own ends.

As Christopher Lasch has suggested, achieving the promise of democracy in twentieth century America has come to mean that government, whether in conservative or liberal guise, should foster material progress (Lasch, 1979, 1984, 1991). This attitude has contributed to the growth of unbridled individualism, the product of a consumer society. No longer is the principal purpose of work to produce high quality, durable goods that are the mark of excellent craftsmanship; rather, it is to enable the worker to consume the goods he or she makes or use the services he or she provides. Democracy in America has been further distorted by recent abuses of governmental power. Thus, politics is seen as a dirty business, politicians are viewed as scoundrels, or at least of questionable character, and Americans are increasingly unwilling to engage in public affairs, all of which threaten democracy.

A way out of this quagmire is to conceive of a broader notion of democracy, one that encompasses government and society, and that enables the individual to achieve excellence in whatever she or he does, but particularly in the practice of politics. If democracy is seen as a form of associated living for the purpose of promoting individual achievement, then politics becomes the business of according equal rights to all citizens and creating the conditions under which human abilities can be cultivated to their highest level. This form of democracy combines the Aristotelian notion of virtue as individual excellence with the ethical concept of democracy as a way of life exposed by John Dewey. It tries to escape the emphasis on technique of the modern world by promoting the ancient ideal of *phronesis*, or practical reason directed toward moral perfection, it avoids the social restrictions of the ancient world by employing modern ideas of citizenship and equal rights; and it presupposes the interdependence of corporate society and its effect on modern life.

In order for democracy to become a way of life, certain conditions must be met. First, communities must be formed through effective communication, shared social ideals, and a commitment to solve common social problems. Second, local communities must communicate with and share in the common social ideals of the larger society. Third, although the particular structure of democratic government may vary, in all cases its ultimate purpose must be to create the good life by conferring equal rights and providing for human excellence. Fourth, the highest obligation of the citizen must be to engage in the practice of politics-that is, to participate in public life. Fifth, all citizens must be educated for participation in that way of living in order for the political conditions of democracy to be met.

The final condition of a democratic way of life brings us back to the problem of education in general and schooling in particular. If we are going to educate citizens for democratic living, what should our schools be like? Furthermore, should education be left solely to the schools? In answering these questions, I would like to examine two alternative schemes for citizenship education.

Recent proposals for the return of education have revived the tradition of civic education that centers on reading historic documents and the study of history, geography, and the civics as means of making good citizens. William J. Bennett, for example, published a series of monographs while he proposed to educate young citizens through a social studies curriculum that was to begin in the elementary school and continue through the junior year of high school. The elementary curriculum would start with myths, stories, fables, and biographies designed to lay a foundation for the formal study of history, geography, and civics. From the fourth grade through high school, students would take a series of courses in American and world history, geography, and American government (Bennett, 1986, 1987, 1988).

Unfortunately, this reform proposal suffers from the historic problem of civic education: it is too abstract. The social studies disciplines are studies apart from related disciplines, and there seems to be no connection between the formal study of history, geography, and civics and the actual problems of citizenship. Although Bennett emphasizes the important skills of reading and writing in social studies, he has no suggestions for enabling students to test their learning on public issues. His recommendations for the practice of citizenship are limited to a few civic tasks in the early years of elementary school. Yet he believes students should be "*learning* science by *doing* science" Bennett, 1986). His proposed science curriculum includes laboratory work for ". . . underlining and illustrating facts and principles of the scientific method, and demonstrating that order and sense may be made from the results of careful experimentation" (Bennett, 1987). If learning about society and the obligations of citizenship is to be as meaningful as learning about the physical environment, then students must have an opportunity to synthesize and apply their knowledge of the social studies.

An alternative to Bennett's civic education is called education for public responsibility. As the principal means of initiating the young into the democratic way of life, this scheme for citizenship education combines the Aristotelian concern for practical reasoning aimed at moral perfection, particularly in politics, with the Deweyan concern for problem solving at the heart of the democratic process.  It offers the student opportunities to engage in the art of politics by posing social problems for them to solve.  It emphasizes the importance of individual responsibility and social obligation through actual civic service.

Education for public responsibility begins in the first years of schooling and continues through high school.  Its curriculum includes formal study of the social studies disciplines, regular engagement in solving social problems, and shared responsibility for the civic needs of the classroom, school, and society.  Each year, students develop into the social studies as a part of their initiation into the culture and as a means of developing a sense of judgment to be used in solving the public problems put before them.  They also are obligated to perform various civic tasks in their classrooms in the early years and in their school and community as they become older and more mature.

Their formal studies begin with American folklore and music, the patriotic symbols and events of American history, and the geography of their community.  In the middle and late years of elementary school, students are introduced to American history, geography, literature, and fine arts in an integrated program that maintains the integrity of the disciplines while demonstrating the interrelationship of their content.  The early years of the secondary school are devoted to an integrated study of the history, geography, literature, and fine arts of western civilization and of at least one non-western culture.  In the last three years of the secondary school, students take work in American history, with a political and geographical emphasis, American government and international relations, and the problems of democracy.  The study of the problems of democracy completes the social studies program and the problem-solving dimension of an education for public responsibility.   Students form communities and political bodies to deal with actual public issues that draw on what students have learned throughout the school curriculum and that enable them to develop the broad outlines of solutions.   Prior to this time, they have been challenged with increasingly complex social problems as an integral part of the social studies curriculum.

The final dimension of an education for public responsibility is the performance of civic tasks.  As previously noted, young citizens do various civic tasks in their classrooms, school, and community from the earliest years of schooling.  In their last year, individual students or student groups design and carry out a civic project under that guidance of members of the community.

Education for public responsibility avoids the pitfalls of Bennett's civic education.  It considerably reduces the abstract nature of civic education by incorporating concrete social problems into the formal study of the social studies disciplines and by engaging students in civic tasks throughout their schooling years.  It also helps students begin to synthesize their knowledge of America and the world by correlating the social studies disciplines with other related disciplines as they are being taught.  At the same time, students gain skill in the exercise of judgment about public issues and practice at the tasks of public service in cooperation with the adult citizens of the community.

Cooperative public service is the final step in meeting the first condition of an education for public responsibility.  The second condition is that adult  citizens must see the example for the young by practicing  the art of politics.  They must engage in some form of public service if the school projects their children do are to have any real meaning.  They must stop shirking their civic responsibility to vote.  Voting is not a privilege in a democracy; it is a citizen's duty.  Consequently, adult citizens must participate in the political process thoughtfully and demonstrate its importance to the young by including them in discussions of public issues.  But this obligation cannot be met so long as citizens are willing to allow politicians to undermine the political process.  In order to exercise their judgment effectively, citizens must demand rational arguments about public issues from their political representatives and they give those arguments serious consideration.  They also must demand that politicians stop wasting time on image-making and devote their efforts to thoughtful debate about the business of the state.

Clearly, it is essential for the entire community to engage in education for public responsibility. The school must lay the intellectual foundations of citizenship and develop practical skill in the art of politics, and the citizenry must participate in public life. If excellence in politics were to become the highest practice for the citizen, then the moral stature of public responsibility would be demonstrated, the work of the school in educating citizens would be meaningful and effective, and the conditions most necessary for democracy to become a way of life would be achieved.

# References

Bennett, W. (1986) *First Lessons: A report on Elementary Education in America*, Washington, D.C., U.S. Department.

Bennett, W. (1987) *James Madison High School: A Curriculum for American Students*, Washington, D.C., U.S. Department of Education.

Bennett, W. (1988) *James Madison Elementary School: A Curriculum for American Students*, Washington, D.C. U.S. Department of Education.

Lasch, C. (1979) *The Culture of Narcissism: American Life in an Age of Diminishing Expectations*, New York, Warner Books, Inc.

Lasch, C. (1984) *The Minimal Self: Psychic Survival in Troubled Times*, New York, Warner Books, Inc.

Lasch, C. (1991) *The True and Only Heaven: Progress and Its Critics*, New York, W.W. Norton & Company.

National Commission on Excellence in Education (1983) *A Nation at Risk: The Imperative of Educational Reform: A Report to the Nation and the Secretary of Education*, Washington, D.C., U.S. Department of Education.

# Chapter VII

# Women and Education: In what ways does gender affect the educational process?

Jo Anne Pagano

Janet L. Miller

# Jo Anne Pagano

During the last decade, public discourse on education came to be increasingly dominated by the sentimental and nostalgic social and political agenda of the Reagan administration. Driven by certain economic imperatives, and enthralled by America's 1950's television image of itself, Reaganite intellectuals issued manifesto after manifesto reasserting faith in and commitment to an America in which all the moms wore shirtwaists and baked cookies, all the dads put their college educations to work earning good money, and all the kids did their homework and learned from their parents' fine examples to be good citizens. E.D. Hirsch rang praise for the successful and hardworking, thoroughly assimilated immigrant. Diane Ravitch persuaded many that the Civil Rights Movement unnecessarily disrupted the smooth and incremental progress toward racial equality taking place in legislature and courts. Allan Bloom mourned the idyll of upper class boys wandering among the groves of academe, now overrun with feminists and other philistines. For all of these scholars, and others such as Lynne Cheney and Chester Finn and their military commander, William Bennett, the promise of America education had been betrayed by apostates of the canon. We are *no longer* culturally literate; we did not share vision or values and our cultural and educational disorder had brought us to the ruin of falling test scores and a falling dollar.

The tale they all tell is one of a past in which all Americans had access to the social and economic reward structure, in which all entered a cultural conversation organized by common history, knowledge, and understanding. It was a time in which all American could have identified, "Remember the Maine," The Monroe Doctrine, "Tippecanoe, and Tyler, Too," and had read Shakespeare and *Moby Dick*, some of the Bible and some of Plato, and knew the world's geography. Americans were literate, numerate, hard-working, and neighborly; schools were doing their job. But this, as we all know, is not an empirical description of the past. Yet even those who are most disadvantaged by it, are often mesmerized by this image of America; it retains a powerful hold on our imaginations. In our imaginations, we are all the same, therefore, all equally worthwhile. This is a version of the prelapsarian dream of original unity, before Adam and Eve knew that there was sex. As assertion of the importance of our differences, threatens America's dream of itself. To ask in what ways gender affects the educational process may provoke in some the struggle to sink deeper into sleep and cling to the dream.

Some will meet this question with surprise. Their unconsidered response will likely be a "No." Now these readers are not making an empirical claim, although their own educational experiences may have be beguiled them into thinking that they are. On the contrary, they are saying that gender *ought* not to affect the educational process. They have absorbed the values of their education, values which sustain a regime of enforced homogeneity. As we know now, the dark side of the expansion and democratization of education in this country was the impulse to appropriate and domesticate all who threatened to challenge America's nineteenth century pastoral vision of itself. Those contemporary educational criticisms which have captured the imagination of so many, and to whom, among others, the questions raised in this book are directed, are efforts to recollect the nineteenth century's image of itself and are symptoms of a nostalgia for an edenic America that never was— an America in which race, class, ethnicity, and gender didn't matter.

Some will meet this question with a shrug and a knowing leer or sneer. I imagine Richard Bernstein, wise outsider and chronicler of the MLA and other academic meetings for readers of THE NEW YORK TIMES. He seems to think mention of certain topics of research and certain titles on programs sufficient to impugn the intelligence and integrity, not to mention the sanity, of the scholars associated with such topics and titles. Any paper with the word "difference" is a target for ridicule simply by virtue of the presence of the word "difference." "Sex" is another such word. The word "difference" employed in a title of any novel written in England during the eighteenth or nineteenth centuries is likely to be met with high hilarity. Its like saying the word "underwear" to an eight-year-old boy.

I meet this question with perplexity. This is one of those questions, the raising of which, is likely more interesting than any response I can imagine. Its having been raised may teach us about ourselves as other questions come crowding, pushing and shoving their ways into our minds. Why is the question formulated as it is? Certainly it teaches us that women and gender are perceived as situated precariously in educational debates. Why do we inquire instead into the ways in which the educational process affects gender? Whose conception of gender are we talking about? Whose gender is a stake in our investigation of the effects, if any there are, of gender on the educational process? And what do we mean by "educational process?"

It seems obvious to me that gender *ought* to have an effect on the educational process, just as it seems obvious to me that the educational process has an effect on gender. Regarding those two claims, I find nothing new for me to say. We've all said what there is to say many times before. That sex and other differences correlate in various ways with school performance has been well-documented, and the conclusion that our teaching ought to acknowledge the difference that difference makes seems unimpeachable to me. That academic achievement is more likely when the mode of teaching connects with the student's cognitive orientation is desirable if our goal is universal educational achievement. Equally obvious is the conclusion that it is desirable for human beings to orient themselves toward multiple axes of experience and cognition, that is desirable that we learn to think and feel the complexity of complex questions.

I suspect that, appearances to the contrary, I am not being asked to say really how gender affects the educational process. Were I to attempt to do so I should be met with yawns from those who agree with me and ridicule from those who do not. I suspect that I am being asked instead to argue that the question is itself a sensible one and that taking it seriously would yield educational benefits.

Still, I am perplexed by the question as it is articulated. For it seems that our interest isn't talking about gender and education at all, but about women and education. It seems curious that questions of gender should be so exclusively assimilated to my own sex, when masculinity is clearly equally implicated in the educational process. It seems that women are the problem, not gender. When this question is so formulated as it is, certain expectations are sown. Foremost among these is the expectation that we will be talking about and perhaps sentimentalizing "women's ways of knowing." But we learn to be women, *and* we learn to be men. Women have certain cognitive and affective dispositions, *and* so have men. Why should gender effects be an issue in thinking about women's education only? An association among women and gender and education neglects the gendered nature of male knowledge. It can suggest to some that education as we know it is fine for men. Then women remain the problem, and the resistance to feminist and other theoretical analyses that employ the concept of difference is predictable. The question is, "Why can't a woman think more like a man?" The educational problem of those of us who teach women becomes then a problem of teaching them to be more like men in their cognitive approaches to the world. The problem of gender articulated as a question involving women and education only, can then be read as a problem of special pleading, rather than as a general problem of human knowledge and relationships. Moreover, it ignores the fact that many women can think more like a man than some men. That is many women are more oriented to abstraction and principled thinking, the sort of thinking usually associated with men, just as many men are more oriented to relational and contextual thinking. The point is that our approaches to education valorize the former and discount the latter. The first is called "thinking;" the second is called "feeling." The point is that we *ought* acquire both orientations, whether we are men or women, and that our educations ought to encourage our development in both domains.

I have a Ph.D., and I have a shameful memory of my behavior in a seminar I took as part of my program. The course was in the philosophy of science and one required of all Ph.D. students. That semester there were two women enrolled in the course. One day, the other woman presented to the seminar her research project. Her framework was ill constructed, and her methodology logically flawed, and I, along with the male students and the instructor in the seminar let her have it. Each time she tried to respond to a criticism, one or the other of us would point out the irrelevance of her considerations to the logic of our arguments. Before the afternoon was over, she left the room in tears. I was a good student, and it didn't occur to me to regret my part in pushing her to that point. I was scornful of her taking criticism so personally, of her thinking like a woman. I was disinterested, objective, and analytical—a scholar. I responded to the work and spoke in the normal style of academic exchange, and I humiliated another person.

I am culturally literate. I can identify most of the items on Hirsch et al.'s list. I've studied classical as well as contemporary philosophy. The literary canon so jealously defended as source and sustenance of our highest and most noble aspirations is featured prominently in my educational history. I appreciate music and art, I can engage in intelligent discussions about science, and I can do some math. I have a good sense of history, and my S.A.T. and G.R.E. scores were very high. And yet these seem not to have made me a better person. This is not to deny that they can help.

At stake in all educational debates is the sort of person education should produce. They are moral issues, and not simply matters of skill and content. Our education ought to help us to be better persons. Decisions regarding the sort of education we want, are decisions regarding the sort of world we want to live in. The cultural literacy that is the outcome of a canonical education seems not to have accomplished much in the way of making this a better world. The social problems and global tensions which motivated the 1983 *Presidential Report on Excellence in Education* have escalated. The magnitude of unemployment, homelessness, world starvation, drug and alcohol abuse, child abuse and other violent crimes, declines in economic productivity has increased since then, as has the threat and actuality of war. This despite some reported rises in standardized test scores. The education that men and women receive is fine for neither men nor women.

What does all of this have to do with original question regarding gender and education? Simply that we associate certain traits and styles of thinking with women; that we relegate to women's work the labor of reproduction—the labor of sustaining and nurturing life, of caring for others. This is the labor Virginia Woolf called unpaid-for, and therefore despised labor. Feminist analyses and educational proposals in recent years have urged us to think of education not only in terms of production, whether economic or intellectual, but in terms of reproduction as well. Feminists argue that the world will be a better place and ourselves better people only if we can take multiple perspectives and orient ourselves simultaneously to the claims of caring and the claims of reason. Why should anyone find such a project threatening, and respond to research with a sneer?

Those who dominate educational discourse often respond violently to the suggestion that such should be our educational goals. I suspect that the strength of protest is related to the magnitude of the anxiety provoked by such suggestions. I suspect that for some it is an anxiety of control. For others it is an anxiety of responsibility. If we are forced to acknowledge that our education is rooted in a set of values and perspectives, *and* that those values and perspectives are neither universal nor obviously humane, then we shall have to take responsibility for the values and perspectives we choose to teach from.

My perplexity will now be seen to betray a certain disingenuousness. I teach at a university that has admitted women for twenty years only. We are not yet coeducational. Many of my colleagues do, however, have a will to coeducation as they do to enlarging in general education program. I am committed to this program and think that it makes us stand out from other colleges and universities of our sort. Now many may read the words "core program" and "general education" and immediately place us alongside Bennett and Bloom, Hirsch and Ravitch, et al. But what we have tried to do is enlarge the notion of the core such that the work of those outside the "canon" is not encountered as eccentric to the core, but as part of it, as part of the conversation that sustains the core. In the present political climate, our program disturbs some of our students and some of our colleagues. When some think of a core curriculum, they immediately think of dead white European males, to repeat a pretty worthless and finally unrevealing phrase.  At Colgate, there are some who worry that general education is made to serve an idealogical agenda, and when they say "ideological" they mean "left-wing."  The inclusion of so-called "nontraditional" works seems to evoke that charge.

Our program is made up of four courses taken by all students.  I chair one of them.  It's called "The Modern Experience in the West" and is situated in the nineteenth century.  Being sensitive to the politically charged climate, to the polarization among students especially, I invited a "conservative" outside speaker to make the point that the point is to learn to listen and speak across differences, to understand that whatever our affiliations, the continued existence of ourselves and even our planet demands that we recognize a common interest.  As I look at the word "conservative," I see how very little that that tells us.  For he is a considerably more complex person and thinker, and no more "conservative" than I am "liberal."  Certain designations no longer delineate the complexities of contemporary cultural politics, a scene redrawn partly as a result of research in questions of gender.

Our speaker was a very angry man.  He is particularly angry with feminists and lesbians.  It's interesting that I know that since women were not the topic of his lecture.  Yet women were more present in his lecture than was the figure about whom he was lecturing.  I was uncomfortable, but I learned something important.  I learned, I think, why Bloom and Bennett, Hirsch and Ravitch and Cheney are so angry.  They have not, as our visiting lecturer has not, as too many scholars on the political left as well have not, grasped the difference between scholarship and advocacy.

When we ask in what ways gender affects education, or in what ways education affect gender, we are suspected of violating standards of objectivity and disinterest.  They assure immediately that we will cook the data—a fitting way to talk about research about women, I suppose.  But it's a delicate line.  As a student, I was exposed to all sorts of studies and "-ologies" that taught me, objectively and disinterestedly, against my own experience, that women are, in more ways than I can count, inferior.  I call that advocacy or idealogical research.  We should pause a moment to notice that simply to announce our topic as "Women and" is to be met raised eyebrows.

Part of the problem is that women's studies and the various racial and ethnic studies programs in this country are grounded in advocacy movements. But they have not remained there. We understood that advocacy required a basis. We needed to understand, intellectually, theoretically, empirically, questions of sexual difference in the contexts of our disciplines. This is knowledge with a passion, but no mere advocacy. There is a difference. Passion does not entail irresponsibility.

The educational challenge in the forseeable future will be to teach people to acknowledge and understand their own passions, their own advocacy positions, without becoming reduced to them. It's that that we have learned from women's studies. My guest, however, chose to understand his life, his work, endangered by our own. It seems clear to me, that gender is implicated in education, and that education has everything to do with gender. When I say, "Let's talk," he hears, "You're wrong." And as far as I can tell, that translation rests largely in his knowledge that I teach women's studies courses.

The real trick is to learn to do more than one thing. I find my teaching of canonical works immeasurably enhanced when I put them in conversation with noncanonical works, just as I find my students' understanding of print texts complimented by visual texts. Similarly, noncanonical works become richer when they are located with respect to canonical traditions. And now another distinction seems problematic, and that is the distinction between canonical and noncanonical. It does, after all, seem possible to do more than one thing at a time. It does, indeed, seem possible to acknowledge differences and to locate ourselves in communities and traditions larger than our differences. Virginia Woolf once said that poetry must have a mother and a father both. We should take our lesson from her.

# Janet L. Miller

In the summer between fifth and sixth grade, I spent a lot of time hoping that I would get Mr. Brucker as my sixth-grade teacher. He was the best - everyone wanted to be in his class, because he was tough yet funny, serious yet caring. At least that's what all my friends said, and I couldn't doubt their wisdom, let alone my own fifth-grade observations of this teacher who always spoke gently to us amidst the shrieks and giggles that filled the hallways of our elementary school.

One hot July afternoon, as I was leaning out the front door, watching for my father to come home from work, I saw Mr. Brucker trudging up out front sidewalk, lugging what looked to me like a suitcase. My heart pounding, I ran into the kitchen and announced breathlessly to my mother that my wish had been granted. Mr. Brucker was here, and that must mean that I had been assigned to his sixth-grader class.

What I found out later, as he sat sipping ice water and talking with my parents in the living room, was that Mr. Brucker was selling encyclopedias during the summer in order to make enough money to support his family through the vacation months. His visit to our home had nothing to do with my assignment to his sixth-grade class. We were part of his neighborhood sales route, a route that meandered through the steel-girded south hills of Pittsburgh. And the encyclopedias, ordered by my parents only in response to my pleading eyes, I'm sure, arrived just coincidentally with the school notice that indeed placed me in Mr. Brucker's prized sixth-grade classroom. But my anticipation, my desire to be in his class, and my eager participation in all aspects of the classroom community that Mr. Brucker constructed with us that year have everything to do with my learning and subsequent re-learning and teaching as a woman.

What I already had learned, way before that summer between fifth and sixth grade, was that Mr. Brucker was prized among students and parents alike, not only because he indeed was a kind, caring, and enthusiastic teacher but also because he was the only male teacher in Sickman Elementary School. The other three sixth-grade teachers, all women, were supposedly equally as good as Mr. Brucker, or so the neighborhood lore implied. But to have a man as a teacher, in that last year of elementary schooling that still sanctioned childhood play even as it prepared us for the grown-up demands and rigors of junior high school, guaranteed for us the rites of passage into the rules and structures of the disciplines and forms of educating that would lead us into our appropriate roles and places as men and women. If we learned those rules and forms well, we perhaps could take our places in a society that could well extend beyond those burgeoning industrial hills that sometimes seemed to hem in, to constrain our parents' and thus our own visions of possibilities.

As I began that sixth-grade year, nervous and excited, I immediately could see why Mr. Brucker's reputation for posing such possibilities was so solidified within our community. We all, boys and girls, were charmed by his spontaneous grin and his willingness to join us in every aspect of our classroom life. In his spontaneity, he did not separate our learning from his teaching, and so, instead of sitting behind his desk, as so many of our earlier teachers had done, Mr. Brucker would straddle a chair as he coached us in our multiplication and division drills. He would leap from one side of the room to the other, foreshadowing the game show host as he attempted to keep our screams of excitement under a roar level during our spelling bees or math team contests. He was the sixth-grade pied piper, his glasses always slightly askew, and his tall lean body perpetually  braced against the crush of students who constantly surrounded him as he tried to lead us through the tangled passageways of childhood and into that clearing known as "real school."

But, even as much as he talked to us about how junior and senior high school would be different from what we were sharing that year, and how we needed to prepare ourselves for those serious undertakings, I always had the feeling that Mr. Brucker never quite believed that was how it had to be. And so, I also experienced in that year some of the disruptive and contradictory positions that Mr. Brucker occupied within our particular elementary school culture. What I am still learning about are the ways in which those contradictory positions contributed to, affected, and ultimately disrupted many of my own contradictory understandings about myself as a female attempting to learn and later to teach.

I was aware, in that sixth-grade year, not only of some of the differences that Mr. Brucker as teacher represented for me, but also of some of the differences that characterized the kids in our class. Even though most of us lived within walking distance of our school, we girls who had known each other for a few years did not walk home with the new girls in our class who were part of the group known as "the hill" kids. Even though most of my friends' fathers worked in the steel mills and most of their mothers worked at home, these new kids were part of a growing community of men and women from Appalachia who had recently moved to Pittsburgh to get jobs in the mills. There was a separation between the "old" and "hill" boys too, and I could see that Mr. Brucker tried to include these kids in every team event or partner activity that he proposed in class. And because this seemed important to him, I too tried to talk with my friends about including these kids in our daily school rituals.

In a way, I might have wanted to work toward such small attempts at inclusion because I felt different from my friends, in some ways. My mother, instead of staying home to care for my sister and me, needed to work a full-time job to help with family finances. She worked not in the mills, like some of the "hill" kids' mothers, but in a real estate office. And so I appreciated Mr. Brucker's discussion, in our unit on careers, of possible jobs that we girls might want to consider. He didn't just assume that we or our mothers would want or be able to stay at home in order to raise our children, and I remember that we girls talked, hanging from the monkey bars during recess that afternoon, about what we really might want to do in our lives besides be mothers. I, of course, had already determined that I wanted to be a teacher, just like Mr. Brucker.

But I was also learning that, even if I were to teach, and even if I were to explore with my students some of the alternative ways of living and thinking that Mr. Bruckers' gentle visions encouraged, I still would not be a teacher just like him. As we worked our ways through geography and grammar lessons, and built clay replicas of the Panama Canal, replete with water-tight

locks, and recited declensions, I began to notice that the other
sixth-grade teachers, the women, would often appear at our
classroom door—to plead for our teacher's help in calming two
students who were fighting in the lunch room, to ask him to
open one of the old and constantly stuck windows in the room
down the hall, to watch our class radio productions every few
weeks, where we introduced and shared with classmates,
through recordings and our own handwritten scripts, our latest
research on Verdi's *Aida* or on the coal mining industry.

Mr. Brucker was the leader of Sickman School, whether he
wanted to be or not. I think now that he tried in some ways to
resist that role, and in our class, he constantly was encouraging
us all, girls and boys, to consider possibilities for ourselves that
did not automatically occur to many of us as we trudged home
each afternoon through the ever-present yet gentle grayness of
our steel town's southern hills. He challenged us girls to move
beyond stereotypic images of ourselves that we reinforced every
recess in our jump-rope and hopscotch play, for example, by
insisting that we be part of the class kickball team. I still
remember his gleeful yelp when I kicked the ball over the fence
for my first-ever home run. He insisted that, on rainy days, the
boys and girls play in the jacks tournaments that he set up for us
during lunch and recess times. And he pushed us all in class,
always asking us for another possible way to figure out the
current math problem. But, even as he was attempting to
disrupt our already deeply internalized conceptions of ourselves
as gendered beings, as girls and boys who should fulfill certain
socially constructed roles within our public and private worlds, I
think that what I was learning in sixth grade had more to do
with my desires to please this teacher rather than to emulate the
disruptive and challenging perspectives that he perhaps was
attempting to enact in his teaching. And in my desire to learn
his acceptance and approval, I was learning the sanctioned
forms of gendered relationships, discourses, and curriculums
that structured and framed the lives of both Mr. Brucker and
myself.

To please Mr. Brucker meant that I had to take some risks; I
had to work to overcome my shyness about speaking up in class
and I had to be willing to attempt to move beyond giving only

the "right answers."  He pushed us all not only to frantically wave our hands in our moments of certainty but also to offer explanations for those answers that we thought might be possible within each of our multiple points of inquiry.  And, with that kind of encouragement, I was able, slowly, to participate in our class exchanges and debates and to articulate the connections that I could make among the various threads of our sixth-grade curriculum.  I was enlarging my own capacities to enter into the official school languages of our textbooks as well as into the unofficial languages and relationships that signaled our connections to one another as we studies and learned together in the effusive sixth-grade community.  And yet, as the year wore on, even as I was becoming aware of those connections among Mr. Brucker, the work our classroom, and ourselves as his students, I also was becoming increasingly aware, as the "hill" kids kept walking home in their own group, and as the boys more and more claimed their apparently rightful priorities in grabbing Mr. Brucker's attention on the softball field as well as in our classroom, of the differences between and among those relationships.

I was aware, certainly before sixth-grade, that the official languages of schooling were valued more than the discussions and bantering that characterized much of our interaction in Mr. Brucker's class.  Even though I think that he clearly valued our dialogues above the facts that filled our textbooks and our "official" recitations of those disparate fragments of information, Mr. Brucker tried, for our own good, he said, to separate us as well as himself from the personal, intimate worlds that permeated our casual yet interrelated conversations about such topics as the geography of Western Pennsylvania, the economic interdependence of the industries that grew out of our "steel city," and the work in which many of our parents were engaged.

We knew that we had to "settle down" when his voice would modulate into the somber and serious lower register, and when he would unfold his long, lean frame into his chair that he positioned in the center of our double-layered concentric-circle desk arrangement.  And then, even though our conversations had been filled with information we had gleaned from parents, siblings, friends, about what it was like to work in the mills, or to forge new communities in these still forested hills, or to worry about how to feed and care for children when lay-offs hit, we began to recite the facts of our textbooks, as Mr. Brucker questioned us in rapid-fire order.

I had become adept at such memorizations and recitations, having learned early in Mr. Brucker's class that such performances earned his praise. I think that we all worked at moving through such rote activities as quickly as possible so that we could get to the real parts of our learning, for I think now that we all recognized, even in sixth-grade, that the textbooks never captured the depths or complexities of our own stories. And I noticed that, even as I could recite lists of economic connection that tied our lives together, for example, there was no mention of the kind of bookkeeping and auditing work that my mother did in her job, or of the incessant housework that she, my sister, and I battled each night when we arrived home. The only women we had read about in our history books were Clara Barton, Florence Nightingale, and Jane Addams, and then we only knew of them through descriptions of their extensions of socially-sanctioned women's work.

And so, I learned that, even though the stories of our daily lives were the ones that Mr. Brucker asked about on the playground or during our lunch breaks or during the conversations of our class, he gave official recognition, official school praise, for those facts about Clara Barton as nurse during the Civil War, or about the geography of western Pennsylvania. Thus, as much as I learned from Mr. Brucker about the value of our connections and conversations, I also learned that, in order to receive the sanctioned merits of schooling, to receive his official acknowledgement and approval, I had to talk with others' words, to speak in the modulated serious tones of others' understandings, to memorize others' stories, to replicate others' knowledges. And in doing so, I neglected or repressed the unofficial, the desires inherent in our stories, our personal conversations and relationships that were at the heart of Mr. Brucker's teaching, and yet were separated as much from his conceptions of official knowledges as were my replications. And in my ironic desire to please, to receive authorization, I became Other.

I realize that this story too is only a partial telling, a story pieced together from myriad memories and recreated through the lenses of subsequent multiple experiences, conceptualizations, and enactments of teaching and learning. In this particular telling, however, are examples of the ways in which dominant educational constructions of gender, in which men teachers were more important, more valid in their associations with and transmission of official knowledge than women teachers, for example, undergirded my initial understandings of learning, curriculum, and pedagogy. In this telling, too, are vestiges of the ways in which those gendered conceptions of appropriate teaching and learning stances still manifest themselves in my educational work. I struggle still to hear my own voice, my own constructions and understandings of knowledge as emanating, in complex and changing ways, from both the personal conversations as well as the public representations of those knowledges. And as I grapple with those still institutionalized dichotomies, I still see Mr. Brucker also wrestling with what he seemed to perceive as artifical separations of our public and private knowledges about our worlds and our relationships to one another. He chose, for many reasons that I guess still substantiate many teachers' transmissions of others' knowledges, to officially support school knowledges, while, in his interactions with us, to offer us visions of other possibilities for ourselves. But I was so embedded in my own already internalized gender role as "good girl," seeking approval and thus replicating his official choices, that I missed, for years, the discrepancies between Mr. Brucker's pedagogical and personal representations of curriculum and learning.

While I do not claim my experiences or understandings as universal for all girls and boys who were educated in the United States during the 1950s, I do think that aspects of static role expectations for both teachers and students, of curriculum conceived as objective and measurable knowledge, and of teaching and learning as separated from the knowledges generated by individuals' relationships and interactions reflect those dominant constructions of gender that, for many, have separated and prioritized educational processes and experiences.

Thus, as we who educate now attempt to understand curriculum as representation of particular historical, social, economic, and political intersections in individuals' lives, we also view those intersections as mediated by multiple constructions of gender, race and class. As we engage in debate with those who argue for stable, unified canons that supposedly represent consensus on singular and universal traditions, we can point beyond inclusions of women's voices and works as a unitary representation, for example, and toward the multiple and shifting nature of those voices and their positions across various discourses which historically and currently constitute their lives in and out of school. Thus, it is important, but not sufficient to speak of elimination of sexism or sexual harassment  in classrooms or of inclusion of minority voices into textbooks. It is important, but not sufficient to note how women are now integrated into educational institutions as students, teachers, administrators, as well as subject of scholarship. It is important, but not suffcient to point out the discrepancies, the separations between what counts as official school knowledges and what students and teachers construct daily as knowledges lodged in their interactions as well as their silences. We must scrutinize and work to change the very constructions of institutions, of disciplines and their representative curriculums, and of men's and women's internalizations of the gendered divisions and separations that historically have characterized educational processes, if we truly wish to work toward the creation of just and humane educational communities.

John Brucker's sixth-grade class provided me with a site for reflections and reconstructions of my own desires as a young girl, a student, and a teacher. As I work to understand the multiple ways in which the complex interactions of that year continue to both reflect and construct my conceptions of teaching, learning, and curriculum, I also am working to reconstruct my own versions, (now acceptable to me as possibly even subject to change), of myself as teacher, as learner, as knower. And while I still wonder what he might think of this particular version of our sixth-grade year together, and how he might construct his own stories of that year, I no longer need Mr. Brucker's permission to tell this particular tale.

# Chapter VIII

# Race and Education: In what ways does race affect the educational process?

Cameron McCarthy

Christine E. Sleeter, Walter Gutierrez,
Clara Ann New, Susan R. Takata

# Cameron McCarthy

Recent deterioration in race relations on college campuses in the United States has not received much attention from curriculum theorists or sociologists of education (McCarthy, 1990). Indeed, while the latter have been overtaken by events, university administrators have been busy defending the overall moral integrity of their institutions suggesting that incidents of racial hostility towards minorities are mere random acts of prejudice and not indicative of university policy or institutional practices. University officials have therefore been careful to throw up a blanket of ideological protection around embattled colleges. They insist that these educational institutions are largely free of the kind of racial intolerance and bigotry that may be found in the rest of society (Viadero, 1989). What sense are we to make of these developments? How are we to understand the current resurgence of racial antagonism in American educational institutions of higher learning?

In this essay, I will challenge these mainstream understandings of the relationship of racial antagonism to educational institutions in the United States. In what follows, I will make use of the work of African-American novelist and essayist, Ralph Ellison. Ellison's discussion of racial exclusion in his novel *Invisible Man* (1982) serves as a point of departure for my analysis of developments in race relations in education and society over the last ten years or so. The resurgence of campus racism within this period is, in my view, symptomatic of broader patterns of racial selection and exclusion taking place in educational and social institutions in this country.

In the prologue to Ralph Ellison's *Invisible Man*, the hero of that novel points us urgently to his alienated condition in a racist American society. To be a Black in America, Ellison contends is to be existentially alien, to be existentially absent at the dinner party, to be in the Dostoyevskian sense, existentially underground. Ellison's protagonist asserts the following:

> I am an Invisible Man. No, I am not a spook like those who haunted
> Edgar Allan Poe; nor am I of your Hollywood-movie ectoplasms. I am a
> man of substance, of flesh and bone, fiber and liquids—and I might even
> be said to possess a mind. I am invisible, understand, simply because

people refuse to see me.  Like the bodiless heads you see sometimes in circus side-shows, it is as though I have been surrounded by mirrors of hard, distorting glass.  When they approach me they see only my surroundings, themselves, or figments of their imagination—indeed, everything and anything except me.

By pointing us to the existential condition of black people in America, Ellison had led us to an important insight into the way racism operates.  For in *Invisible Man*, Ellison had drawn our attention to the ordinariness, the easy, every day quality of white exclusion of Blacks from participation in the mainstream life of American society.

Drawing on Ellison's insights, I want to argue that racism benefits Whites in their everyday encounter with Blacks in, for example, patterns of selection and recruiting in the university, in patterns of selection of what is good knowledge in the university, in the patterns of selection of who shall be in what fraternities and sororities and so on.  Racism is therefore systematic, structural and institutional.

White Americans irrespective of their personal beliefs, materially benefit from a racial structure that privileges "whiteness" in every social and cultural sphere—in the market, in housing and residential patterns, in educational institutions, in the media, and in the classroom.

An illustration might help here.  A few years ago, when black students at the University of Wisconsin protested the Phi Gamma Delta fraternity's use of an offensive effigy of a Fiji Islander to advertise its May 2nd Fiji Island Party, the president of that fraternity contended that he was, quote, "very surprised at the racist accusation" (*Badger Herald*, Sept. 9, 1987).  He continued, "We've had the Fiji Party for about forty years with no complaints."  This kind of defense of an act of racial hostility is typical.  It raises the issue of the regularity, familiarity, and the obviousness of racial differentiation that Ellison (1982) pointed us to in *Invisible Man*.  For forty years the Phi Gamma Delta fraternity at the University of Wisconsin conducted a grotesque, racist, White exclusionary ritual virtually on the university campus, and nobody noticed.  White students, according to one sympathetic newspaper columnist, "were just having fun."

Twenty-five years after the landmark Civil Rights Act of 1964, schools and universities are experiencing what many educators now characterize as "a disturbing resurgence of prejudice" (Viadero, 1989, p.1). According to the National Institute Against Prejudice and Violence, incidents of "intergroup conflict" have occurred at more than 160 colleges between 1986-1990 (McCarthy, 1990). Particularly notorious was the October 1986 beating of a black student at the University of Massachusetts at Amherst after an argument about a World Series game turned into a racial attack, with a crowd of some 3,000 Whites chasing twenty Blacks. Other incidents of gross racial or ethnic insensitivity have occurred at southern universities. At the Citadel Academy in South Carolina and at Tulane University in Louisiana there have been cross burnings and racial obscenities. Back in the North again, in January 1989, the Zeta Beta Tau fraternity at the University of Wisconsin held a mock slave auction in which pledges painted their faces black and wore Afro wigs (Steele, 1989; Tifft, 1989).

University officials and administrators have tended to act as apologists for these instances of blatant racism suggesting that these racial hostilities are merely examples of individual prejudice and authoritarianism. But I want to point us in a different direction. The racism of white fraternities on university campuses is constitutively linked to the everyday educational and social experiences of minorities in education and society in this country. I therefore want to draw attention to the sociocultural-cultural and constitutive rules that define the very existence of fraternities. The sociocultural and constitutive rules that make fraternities intelligible and give these organizations common sense racial meaning. The very raison d'etre of the fraternity is that of producing a white exclusionary identity. This is powerfully expressed in practices of selection for membership and the observance of nativistic white rituals. In this sense, white dominant fraternities and sororities formally and symbolically resemble white supremacist groups like the Ku Klux Klan or the Aryan Society. They exist for the affirmation of white identity often at the expense and to the exclusion of Blacks and other minorities. Let me give some examples of what I mean.

In an open letter, quoted in the *Nation*, the grand president
of Kappa Alpha Theta (the oldest women's sorority) defended
the right of exclusion and selection for her sorority this way:

> We have alumnae who are reluctant to recommend any one other than
> the traditional White, Anglo-Saxon Protestant.  And this is their right.
> The purpose of the recommendation system is to give alumnae the
> opportunity to highlight personal friends and the daughters of friends,
> not to provide a "ticket" for everyone [Lord, 1987, p. 13].

A few years ago, the members of the Michigan chapter of the
Sigma Alpha Mu, held a "jungle party." At this event, members
of the fraternity painted their bodies black, wore tribal paint,
and placed rings through their noses.  After the *Michigan Daily*,
the campus newspaper, ran photographs of this event, black
students protested.  Here again, the president of the Michigan
Fraternity claimed to be "stunned." He contended, much like
the president of the Phi Gamma Delta in Madison that "It is
difficult to know how minorities feel about certain practices"
(Lord, 1987, p. 12).

Racial assaults on black students of this kind are increasing all
over the country, and particularly in northern university systems
that, in the 1960s, had declared themselves refugee-shelters for
black folk fleeing racism and segregation in the South.  This of
course is not to say that disturbing examples of racism do not
continue to define life in southern universities.  For in many
ways the university represents an extension of the plantation
system.  But we must be careful not to treat these events as
individual, random incidents of racial prejudice.  The racial
excesses of white fraternities exist as a material symbol for a
university system and a society that have retreated from the
promise of racial equality and the moral consensus for social
amelioration that had been mobilized during the 1960s.  It is
important that we begin to see the links and connections
between what is going on in the margins (or what University
officials would like to have us believe are the margins) of college
campus life and political developments taking place in society as
a whole.

A set of cultural, political, and economic dynamics that we
have come to associate with the Nixon Administration but more
definitively with the administrations of Ronald Reagan and

George Bush lies at the heart of the matter. Reagan's ascendancy to power in the 1980s coincided with a ground swell of racial reaction within the white community in the United States to the perceived excesses of state welfarism—a state welfarism that in the view of conservative Whites had made working class Blacks and women the beneficiaries of the hapless white American tax payer (Omi & Winant, 1986). From the inception, Reagan administration officials sent out their signals loud and clear when they began to flesh out aggressive conservative social policies which centrally targeted the civil rights gains of women and minorities. The Reagan administration, through the activism of the justice department and other apparatuses of the State sought to challenge and reverse affirmative action quotas in industry and slow down the project of social reform that had been set in motion in previous decades. In short, the conservative restoration fostered by the Republican administration of the 1980s provided buoyant support for a broad expression of racial resentment towards minority causes. This is what Omi and Winant (1986) describe as the "white male back lash." There was at least one area of continuity in foreign and domestic policy: the Reagan government not only beat up on small Third World nations like Grenada and Nicaragua, but sought to punish the "enemy within"—Blacks and other disenfranchised groups. Not only were neoconservative groups emboldened, but white supremacist groups such as the Aryan Society and displaced white youth such as the "skin heads" were given a practical and moral boost. This brings us right back to the fraternities and the sororities once again. The resurgence of supremacist organizations in the eighties parallels a similar resurgency of white fraternities and sororities. According to Lord (1987), fraternity membership doubled in the decade of the 1980s—even though the full-time undergraduate population increased by only twenty percent, up from five million in 1977 to six million in 1987. Membership in the sororities has also grown by over 30 percent within the same period. On campuses where chartered sororities never existed—Yale, Princeton, the University of Chicago—new chapters have been "colonized" (an interesting choice of verb by a group made up predominantly of White Anglo-Saxon Protestants).

But let us continue with the broader picture of the effects of the conservative restoration in the 1980s. In industry and in the university system, and most glaringly with respect to the courts, priorities for addressing inequality that had been pushed forward in the 1960s now have been severely scaled back or have fallen in abeyance. A trend towards a radical reversal and stagnation in the fortunes of minorities has set in. For example, in the last decade or so, overall unemployment has averaged 15.2 percent for Black Americans. The unemployment rate for Whites during the same period is under 6.0 percent. In 1986, the median income for black families was 57.1 percent of that of white families—some three percentage points less than it was in 1970! The Alliance Against Women's Oppression (1983) contends in one of their discussion papers that black mothers are four times as likely to die at child birth as white mothers. Black and Native American infant mortality rates are currently higher that those of Third World countries such as Barbados, Costa Rica, and Trinidad and Tobago.

This pattern of severe black disadvantage is also reflected in the statistical information now available on racial inequality in schooling in the United States. Hann, Danzberger, Lefkowitz (1987), the authors of *Dropouts in America*, contend that in 1986, 40 percent of Hispanic and 26 percent of black students had dropped out of school compared with 13 percent of white high school youth. Today, there are fewer black high school graduates entering colleges than there were in 1976. In the decade or so, since 1976, the proportion of black high school graduates who go to college has declined from 33.5 percent to 26.1 percent. And of those black students who make it to college, only 42 percent of them continue through to graduation (Sudarkasa, 1988).

These developments are symptomatic of the effective deprioritization of minority interests and the steady racialization of the state's social and political agendas as formulated by successive conservative US administration in the 1980s. This has been the case in areas that are of special importance to African-Americans and other minorities such as higher education. Figure 1 illustrates and summarizes patterns in state policies with respect to the issue of inequality in higher education. Policies of the 1960s are compared with those of the 1980s.

**Figure 1:  Trends in State Policy Toward Minority Education**

| Higher Education | | |
| --- | --- | --- |
| 1960s | Versus | 1980s |

1. In 1964, the Economic Opportunity Act authorized the funding of work-study programs to assist academically disadvantaged students.

2. In 1964, the Civil Rights Act was passed prohibiting funding to institutions that discriminate on the basis of race, thereby mandating that colleges and universities open their doors to minorities.

3. Under the Higher Education Act of 1965, work-study program were expanded, a program of need-based grants was established, and federal assistance to struggling Black colleges was provided.

4. In 1968, the trio of outreach and academic support programs (Upward Bound, Talent Search, and Special Services for Disadvantaged Students) was created.

1. In 1980, incoming President Reagan declared his hostility to federal involvement in education and suggested that the Department of Education should be abolished.

2. In 1983, the Reagan administration provided tax exemptions to private institutions—like the Bob Jones University, that practice elitism and discrimination.

3. In its first four years, the Reagan government used the material and legal resources of the Department of Justice to contest affirmative action programs and busing.

4. In 1988, the severity of cutbacks initiated by the federal government was felt, particularly in the area of college work-study programs upon which many minority students depend for supplementary income while they are in college.  Funding for these work-study program decline by 22 percent during the 1980s.

These statistics are indeed disturbing.  But much of current research and social policy continues to "blame the victim." Mainstream educators and sociologists of schooling reduce the complexities associated with racial inequality to one overwhelming theoretical and programmatic concern:  the issue of the educability of minorities.  In these accounts, the central task has been to explain perceived differences between black and white students as reflected in differential achievement scores on standardized tests, high school drop out rates, and so on. Explanations of black "underachievement" are consequently situated within pathological constructions of minority mental capacities (Jensen, 1981; Dunn, 1987), child rearing practices (Bell, 1975), family structures (Moynihan, 1965), and linguistic styles (Hess & Shipman, 1975).

But "Black Underachievement" is an ideologically convenient place to attempt to bury more difficult questions regarding social inequality and racial differences in the United States.  In a societal context in which Blacks are treated as "aliens" or "intruders" in their own country (as Naipaul [1989] argues in *A Turn in the South*), educators continue to talk about educational institutions as if they were effective fortresses against a hostile racial environment.  This is a naive and forlorn hope.  As is evident from the examples of racial hostility discussed at the beginning of this essay, educational institutions in the United States are not immune to manifest acts of racism "observed and experienced outside the school door" (Troyna, 1984, p. 115). What I want to argue then is that the persistence of racial inequality and the increasing evidence of racial antagonism toward minorities in this society present educators and educational institutions with a series of moral dilemmas—indeed, with a proliferation of crises of legitimation.

To begin with, "Black Underachievement" constitutes a crisis of legitimation because it throws into question the meritocratic credibility of the educational system and the professional competence of educators and policy makers.  For minorities who are persistently tracked into non-academic futures, the liberal democratic remonstration that schooling is a neutral setting in which everyone has a "fair chance" is thrown into real suspicion and doubt.

Second, the rather naive assumption that mainstream educators hold that educational attainment and credentials are direct routes to occupational success and social mobility is often contradicted by the experience of black school leavers and college graduates in the job market. Troyna (1984) and Blackburn and Mann (1979) in their incisive analyses of the British job market scene explode the myth that there is a necessary "tightening bond" between education and the economy. In his investigation of the fortunes of "educated" black and white youth in the job market, Troyna concludes that racial and social connections rather than educational qualifications per se "determined" the phenomenon of better job chances for white youth even when black youth had higher qualifications than their white counterparts. The tendency of employers to rely on informal channels or "word of mouth" networks, together represent some of the ways in which the potential for success of qualified black youth in the labor market is systematically undermined. Carmichael and Hamilton (1967), Marable (1985) and Crichlow (1985) have made similar arguments about the racial disqualification of black youth in the job market in the United States. This is what John Ogbu and Matute-Bianchi (1986) call the "job ceiling."

A third crisis is being precipitated in educational institutions in this society as school populations and university populations become more and more ethnically diverse. For instance, forty-six percent of the students in Texas schools are black or Hispanic. In the twenty-five largest systems in the United States, the majority of students are now minorities (*Education Week,* May 14, 1986). These demographic changes raise profound questions about school knowledge; particularly the wisdom of maintaining the rather unventilated dominance of the Anglocentric curriculum in our educational institutions. The Anglocentric dominance in the American school curriculum is rapidly being overtaken by the concrete event of the emergence of racialized "others" (immigrants from Africa, Asia, and the Caribbean, and indigenous minorities) in major cities in the United States.

Fourth, teachers and educators are presented with a crisis of legitimation with respect to the whole project of integration itself. In a context in which the state has reneged on the promise of racial equality raised in the Johnson and Kennedy administrations, teachers and educators are being bombarded with new and contradictory demands. They are being asked to generate an ethos of harmony and equality at the same time that they are having to respond to increasing governmental pressure to foster competitive individualism and "excellence" in schools. In many ways, federal policies within the last decade of cutting back on financial support for the higher education of low-income students have sent out a message that has been highly destructive for the education of minorities. In a period when rewards and resources are becoming scarce, the gap between winners and losers is widening. Black youth have fallen victim to a system that says: YOU ARE NOT A PRIOR-ITY . . .YOU DO NOT REALLY MATTER.

# References

Alliance Against Women's Oppression. (1983). "Poverty not for women only: A critique of the feminization of poverty." *AAWO Discussion Paper 3*. San Francisco.

Badger Herald. (1987, September 9). "The Fiji Island affair." *Badger Herald*, p.1.

Baldwin, J. (1986). *Nobody knows my name*. New York: Dell.

Bell, R. (1975). "Lower class negro mothers' aspirations for their children." In H. Stub (ed.), *The sociology of education: A sourcebook* (pp. 125-136). Homewood, IL: The Dorsey Press.

Blackburn, R. and Mann, M. (1979). *The working class in the labour market*. London: Macmillan.

Carmichael, S., and Hamilton, C. (1967). *Black power*. New York: Vintage.

Crichlow, W. (1985). *Urban crisis, schooling, and black youth unemployment: A case study*. Unpublished manuscript.

Dunn, L. (1987). *Bilingual Hispanic children on the U.S. mainland: A review of research on cognitive, linguistic, and scholastic development.* Circle Pines, Minnesota: American Guidance Service.

*Education Week.* (1986, May 14). "Here they come ready or not: An *Education Week* Special Report on the ways in which America's population in motion is changing the outlook for schools and society." *Education Week,* p. 28.

Ellison, R. (1982). *Invisible Man.* New York: Random House.

Hann, A., Danzenberger, J., and Lefkowitz, B. (1987). *Dropouts in America,* Washington, D.C.: Institute for Educational Leadership.

Hess, R. & Shipman, V. (1975). " Early experience and socialization of congitive modes in children." In H. Stub (Ed.), *The sociology of education: A sourcebook* (96-113). Homewood, IL: The Dorsey Press.

Jensen, A. (1981). *Straight talk about mental tests.* New York: Free Press.

Lord, M. (1987). "Frats and sororities: Greek rites of exclusion." *The Nation,* 245 (1), pp. 10-13.

Marable, M. (1985). *Black American politics.* London: Verso.

Moynihan, D. (1965). *The negro family: The case for national action.* Washington, D.C.: United States Department of Labor, Office of Policy, Planning, and Research.

McCarthy, C. (1990). *Race and curriculum.* London: Falmer Press.

Naipaul, V.S. (1989). *A turn in the South.* New York: Vintage.

Ogbu, J., and Matute-Bianchi, M. (1986). " Understanding sociocultural factors in education: Knowledge, identity, and school adjustment." In California State Department of

Education (Ed.), *Beyond language: Social and cultural factors in schooling language minority students* (pp. 73-142). Los Angeles: Evaluation, Dissemination and Assessment Center, California State University.

Omi, M. and Winant, H. (1986). *Racial formation in the United States.* Boston: Routledge and Kegan Paul.

Sudarkasa, N. (1988). "Black enrollment in higher education: The unfulfilled promise of equality." In National Urban League (Eds), *The State of Black America, 1988* (pp. 7-22). New York: National Urban League.

Steele, S. (1989, February). "The recoloring of campus life: Student racism, academic pluralism, and the end of a dream." *Harper's Magazine*, pp. 47-55.

Tifft, S. (1989, January 23). "Bigots in the ivory tower." *Time* p. 28.

Troyna, B. (1984). " Multicultural education: Emancipation or containment?" In Barton, L., and Walker, S. (eds) *Social Crisis and Educational Research* (pp. 75-97). London: Croom Helm.

Viadero, D. (1989). "Schools witness a troubling revival of bigotry." *Education Week*, May 24, p. 1.

# Christine E. Sleeter, Walter Gutierrez, Clara Ann New, Susan R. Takata

Muchos padres hispanos que inmigraron y continuan inmigrando a los Estados Unidos a través de muchos años, nunca pensaron; ni siquiera se dieron cuenta de las grandes dificultades que ellos encontrarían el tratar de educar a sus hijos en este país. El sueño dorado que les impulsó venir a este país fue la creencia que aquí todo es fácil, todo es bueno, todo es gratis, todo es posible y todo el mundo es rico y educado. ¡Qué triste que todo este sueño dorado se rompa en pedacitos al contacto con la realidad de la vida, la cultura, la educación, el idioma de este país! Pronto estos padres se despertaron y se dieron cuenta que nada entedieron y que todo fue una ilusión. ¡En verdad, un sueño y nada más!

Isn't this passage inaccessible for many readers? It is the same in reverse for many students who are not Anglo. American schools and the American population in general are rapidly becoming increasingly racially diverse. By the year 2000, 39% of the U. S. population will be minorities. Just the Hispanic population alone, from 1976 to 1987, increased more than 70%. Between 1980 and 2000, the Asian American population will have tripled. Often Whites believe that the best way to deal with this is to ignore race and try to be colorblind. That means in the process ignoring important factors such as how different people make and communicate meaning. Or, educators leap onto "quick fix" solutions that really do not change anything.

The investment of energy, money, and cultural resources in the education of citizens is necessary and recognized by any civilized country. But to deny a full and rich education to some based on their race and culture is chaotic and brutal, not to mention unproductive; it breaks the spirit of democracy and undermines civilization itself. It is important for Whites to realize that they (or we, depending on one's frame of reference) have tried to "hog" the resources of this country since its inception, and have built institutions and beliefs about people that perpetuate unfairness and discrimination. Dealing with this is very painful for Whites, but necessary if we are to build a just society in the future that provides access to a quality life and personal freedom for *all* its citizens.    In this essay we will critique current approaches to addressing diversity in schools, then discuss some complexities of race and culture in the education process.

**Diversity as a "PR Piece"**
Discussions about diversity in schools and universities provide an example of "new" approaches to thinking about race that really are not new at all.   In recent years, racist flyers and graffiti, name-calling, self-imposed segregated groupings (sticking with one's own kind) and fraternity pranks targeting particular racial and ethnic groups reflect the continued intensity and persistence of racism in schools and on university campuses.   In an era of scarce resources, there is fierce competition for admissions, financial aid and other educational goods and services.   Such scarcity has fostered this new racism.   There is a threat of a power shift that was once dominated by Whites, as the minority is in the process of becoming the majority.   The new racism is one response to this major social change soon to reshape American society.

In response, many schools and universities are designing for "diversity."   Diversity is all about who should be "privileged" to the American Dream.   Designing for diversity may be seen in the celebration of Black History Month or Native American Awareness Week, the development of ethnic studies courses, the hiring of more minority faculty and staff, and the admission of a more diverse student population.   These things are done supposedly to clarify our understanding of racial and ethnic issues.    But, is it realistic to expect new understanding to develop during a festival or a semester's course?   Some students will change, while others will hold more tenaciously onto their prejudices and racist ideas.    There is a backfiring effect of ramming diversity down the throats of students, who take such courses out of resentment and anger at another "required" course.   The students ask, "who needs it?"

In the 1960's the focus of intense racial conflict was on access to quality education, university admissions policies, and ethnic studies; in 1992, the focus remains the same.   Very little has changed for minorities.   Is "Diversity" just a public relations scam of the 1990's? Although some see progress made, others see a frightening trend backwards. The ultimate bankruptcy came in 1974 with the Bakke decision, in which white males became victims of discrimination. More recently, Harvard University is accused of implementing an affirmative action policy for the rich (the practice of admitting the children of alumni). Then there is the false appeal to making it "on your own" or the "rugged frontier theory." The argument goes that to accept help is to lower one's self esteem. But help in any form, to undo the damage done, is essential to continued progress. In the '90's no one is making it "on their own." Are we really designing for diversity?

Education in the United States has undergone profound changes in the last several decades. Because education is the main vehicle out of poverty, open door admissions and affirmative action programs offered seductively quick solutions to the problem of equal access. Legal barriers to access based on race and gender were struck down, and society breathed a collective sigh of relief that discrimination has now ended. In other words, societal responsibility for oppression ended at the door to schooling with the charge that schools and the academy take up the challenge of educating those now within its ivy covered enclosure. But minority access to education has several built-in institutional biases reflective of a racist system.

Some believe that education is the cure-all solution to society's problems. But education did not create today's economic situation. The dilemma of education today merely mirrors the dilemma of our society. By 1990 it is clear that getting into schools and universities is only the first step. Because of institutional discrimination, women and minorities have been less successful getting out and on into other societal systems.

## The Embeddedness of Prejudice

The immediate and long-term influences of oppression based on race were documented in excruciating candor in the book entitled *Something of Value* (Ruark, 1955). The premise (and conclusion) states that when you take everything from a people, you had better give them something of value; hence, the Mau

Mau came into existence.   South Africa has never been the same.

The notion of race is socially constructed, based on our ability to identify by sight people whose ancestral origins were on different parts of the globe.  As a social construct, race has served to reinforce extreme opinions and biases held by some educators, and to condition significant segments of the population to accept passively inequality based on skin color as an incontrovertible way of living and learning in America.  The fabric of prejudice is so delicately interwoven into attitudes, pedagogy and resulting behaviors that the mere suggestion that impaired academic achievement might stem from racist practices invokes responses akin to those attributed to the main character in a fairy tale called "The Emperor's New Clothes." Blinded by his prejudices, the Emperor paraded through the streets in the nude because he was so thoroughly conditioned by his tailor—who was too insignificant to lie to him—to believe that he wore invisible clothes that were magnificent to the human eye.

American society, too, has continued to ignore the problematic consequences of attempting to enforce colorblind notions upon those who benefit from oppression, and those who are perpetually victimized.  Race, as well as color, has extensive ramifications which exist without meaning or reference to the intrinsic person, but which can exert painful day-to-day impact upon students of color as they struggle in the quest for identity, and frequently result in colossal self-denigration.  Depending upon the length of life, for example, a person whose lineage can be traced to African origins has borne as many as five socially imposed designations:   Colored, Negro, Black, Afro-American and African-American.  Unlike white students, for whom the connotations of race appear to remain constant and positive, the capricious ambiguity inherent in this group-naming process produces confusion and lack of self-worth in Americans of color.

Diminished estimation of self-worth has been found to correlate with lower academic achievement and other manifestations of undesirable behavior on an interpersonal level.  When race is utilized as the dominant measure of worth for an American, that is, race determines what, when and how students experience education, it is small wonder that students of color and disadvantaged Whites exhibit severe feelings of worthlessness, helplessness, anger and isolation. In classrooms where varied ways of knowing, believing, assessing and behaving are considered to be innate deficiencies rather than cultural differences, the tendency for teachers to rely heavily on well inculcated systems of racism is great. One result is the statistically improbable numbers of school suspensions issued black males, and the disproportionate numbers of students of color placed in exceptional education programs, such as those for the mentally retarded, learning disabled, and emotionally disturbed.

A glaring example is that of a black male who was retained in the same kindergarten class for six semesters because the teacher was unable to elicit acceptable responses from him on a standardized IQ test. Instead of connecting related pictures by a single line, the student—who was an accomplished caricaturist—would add another related picture and circle the three (or more) concepts. This thought process was replicated in each battery of the test. The teacher attributed this behavior to his being black, as the other members of the primarily white class followed the manual instructions explicitly. Since this youngster was generally reticent and did not participate in class discussions, the teacher assumed that his quiet demeanor signified lack of comprehension, and his "bizarre" responses on the same test for six semesters justified her beliefs.

Similar encounters may be observed consistently, due to the ignorance and racism that permeates the educational arena, where the popular remedy seems to be a steady proliferation of stigmatized programs that exclude students based on race. It appears that placing the blame on race is far more palatable than examining the players who are participating in the arena, in that benign attention can be given to the students and school can continue as usual.

## Institutional Racism

Most people equate racism with individual prejudice, but it goes far beyond that. Institutional racism comes about when a group of people have the power to enforce their prejudices by creating social institutions to buttress their privileges. Over the course of America's history, until recently we have had a dual system of institutions: those for people of European ancestry, and those for everyone else. The segregated school system was an example. Further, this dual system maintained white control over wealth and power, and at various points in history, helped Whites extend their control through conquest. For example, the Southwest was part of Mexico until the U. S. took it over through war, following which Anglos took land from Mexicans living on conquered territory by manipulating property laws and taxes.

It has been only since 1954 that this dual system of institutions was declared illegal by the Supreme Court. However, 1954 was preceded by over 400 years of constructing a dual system. Therefore, legal declaration that race is no longer to be a legitimate factor for allocating access to jobs, housing, education, and so forth, only began to dismantle institutional racism. Legalized racism was replaced by more subtle forms of racism.

For example, the school curriculum has been constructed around the European and Euro-American experience: history moves from Europe to the East Coast of the U. S. and west from there; most literary, musical, and art figures taught about are white; and European notions of linear progress and conceptions of circular time and mastery of the natural world are taught (as opposed to, say Native American conceptions of circular time and living in harmony with the natural world). While a few heroes and contributions from other groups have been added, the curriculum remains essentially Euro-centric. Students are regularly tested for their mastery of it, then rank-ordered, and sorted into ability groups and tracks for different instruction. Those who enter school most familiar and comfortable with a Euro-American perspective about the world tend to leave school well prepared for the best college and life opportunities. This is institutional racism; children are not overtly denied access to instruction based on their race, but instruction is still organized in such a way that white students, on the average, profit most from it.

White Americans often confuse race with white ethnicity, and wonder why Americans of color are experiencing difficulties that go beyond those of their white ethnic ancestors. The main difference between race and white ethnicity is skin color and other visible differences, and their use both historically and currently. During the period of colonization, Europeans destroyed as best they could the cultures and peoples of Africa and the Americas, enslaving Africans because their skin color allowed easy identification of slaves. When Eastern and Southern Europeans immigrated to the United States, they were not immediately accorded the privileges of White Americans, and did face considerable persecution and discrimination. But they succeeded, as Omi and Winant (1986) put it, in drawing "the color line *around*, rather than *within*, Europe" (p. 65). Further, they were able to bring with them families and communities that could remain intact and provide economic and cultural resources for survival and growth.

In contrast, African, Native American, and Mexican families and communities were attacked with intent to destroy over a long period of time, and to some extent, such policies are still intact. For example, the Chinese Exclusion Act of 1882 specifically prohibited immigration based on race, and in the process splintered many families by preventing them from joining their men who had already immigrated to the U. S. A bachelor society developed, and Chinatowns today are still impoverished partly as a result. As another example, Whites today are agitating for the termination of Native Americans' treaty rights, while on many reservations natives experience a high rate of disease and unemployment, leading to self-inflicted death and alcoholism. Adequate health care and health insurance are unavailable for low-income Native Americans, African Americans and Latinos, resulting in high infant mortality rates and shorter life spans than Anglos experience. African American males can look forward with greater likelihood to spending their young adult years in prison than in college.

## Race, Culture and Language

Racism is made to appear legitimate by trying to convince Americans that the most worthwhile culture and knowledge comes from Europe and Euro-Americans. The teacher who believes that regards children who are not white as culturally impoverished.

One need only immerse oneself in the language, philosophy, art, and accomplishments of a non-white group to realize that such a teacher is the one who is culturally impoverished. There are fundamental *cultural* and *language differences* in what students bring with them to school, that are based in their racial or ethnic roots. For example, the Hispanic style of learning is to be dependent on the caring teacher. In Hispanic cultures people work together rather than independently, so Hispanic children often wait to secure a personal relationship with the teacher and other students before attempting to complete a task. The teacher needs to be aware of the sensitivity defining how many Hispanics learn best. As another example, the syntax of the Spanish language is broad, open and free in its structure. The English language is restrictive, it is economic in word usage because Anglo thought is different from Hispanic thought. To an Anglo who does not understand this, a Hispanic student might appear to talk around a point imprecisely; conversely, to a Hispanic student, an Anglo may appear to speak too bluntly and even rudely, and to move through with ideas with excessive speed.

Our nation's educational system has been the subject of much negative attention over the past few years, and nowhere is this more deeply felt than in minority communities, who view education as the main road out of poverty. For example, about 45 percent of Hispanics are expected to drop out of high school, according to former Secretary of Education Lauro Cavazos. Alarming statistics link low levels of education with high incidence of teen pregnancy, unemployment, and even suicide among minority youth. A lack of roots or identity can impede the academic development of a child, and the risk is even greater when coupled with low economic status. Many minority parents, faced with racism and low paying jobs, compromised their ethnic identity for a chance at the American dream. As a result, a significant number of language minority babyboomers never learned their parents' language nor gained an understanding and appreciation of their heritage. They are often more familiar with negative and limiting stereotypes projected through the media than they are with poets, thinkers, and leaders who shared their ancestry.

Bilingual and multicultural education should provide the deep understanding of the minority student's roots, culture, heritage, people, and the people's ambitions.   Of course language minority groups have to learn English, and as quickly as possible, in order to survive.  But these are necessities, not blanket exclusions.   Most language minority people cannot forget their language, nor do they want to.  Language itself encodes values, literary works, and world view.   To learn a second language is to open new horizons; to lose one's first language is to sacrifice one's identity and roots.

Connection with one's ethnic and racial ancestry will give a student roots.   Roots and education can be combined in an effort to give minority children motivation for the future by teaching them about their language, their heritage.

A well designed bilingual and multicultural approach to education can help minority children to stay in school and grow.  The country's changing racial and ethnic composition will demand sweeping changes in the delivery of education.  Minorities are disenfranchised.  Demographics will dictate that most people, especially those in positions of power, understand, accept and even encourage cultural diversity.   Schools should concentrate on changing themselves, developing the capacity to serve all students, instead of consistently trying to change the nature of the students.

**Conclusion**

Teacher education programs are critical points of departure for aspiring educators whose socialization tends to be disparate from the populations that they will be entrusted to teach.  As such, it is imperative and incumbent on teacher education personnel that curricula prepare teachers to interact successfully with and diligently teach students to become aware of different styles of intellectual acumen, and to be adept at helping students recognize and reject attempts to exploit them because of their race.  This is hardly a simple endeavor, as it entails self-exploration and objectivity which bring curriculum content and pre-teachers together without violating either for *all* citizens.

# References

Omi, M. & Winant, H.  (1986).  *Racial formation in the United States*.  New York: Routledge.

Ruark, R. C.  (1955).  *Something of value*.  Garden City, NY: Doubleday.

# Chapter IX

# Socioeconomic Class and Education: In what ways does class affect the educational process?

**Joseph W. Newman**

**William Stanley**

# Joseph W. Newman

Most Americans take pride in our nation's efforts to educate children from all socioeconomic backgrounds, and there is much to admire in our commitment to sending all children to school. We should be concerned, however, that once the students get to school, social class plays such a strong role in their success—or lack of it. As pleasant as it would be to pretend schools take in students from diverse backgrounds and give then all the same opportunities to succeed, that simply does not happen. It is easy to underestimate the effects of social class on education because social class is such an under-developed term in our national vocabulary. Social class is a concept Americans talk around rather than talk about.

In fact, we often talk more openly and pointedly about race, religion, and (to a lesser degree) gender—the subjects of other chapters in this book—even though we claim the discussion makes us uncomfortable. When we discuss race, religion, or gender with a group of friends, educational issues often come to the fore. We may talk about school desegregation, for exam-ple, or prayer in public schools, or female cadets at West Point. The news media give us at least a surface awareness of these issues, for they are part of our nation's political conversation. The courts constantly call our attention to race, religion, and gender, for there is a well-documented record of discrimination based on these factors in the schools and throughout society.

Americans regard social class as a different kind of factor. Do poor children *as a group* receive unfair treatment in school? We may be hesitant to answer yes. The courts, too, have hedged their answer, for judges usually do not consider social class a factor comparable to race, religion, or gender in discrimination suits. Try discussing social class with a group of friends, and notice how the conversation wanders, most often into race or ethnicity. Educator and civil rights activist Mary Frances Berry contends the media show little interest in poor people without an added minority "teaser." Stories about poor black people, poor brown people, or poor red people get attention, she says but "nobody cares about poor Whites—not even poor Whites."

Who are the poor?   Answering that question helps explain our reluctance to confront social class head on.  A poor person is somebody else, many white Americans want to believe.  Yes, African Americans, Hispanic Americans, and Native Americans are disproportionately poor.  That is, compared with the total population, a much higher percentage of the people in these groups are poor.  When we try to understand their plight, we cannot ignore the continuing racial and ethnic discrimination they face.  But U. S. Labor Department figures show almost 70 percent of all poor people are white.  The reason is almost 80 percent of the population is white, and even though Whites have a lower incidence of poverty than the total population, Whites still constitute the largest group of poor Americans. Statistically, the typical poor family in the United States consists of a white woman—a female head of a household—and her children.  Trying to understand this family's plight. We cannot ignore continuing discrimination based on gender.

Although social class is tightly interwoven with other social forces discussed throughout this book, class has a powerful impact in its own right.  As Americans we cannot afford to pretend our nation has avoided the social stratification we like to criticize in other nations, for the United States too has social classes, a class structure that exerts a strong influence on the process of education.  Socioeconomically, some Americans are more equal than others, and this chapter explains how inequalities in education mirror inequalities in social class.

### Unequal Children, Unequal Schools
Consider how the circumstances of a child's birth influence the kind of school the child attends.  This example makes use of a model sociologists have developed and refined since the 1920s, a five-tiered class structure based on such factors as income, occupation, education, and housing.  A child born into the *upper class* (the top 2 percent of the population) or *upper-middle class* (the next 15 percent of the population) usually experiences American education at its best.  This child's family literally goes shopping for a school.  The child will probably attend a public school patronized by other families of high socioeconomic

status, a Roman Catholic school with a similar clientele, or a selective Independent school.

A child born into the *lower-middle class* (about one-third of the population) or *upper-working class* (another one-third) is likely to attend a neighborhood public school that gets fair-to-good reviews from parents.   Lower-middle class and upper-working class families are still the backbone of American public education, but those who are dissatisfied often opt for a religious school-Roman Catholic or fundamentalist Protestant.

A child of the *lower-working* class (the bottom 15 percent of the population) encounters American education at its worst. Born into a family with a few educational options, this child will almost certainly attend a neighborhood public school dominated by other poor children, a school many students, parents, and teachers regard as inferior.   From the 1960s through the 1990s, the educational label placed on the lower-working class student has changed from "culturally deprived" to "culturally different" to "disadvantaged" to "at risk."   Although educators have tried to make each label less condescending than the one before, whether the treatment the student receives in school has changed along with the label is a subject of intense debate.

**Language and Dialect**

To understand why, consider the issue of language and dialect. Linguists help explain what the casual observer in a school notices:   the lower a student's social class, the greater the differences between the dialect used in the student's home and the dialect used at school.   To linguists, dialect is not at all a pejorative word.   Everyone speaks a dialect—a cultural variation of a language.   Dialects vary in pronunciation, vocabulary, and syntax.   Standard English is simply the dialect of English that appears in grammar books.   No one speaks or writes standard English perfectly.

Students from middle and upper-class backgrounds, though, usually acquire a fairly close approximation of standard English just by growing up with their families and peers. These students come to school with a tremendous advantage, for they already know the "official" dialect of the school.   They can use the dialect to make sense of what goes on at school, from the teacher's morning greeting to the afternoon math lesson.

Students from working-class (especially lower-working class) backgrounds enter school with a double burden, for they must try to learn a new dialect at the same time they are trying to understand the formal and informal operation of the school. Their task is much more difficult than the one middle and upper-class students face. Evaluated against *norms*, standards that by definition reflect average performance, working-class students have to try harder just to keep up—they have to run faster just to stay even. Here is one of the most pressing problems of American education.

William Bennett and Chester Finn, secretary and assistant secretary of education, respectively, during the Reagan administration, have definite opinions on how to deal with the problem. The causes of this and other educational problems seem obvious to them: during the 1960s and 1970s, Americans "simply stopped doing the right things." Bennett and Finn are especially critical of educators who, led astray by liberals and radicals, lowered their expectations of students. Academic and moral standards plummeted down a slippery slope. To start doing the right things once again, the schools must saturate students with standard English. Teachers must once again stress corrections in language, for teachers are role models and more: authority figures who must insist on learning. All students will profit from this reversion to tried-and-true methods, Bennett and Finn conclude, and working-class students have the most to gain.

Such proposals, couched as they are in tough but egalitarian rhetoric, have strong political appeal. Bennett and Finn along with *Cultural Literacy* (1987) author E.D. Hirsch, Jr. and education professor Diane Ravitch, are staking out the high ground in America's ongoing educational debates. These conservative critics are billing themselves as traditionalists with a social conscience. They want the best for all students, they say, placing special emphasis on the *all*. Critics on the opposite end of the political spectrum, temporarily outflanked by this maneuver, sometimes find it difficult to counter the democratic posture.

In their efforts to be more egalitarian than the traditionalists, critics on the left must be careful not to apply a double standard. When scholars with graduate degrees and great facility in standard English use their impressive skills to brand standard English elitist, the arguments sound unconvincing at best and hypocritical at worst. Those who owe their own success to the use of the "prestige dialect" should be the last ones to encourage others to reject the dialect as an instrument of "cultural imperialism." Critics can be more constructive by agreeing standard English is indeed valuable, both intellectually—it can help unlock a storehouse of knowledge—and economically—it can help students move up in the social structure.

Bennett, Finn, and other traditionalists quite properly defend the value of standard English, but they offer no new suggestions for helping working-class students grasp the value. The notion that students will learn if authority figures insist they learn is certainly not new. The noses-to-the-grindstone approach has been around for years. But has it ever worked with large numbers of students? Traditionalists believe it has, and they seem nostalgic for a Golden Age of American education, a time when teachers were able to push all students to high levels of achievements by demanding hard work and promising rich awards.

Such an age never existed. There *was* a time when only a few students entered high school and fewer still graduated. According to statistics from the U.S. Department of education, in 1900 only 10 percent of the eligible age group went to high school and only 6 percent graduated. In 1920, 31 percent started and 17 percent finished, and in 1940 the percentages were 732 and 51. These figures are for all 14-to-17 year olds. The attendance and graduation rates for working-class students were much lower. Throughout these years, moreover, teachers complained many students fortunate enough to graduate from high school left with inadequate skills in standard English. Does this sound like the Golden Age of education traditionalists pine for, a time when, according to E.D. Hirsch, schools "effectively taught . . .disadvantaged children under a largely traditional curriculum?" Surely this is not an age we would want to recreate in the 1990s.

Nor would we want to return to the days when it was standard practice in schools to make working-class students feel ashamed of their home dialect. Traditionalists downplay the harsh treatment students suffered in an educational system committed to safeguarding correctness at all costs. Today, linguists know attacking a student's home dialect is the same thing as attacking the student. The suggestion here is not that teachers abandon standard English for "anything goes" approach to language. Instead, teachers can help students learn to use different dialects in different settings. Most people, in fact, shift back and forth between formal and informal language, between standard and non-standard English, depending on the situation. We speak differently in a job interview than at a baseball game. We write differently in a letter to the Internal Revenue Service than in a note to an old friend.

Here is a more realistic gauge of correctness: the concept of *appropriateness*. According to linguist, working-class students need practice in making deliberate choices about which dialect to use in which situation. Some school are having success with an approach that calls on students and teachers to envision specific situations requiring standard English. Students can role-play job interviews, for example, or talk with people from the immediate neighborhood who use standard English in their work and a less formal dialect in most other situations.

More fundamental reforms will be necessary in society, however, in order for these techniques to be more than empty exercises for working-class students. Many students do not view themselves as upwardly mobile. They have difficulty imagining themselves in jobs that demand standard English, for they have already encountered social and personal barriers that, from their point of view, look insurmountable. They see no connection between what the school has to offer and what they will need as adults. Seeing the world through these students' eyes can help us understand why they find the advice to work hard and reap rewards at once laughable and infuriating.

Traditionalists offer little more than a pep talk, an upbeat message that doors of opportunity will open to students who master standard English. Don't give up, traditionalists urge. Don't make excuses for yourself. You can be successful. Much of this advice is not bad *in* itself, but *by* itself—in the absence of political action—the pep talk rings hollow. The traditionalists' political commitment to reducing discrimination and increasing opportunity rarely matches their rhetorical commitment. William Bennett is a perfect example of this phenomenon. He urges poor people to work hard while he opposes legislation designed to reduce discrimination at school and on the job. He challenges working-class students to speak well, fit in, and move up while he supports cuts in higher education grant and loan programs.   Bennett practices double-standard politics of the worst sort.

## Ability Grouping and Tracking

Social class is at the heart of the ongoing debate over ability grouping and tracking, practices so deeply entrenched in American education many people cannot imagine schools without them.   Ability grouping and tracking became popular at the turn of the twentieth century, when schools faced an influx of working-class children.  Since then educators have continued to diversify the curriculum in an effort to accomodate students from different socioeconomic backgrounds.  Some educators, speaking bluntly, have argued working-class students lack both the interest and ability necessary to succeed in school.  They need a special curriculum just to get by.   Other educators, trying to sound less judgmental, have taken the position that all students differ in their interests and abilities.  Only a diversified curriculum can "meet the needs" of all students.  Whatever the justification, the results are clear:  the schools are divided by social class.  Ability groups and tracks in schools reflect socioeconomic divisions in society.

Ability grouping involves placing together students of similar ability for instruction in particular subjects.  Elementary school teachers usually form separate groups for fast, average, and slow readers, for example,  The conventional wisdom among teachers is today's students are too sophisticated for the names teachers once assigned to reading groups: bluebirds, robins, and redbirds.  Invariably, teachers say, students redesignate one of the bird groups buzzards.  In an effort to stay a step ahead, many teacher now allow students to select the group names, and in 1991 the students favored New Kids, Ghostbusters, and Ninja Turtles. Now students have to be more creative to come up with an insulting nickname for one ability group. Popular choices in 1991 were Iraqis and Scuds.

The names in this account are already dated, but the point is not. The lowest group is the one that gets the bad name, for ability grouping puts the label of "losers" on low-group students. Students from working-class backgrounds are more likely that other students to be placed in the lowest ability groups in the first grade, for their home dialect differs more from the school's official dialect. Thus working-class students can acquire a stigma almost at the start of school.

Evidence on the academic effectiveness of ability grouping is mixed, with about as many studies unfavorable to the practice as favorable. The most favorable studies show it offers a slight advantage to students in the top group. The least favorable studies show it does significant harm to students in the the bottom group. Instead of reducing the academic and social differences children bring with them to school, ability grouping seems to increase the differences. As students move through the grades, the gap between top and bottom widens.

After examining the evidence, some educators are looking for alternatives to ability grouping. One promising strategy is *cooperative learning*, in which teachers form learning teams composed of students with different socioeconomic backgrounds and different academic abilities. Students cooperate rather than compete. Faster students help slower students. Teachers assign grades based on a combination of individual progress and group performance. Whether cooperative learning can dislodge ability grouping from its entrenched position in the schools, however, remains to be seen.

When students move from elementary school to middle or high school, tracking helps ability grouping accentuate their differences. Tracking involves placing students in different academic programs, often called college preparatory, general, and alternative/basic/vocational. Sociologists have documented how the tracks reflect the social structure. The more affluent a school's student body, the more emphasis the school is likely to place on college prep programs. Schools with poorer students, by contrast, tend to have smaller college prep tracks and larger general and alternative tracks. In the nation as a whole, college prep programs enroll about 80 percent of upper and upper-middle class students are eight times as likely as lower working-class students to be in their schools' most prestigious track. Enrollment in alternative programs is weighted in just the opposite way, heavier on working-class students and lighter on others.

Tracking promotes even deeper academic differentiation than ability grouping. In ability grouping, all students take a particular subject— reading or mathematics, for example—albeit on different levels. In tracking, students follow different programs that may involve completely different subjects. Students in a high school's college prep track may take four years of math, for example: algebra I, algebra II, geometry, and trigonometry. Students in the general track may take three year: general math, consumer math, and algebra I. Alternative track students rarely take more than two years, typically general math and consumer math. Tracking parcels out science in the same way, with more years and more demanding courses going to college prep students. Tracking usually reserves foreign languages for the same favored students. Even English and social studies, subjects all students take for three or four years, are differentiated because of tracking. While college prep students are learning to write essays and analyze issues, other students are filling out worksheets and looking up answers in the back of the book.

Since the release of *A Nation at Risk* (1983) and a flood of other reports decrying the poor quality of American education, tracking has come under attack by critics from throughout the political spectrum. Today tracking has fewer defenders than at any other time since the 1940s. Tracking does more harm than good, most critics agree, and it does the most harm to working-class students. A consensus is forming that now is the time to reduce tracking.

Debating why tracking is so resistant to change, though, points up differences of opinion among the critics. William Bennett, Chester Finn, and other traditionalists place much of the blame on the education system. The adults in charge of the public schools are allowing students to take the easy way out, traditionalists contend. Even when state legislatures and state boards of education raise high school graduation requirements, teachers find a way to let the weakest students water down their education. To fulfill the two-course math requirement most states have imposed for graduation, alternative-track students usually select the easiest courses available. The same thing happens in every other subject, and teachers who know better stand by and let it all happen. Parents and other citizens must share the blame for this tragedy, traditionalists argue, for we have not held the schools accountable. Now is the time to demand, in Diane Ravitch's words, "the schools we deserve."

All students deserve excellent schools, to be sure, but the traditionalists' arguments are out of touch with the world of the schools, the world students and teachers know from the inside out. Teachers' working conditions are their students' learning conditions, and they are blocking attempts to reduce tracking. Bennett and Finn shy away from discussing such matters, but people who spend more time in schools remind us of the heavy workload teachers carry. It is not unusual for high school teachers to be responsible for teaching five classes of thirty to forty students each—a total of 150 to 200 students every day. Just interacting with so many human beings is a wearying task. After school, there are not enough hours in the afternoons, evenings, and weekends for teachers to do justice to their many other responsibilities, one of which is grading papers. Do the arithmetic and see how much time it would take a high school teacher with the above workload to spend just ten minutes per week on each student's written work. Now put yourself in the teacher's shoes and ask whether it would be possible to double or triple that time in order to give working-class students some of the help they would need to succeed in an academically rigorous program.

### Class, Dollars and Programs

Reducing tracking and pushing all students to their limits are admirable goals, but given current conditions in the schools, the goals are out of reach. Even if teachers were superhuman, they could not compensate for the lack of resource in many schools.

The public schools in the nation's poorest school districts, supported by weak local tax bases, cannot afford many of the programs other districts can. An affluent surburban high school often spends $7,500 per student and offers four foreign languages, six math courses, and eight science courses. Most students in this school take the challenging program Bennett recommends for every American student. Only a few miles away, a rural or central-city high school is able to spend only half as much money per student and offer only half as many courses in each academic area. If schools cannot provide programs, students cannot take them.

Throwing money at problems will not always solve them, traditionalists like to remind us, but without more money our poorest students will never have access to the academic programs that help privileged students become privileged adults. An encouraging sign on the horizon is the success of lawsuits seeking additional state funding for school districts unable to raise enough local revenue to offer quality programs. As these cases work their way through the courts, judges are finally saying what they have been reluctant to say in the past: poor students *as a group* do indeed receive unfair treatment in America's schools.

# William Stanley

**Introduction**

Our society appears to have great difficulty coming to terms with the question of social class (McDermot, 1990). For example, most Americans describe themselves as middle class despite large differences among them in terms of wealth and income. Educator/philosopher Mortimer Adler (1983), has even referred to the United States as a "classless" society. There is a lack of consensus regarding the meaning of social class and the criteria we should use to determine an individual's (or group's) class identity. Class has been determined in many ways throughout history, (e.g., family heritage of an aristocracy), but in modern industrial societies, some combination of the following criteria are likely to be employed: wealth, income, occupational status, educational attainment, housing, lifestyle, cultural orientation, and one's relationship to the means of production. There is also disagreement over the actual nature of social class structure in our society and the extent to which genuine social mobility exists among classes. Finally, how class and education are related in the United States remains a controversial question.

Despite the lack of consensus and occasional assertions of classlessness, most people do understand that classes are a major feature of our society and that there are wide differences of wealth, income, status, culture, and power. Furthermore, most Americans seem to believe that class background has a significant effect on a student's educational attainment and socioeconomic success.

Research on the relationship between class and one's life chances has been underway throughout this century. Some of the results have been unclear or even contradictory. Still, there have been some indisputable findings. For example, the rates for infant mortality and serious childhood illnesses are significantly higher among the poor than they are for the more affluent. Children of the poor also have significantly less access to schooling, both in terms of quality and total number of years completed. And since the level of schooling is highly correlated with occupational status and income, one's class also has a significant affect on attaining each of these goals.

### Some of the Specific Effects of Class on Education

Most educators in the United States, despite their differences, have understood class to have a significant affect on education. Early in this century, Dewey (1916) discussed the negative influence of class on education, as did leading social reconstructionists like George Counts and Theodore Brameld during the 1920's and 30's. Another important contribution to this literature was August Hollingshead's (1949) *Elmstown's Youth* which described the differential treatment received by the poor, middle-class, and upper-middle-class students. James Conant (1961) also noted the negative impact of poverty on education in the postwar period. *The Coleman Report* (1966) is among the most influential studies involving the effect of class on education. Class was found to affect student attitude toward school, classroom participation, level of prior knowledge, and time denoted to homework. Many of Coleman's findings were confirmed by Jencks (1972) and more recently by Wilson (1987). And Ted Sizer (1984), in his book *Horace's Compromise*, made the following observation:

> Among schools there was one important difference, which followed from a single variable only; the social class of the student body. If the school principally served poor [students], its character, if not its structure, varied from sister schools for the more affluent. It got so I could say with some justification to school principals, "Tell me about the income of your students' families and I'll describe to you your school. (p. 6)

Since local control and financing of schooling is still the major form of school organization in this society, social class has a significant impact on the level of expenditure per pupil. One recent estimate contends that, on average, affluent suburban school districts spend approximately $9,000 per pupil compared to $4,500 per pupil in inner city and rural schools. This amounts to a $58,500 per pupil gap in spending over the thirteen years from kindergarten through senior year (Nelson, Palo, and Carlson, 1990). Of course, these are averages and actual amounts will vary from district to district. Nevertheless, it is the case that most districts with a predominantly lower class student body receive significantly less funds per pupil than the districts serving middle or upper class students. The impact of this differential funding can be observed in several ways. Lower class school districts are more likely to have deteriorated school buildings and drab classrooms in need of repair. Generally, such schools are less well supplied, have inadequate science laboratory facilities, and out of date or inadequate numbers of textbooks. Teachers in these schools often have less training and receive lower salaries. The work environment is frequently quite unpleasant, even violent. Crime, drug abuse, and teenage pregnancy rates are higher than in most affluent suburban schools. It is difficult to retain teachers, and many classes are taught by substitutes. Lower class inner-city schools have much higher student dropout rates (50% or higher) compared with the national average of about 25% (McLaren, 1989, pp. 8-10).

There is also evidence that lower class children are more likely to be diagnosed as having learning disabilities and placed in special education programs. The pervasive use of tracking and grouping is also influenced by class with the bulk of lower tracks and groups being populated by lower class students. And once a child is placed in a lower track or group, he or she is unlikely to move to a higher one. Finally, there is evidence that lower class children generally have a harder time learning than do middle class students. I will say more about this as we go on. For now, it should be clear that a lower class background can have a significant negative impact on educational opportunity and future life chances (Darling-Hamond, 1990).

Given the negative effects of class on education, it is alarming to note the evidence for the persistence of hard-core poverty in our nation. During what has been called "the longest period of economic expansion in the post-war period"—1982-1990, the economic gap between the bottom fifth and the top five percent of our population has actually increased, and twenty percent of all children under age six live in poverty (McLaren, 1989, 7-8).

**The Origins of Class in our Society**
Sociologists have posed two main explanations for the existence of class and social stratification in our society: a functionalist (or consensus) theory and a radical (or conflict) theory. There

are many variations of view within each of these theoretical orientations.    However, each general theoretical position reflects a major way scholars have tried to explain social class and its function.  Most important for our purposes, each theory has very different implications for educational practice.

### The Functionalist Account of the Relationship Between Social Class and Education

For functionalists, the existence of social classes or social stratification is an inevitable outcome of the process necessary to stabilize our social system.   Social organization and stability require people to perform many different roles, some far more difficult or complex than others.   In the main, people are induced to perform social roles by extrinsic rewards, especially income and prestige.  The functionalists also believe that human intelligence and skills vary widely and that there are relatively fewer people available for the more difficult social roles (e.g., surgeons, physicists).  The combination of high social need and scarce human resources results in higher income and prestige for certain occupations that satisfy important social roles.  Over time, this process results in a society wherein different groups performing different social roles form classes or social strata defined by income level, education, occupational prestige, housing, lifestyle, and culture.

In other words, the existence and evolution of classes is explained as a natural feature of social organization.  Therefore, it would be both unrealistic and dysfunctional to try to eliminate social classes.  Rather, we need to ensure that our society has genuine social mobility so that people have an equal opportunity to achieve the class position equal to their abilities.  No one should be kept from entering the middle or upper class strata because of his or her race, ethnicity, gender, religion, class origin, or other similar variables.  Functionalist theorists acknowledge that our class system is far from perfect and that racism, sexism, and other forms of discrimination continue to limit social mobility.   In addition, economic decline often reverses the course of social mobility, with the negative consequences of recessions tending to fall more heavily on those in the lower classes.  Nevertheless, functionalists believe that ours is a relatively open society, and we are working to remove the remaining barriers to social mobility.

Public education plays a crucial role in this regard. Our public schools are open to all children regardless of their class background, and educational attainment is highly correlated with future income and occupational prestige. While discrimination limiting social mobility still exists, differential social rewards are generally linked to real human differences in terms of one's ability to make a social contribution. If we accept these functionalist assumptions, then our social stratification can be understood as both natural and fair. As long as our society provides genuine equality of opportunity to all citizens, our present social class system is more properly described as meritocracy and not a society based on a rigid class structure of owners against workers or elites against common people.

## The Radical Account of Class and Schooling

Radical or conflict theorists are far more skeptical than functionalists regarding the inevitability of social classes, at least in their present form. Most radical theorists have been influenced to some degree by Marxism. Early forms of Marxist thought understood modern industrial societies as divided into two major classes, i.e., the dominant bourgeoisie who owned and controlled the economic means of production and the proletariat or industrial working class. Over time, the Marxist interpretation of class (e.g., rejection of the inevitability of a classless society following a successful worker revolution) has undergone major revisions to reflect the significant socioeconomic changes that have occurred since the death of Marx. In fairness to Marx, he never held a rigid or fixed definition of class, understood that modern industrial society was far more complex than a single two-class model, and would have supported the reinterpretation of social class in terms of specific historical conditions.

The important point for radical theorists is that, in general, social classes do not reflect genuine human differences but are the result of unequal power arrangements. Radicals argue that most of the measures (e.g., I.Q. tests, SATs) we use to determine human differences are not objective scientific measures but pseudo-scientific constructs employed to help maintain

control over the lower classes.  Obviously, it is in the interest of
the dominant social classes to have most people, particularly
those in the lower classes, accept the functionalist account of
social classes as necessary and inevitable.

For radicals, the dominant social classes use education to help
reproduce their power and existing social arrangements.  While
this process is never entirely successful, it is effective.  The
dominant classes exercise control over education in several
ways.  First, education is generally organized in such a way as to
reflect present social arrangements.  Schools are hierarchical
organizations with white males holding most leadership
positions and teachers having relatively little power.  Second,
the curriculum is largely designed to support the views of the
dominant classes.  For instance, there is little criticism of the
current social order, and course content mainly reinforces traditional values, economic theory, and functionalist views of
human behavior and institutions.  Third, the very practice of
education is conducted in ways that function to undermine the
competence of the lower classes.  Almost two decades of
research (e.g., Labov, 1973; Bernstein, 1971; Bourdieu, 1973,
1977; Bourdieu and Passeron, 1977) have documented the very
different forms of language used by students with different class
backgrounds.  These different forms, language codes, or
discourses can have a powerful effect, because they either
enhance or diminish a student's potential for gaining from his
or her educational experience.  *Different* discourses do not mean
either inferior or superior as Labov (1973), Bernstein (1971)
and others have demonstrated.  For example, the dialect of
urban black children is no less a complex, meaningful language
code than the traditional middle class dialect of white children
(Labov, 1973; Gee 1988, 1990).

The consequences of using one dialect as opposed to the
other can be devastating.  As sociolinguist James Gee (1988,
1990) explains, the discourse style one brings to school might be
the single most important variable that explains student failure
or success.  Most schools (and school materials like texts, work-
books, films, etc.) feature the mainstream discourse spoken by
the white middle class.  Thus, white middle class students are
inducted into a familiar process of schooling that gives them the

opportunity to practice and improve their linguistic competence. In sharp contrast, most poor children, particularly black and Hispanic students, enter school using a very different discourse inconsistent with the mainstream discourse of the middle class. Students from lower class families must simultaneously attempt to learn a new (middle class) linguistic discourse along with the content of school subjects. It is no wonder that such children tend to fall behind and have higher failure and dropout rates. Moreover, schooling teaches such students, at least indirectly if not overtly, that their mode of discourse is inferior and that they need to learn to speak and write *the* correct way.

I am not suggesting that schools should not attempt to teach lower class (as well as other culturally different) children to become competent users of the standard English of the middle class. Rather, this necessary competence (given our present society) must be accomplished in a very different way which respects the culturally different student's discourse and does not seek to replace it with another. While bi-dialectical competence should be a goal for children of the poor and culturally different, it should also be part of the linguistic competence required of middle class children. This implies a comprehensive approach to language acquisition that includes the study of the literature of culturally different groups, as well as an analysis of language that illustrates how middle class English is merely one possible dialect among others and without any intrinsic structural superiority. On the other hand, culturally different children need to have a realist understanding of the dominant role played by middle class English in our society and how a lack of competence with this discourse can influence their life chances.

The evidence that education helps to reproduce the present class structure does not mean that there is no significant social mobility in our society. Rather it suggests the social mobility that does exist is largely shaped and controlled by the classes with the most power. According to radical theorists, a certain amount of mobility is necessary to keep the lower classes contented, avoid social revolution, and provide evidence for the functionalist position that our society is a democratic meritocracy. In this way, a limited amount of social mobility can function mainly to preserve the present class structure. Indeed, the evidence available indicates that our class structure has not changed significantly throughout most of this century. And as noted earlier, the income gap between the top and bottom classes has actually widened over the past decade of economic prosperity. We must also recall that those who are able to improve their class position (generally) must acquire the values of the higher classes. Thus, the more successful one becomes, the more likely he or she will come to identify with the dominant class view.

**Conclusions**
While the debate continues over the relationship between class and schooling, we can draw certain conclusions. The existence of social classes representing great differences in wealth, income, occupational prestige, and cultural orientation is a dominant feature of our social order. It is also clear that one's class position has a powerful effect on the quality and level of education attained. Lower class children also tend to have more learning difficulties even when placed in high quality schools. In other words, lower class children generally require more educational assistance, yet they typically receive less than their more affluent counterparts.

What remains in dispute is the extent to which the existing class structure is more a natural reflection of human abilities or the artifact of unequal economic, cultural, and political power. Even most conservatives agree that significant barriers exist to social mobility and that these (e.g., racism, and sexism) should be identified and removed. Unlike radicals, however, the conservatives remain convinced that removing artificial barriers to mobility will not eliminate significant social stratification. Conversely, radical educators would like to put such assertions to the test. They wonder what our society and schooling would be like if we eliminated most forms of discrimination and created genuine educational opportunities that did not penalize culturally different students.* Until this occurs we should

---

\* The reader should consider Chapters 7 and 8 for some other perspectives on the links among class, gender, and race.

remain skeptical regarding the conservative (functionalist) assertions regarding the inevitability of our present class structure.

# References

Adler, M. (1982). *The paideia proposal.* New York: Macmillan.

Bernstein, B. (1971). *Class, codes and control: Theoretical studies toward a sociology of language, vol. 1.* New York: Schocken Books.

Bourdieu, P. (1973). "Cultural reproduction and social reproduction." In R. Brown (Ed.). *Knowledge, education, and cultural change.* London: Tavistock, 71-112.

Bourdieu, P. (1977). *Outline toward a theory of practice.* Cambridge: Cambridge University Press.

Bourdieu, P. & Passeron, J. C. (1977). *Reproduction in education, society and culture.* London: Sage Publishers.

Coleman, J. S. et. al. (1966). *Equality of educational opportunity.* Washington, DC: Government Printing Office.

Conant, J. B. (1961). *Slums and suburbs.* New York: McGraw-Hill.

Darling-Hamond, L. (1990). "Achieving our goals: Superficial or structural reforms?" *Phi Delta Kappan,* 286-295.

Dewey, J. (1916). *Democracy and education.* New York: Free Press Edition, 1967.

Gee, J. P. (1988). " Discourse systems and aspirin bottles: On literacy." *Journal of Education, 170* (1), 27-40.

Gee, J. P. (1989). *Social linguistics and literacies: Ideology in discourse.* Falmer Press.

Labov, W. (1973). "The logic of nonstandard English." In N. Keddie (Ed.)., Tinker, Taylor: *The myth of cultural deprivation*. Harmondsworth, UK: Penguin Publisher.

McDermont, B. (1990). *The imperial middle: Why Americans can't think straight about class*. New York: Morrow Publishers.

McLaren, P. (1989). *Life in schools: An introduction to critical pedagogy in the foundations of education*. New York: Longman.

Nelson, J. L., Palonsky, S., & Carlson, K. (1990). *Critical issues in education*. New York: McGraw-Hill.

Sizer, T. R. (1984). *Horace's compromise: The dilemmas of the American high school*. Boston: Houghton Mifflin.

Wilson, W. J. (1987). *The truly disadvantaged: The inner city, the underclass, and public policy*. Chicago: University of Chicago Press.

# Chapter X

# Religion and Education: What role should religion play in the public schools?

E. Wayne Ross

Robert P. Green, Jr.

# E. Wayne Ross

The question of religion in the public schools poses a mine field of controversies.  A series of tensions and conflicts over issues such as school prayer, "creation science," and "secular humanism" in textbooks have defined the debate over the role of religion in the public schools over the past 30 years, with little success in overcoming extreme positions, ignorance, and confusion on all sides of these issues.  Ultimately, the question of what role religion should play in the public schools is a public policy not a religious issue.  The question requires us to take a hard look at national institutions such as the Constitution and public education and involves reflection on democratic principles of liberty and justice.

## Religion, Education and the Supreme Court

The controversial nature of the issue evolved from a series of United States Supreme Court decisions in the 1960s, when state-mandated prayer and devotional use of the Bible in public schools was abolished.  In 1962 in *Engle v. Vitale*, the Court found the recitation of a prayer, developed for use in the public schools by the New York Regents, a violation of the First Amendment of the U. S. Constitution, which prohibits enacting any "law respecting an establishment of religion or prohibiting the free exercise thereof."  The court argued that just because a prayer is denominationally neutral and voluntary does not mean that it is excluded from the limitations imposed by the Establishment Clause of the First Amendment.  A year later, in two separate cases (*Abington v. Schemp* and *Murray v. Curlett*), the Court ruled that enforced Bible reading and school prayer were unconstitutional.  The Court argued that it could not

> accept that the concept of neutrality...collides with the majority's right to the exercise of free religion.  While the Free Exercise Clause clearly prohibits the use of state action to deny the rights of free exercise to *anyone*, it never meant that a majority could use the machinery of the State to practice its beliefs. (cited in Provenzo 1990)

The Court's decision set off a chain reaction that still shows no sign of abating.

**The Public Schools' Response**
After the Court's decisions in 1963, discussion of religious
ideas, themes and influences all but disappeared from the
public schools. The irony is that the Court never intended its
rulings to have this effect. In his concurring opinion, Justice
Arthur Goldberg wrote that "many of our legal, political, and
personal values derive historically from religious teachings" and
thus the court recognized "teaching *about* religion, as distin-
guished from the teaching *of* religion in the public schools."

People in schools worried about the line between acknowledging the role of religion in American society and history and
appearing to favor a particular faith. The fear of parental anger
or court challenge had, by the 1980s, resulted in the disappearance of religion from school curricula and texts. In one study
of sixty representative social studies textbooks used in grades
one through four, none were found to "contain one word referring to any religious activity in contemporary life" (Vitz, 1986).
"When in doubt, leave it out," became the guideline for educators and publishers on issues related to religion in the public
school curriculum.

**What Role Should Religion Play in the Public Schools?**
The exclusion of religion from the public school curriculum has
resulted in movements on at least three fronts to fill the void.
These efforts include: (a) the development of an American civic
religion as a substitute for denominational religion; (b) the
reinstitution of religious practices and instruction in the public
schools; and c) encouraging teaching *about* religion in the public
school. The latter position seems the only tenable one in a
democratic and increasingly pluralistic society.

*American Civic Religion.* The overriding idea in this effort is to
concentrate on values and beliefs that can be viewed as representing the majority of the population and thus forming a
creed, a nationalistic, patriotic religion. American civic religion
in schools discourages critical reconsideration of mainstream
values and beliefs and encourages beliefs such as:

• The United States is particularly favored by Divine Provi-
  dence and American prosperity is evidence of its favored
  status.

- Because American capitalism has produced prosperity, capitalism is to be the economic system of all nations.

- American-style democratic government represents the interests of all citizens and therefore should be the political system of all nations.

- The American President is elected by the people. Therefore we should uncritically trust, obey and support all the President's policies.

This patriotic religion has its roots in the historically Protestant tradition of national civic piety. The focus of this effort is on developing citizenship through the inculcation of "right values" and the purpose is to raise up a future generation of citizens who will guarantee the survival of society—in this case mainstream American society. This approach leads to majoritarianism and attempts to achieve unity within American society at the expense of pluralism.

*Reinstitution of Religious Practices In Schools.* This effort rejects the philosophical as well as political validity of the Supreme Court's decisions regarding religious practices in public schools. Over the past decade the New Christian Right has become increasingly influential in American politics. Some of the most forceful and well organized efforts to reinstitute religious practices in schools have come from religious fundamentalist groups within the New Christian Right, who describe themselves as "anti-evolution, pro-life, pro-family, and pro-school prayer." This movement is opposed to the separation of church and state; the growing secularization of American society; and the current thrust of American education. In so doing, they have rejected the dominant moral and intellectual values of contemporary American culture and society.

The fundamentalist critique of American education is rooted in the belief that there can be no compromise between Christian/religious forms of education and that of the Enlightenment and a contemporary thought (Rushdoony, 1972; 1973). Progressive educational principles, which have their roots in the work of people such as Horace Mann and John Dewey are attacked as being largely responsible for the current crisis in American education.    Tim LaHaye of Christian Heritage College has argued that:

> Free development of oneself has led to selfishness and rebellion on the part of many individuals.    Learning through experience—the foundation of Dewey's experimental educational philosophy—means that one is limited to only one's observations and experience.    The wisdom of "history, learned teachers, and Scripture" are ignored.    By focusing on the present rather than the hereafter, we are distracted from the fact that our life in this world is simply a preparation for eternity.    Finally, learning to cope with a changing world, has the effect of denying that there are absolute truths or "eternal verities." (Provenzo, 1990, p. 10)

The latter point highlights the fundamentalist's rejection of the public schools as an agent of enlightenment and social reform. It is viewed, instead, as a negative manifestation of an increasingly secular society.    The religious fundamentalists' agenda for American education would create an absolutist, intolerant and exclusive public school system.    A system in direct conflict with the pluralistic, tolerant, and inclusive roots of American education.

The fundamentalist critique, as Provenzo has pointed out, is one that deserves serious attention, because it raises important questions about the nature and purpose of schools; the values and assumptions underlying schooling; and how the schools meet the needs of a pluralistic society.    However, while fundamentalists rightly demand tolerance and alternatives on the question of religion and education, they reject them for others and thereby adopt a position inconsistent with democratic principles.

*Teaching About Religion.*    The study of religious distinctions in American society as well as the ways in which religious values intersect with politics and public policy have simply been excluded from the school curriculum.    This is problematic on two counts.    First, it results in a lack of attention to the role of religion in the public sphere.    As Gary Wills (1990) has illustrated, religion has always been at the center of our political crises, which are always moral crises—the supporting or opposing of wars, of slavery, of corporate power, of civil rights, of sexual codes, of "the West," of American separatism and claims to empire. If we neglect to examine the role of religion in these matters, we blunt our ability to understand the past and to critically evaluate a foundational aspect of our public philosophy.

Secondly, silence on issues of religion in schools, far from easing tensions, fosters ignorance and mutual incomprehension among people with widespread religious beliefs and practices and that live in an increasingly pluralistic society. While technology, urbanization, social mobility and universal education all were supposed to eat away at religion, poll after poll in recent years has illustrated the centrality of religion in American life. For example:

- Nine out of ten Americans say they have never doubted the existence of God.

- Eight in ten say they believe they will be called before God on Judgment Day to answer for their sins.

- Seven in ten believe in life after death.

- Ninety percent of Americans say they pray some time during the week.

- More people attend religious services, in any week, than go to all sports events combined. (Wills, 1990)

American religious pluralism now goes beyond the predominance of Protestant/Catholic/Jewish and includes sizeable (and increasing) numbers of almost all the world's great religions (Muslim and Buddhist in particular) as well as a growing number of Americans with no religious preference (between 10 and 12% of the U. S. population).

Teaching about religion in public schools, as opposed to religious instruction, would fulfill a need for fuller knowledge and increased awareness of religious motivation in our history and culture. Greater understanding of key ideas such as freedom of conscience, religious pluralism, religious liberty and the separation of church and state are to be developed. The role of religion in issues of social justice should also be emphasized—including the religious impetus behind the abolitionist movement, the radical populists of the 19th century, the civil rights movement of the 1950s and 1960s, as well as liberation theology and other contemporary social justice movements.

Teaching about religion can also enhance our response to the expanding pluralism within our nation. With both the school and general population approaching a "minority majority" status we are faced with questions of how to create a common vision in which pluralistic diversity is celebrated and religious freedom and freedom of conscience is enhanced.

Conflict and debate are vital to democracy. Yet dialogue on religious values and their intersection with politics, education and public policy has been neglected and the discussion polarized. This dialogue must be fostered if we are to avoid both the blind patriotism of a civic religion and the absolutism of the religious right while advancing a democratic vision within an increasingly pluralistic society.

# References

Provenzo, E. F. (1990). *Religious Fundamentalism and American Education.* Albany: State University of New York Press.

Rushdoony, R. J. (1972). *Intellectual Schizophrenia: Culture, Crisis and Education.* Philadelphia: The Presbyterian and Reformed Pub. Company

Rushdoony, R. J. (1973). *The Messianic Character of American Education: Studies in the History of Philosophy of Education.* Nutley, NJ: The Craig Press.

Vitz, P. C. (1986). *Evidence of Bias in Our Children's Textbooks.* Ann Arbor: Servant Books.

Wills, G. (1990). *Under God: Religion and American Politics.* New York: Simon & Schuster.

# Robert P. Green, Jr.

As political scientist John Kenneth White (1988) has so persuasively argued, Ronald Reagan was a master of the new politics of
old values. At a time when a majority of Americans believed
"we were better off in the old days when everyone knew just
how they were expected to act," when two thirds felt
"everything changes so quickly these days that I often have
trouble deciding which are the right rules to follow," and over
seventy percent thought that "many things our parents stood
for are going to ruin right before our eyes," Ronald Reagan
provided an antidote. Painting a Norman Rockwell-like vision
of America with his rhetoric, Reagan appealed to the traditional
American values of family, work, neighborhood, peace, and
freedom. Reagan was effective because he recreated a romantic
vision of America that Americans wanted to believe in—even if it
had never existed. Unfortunately, as Democratic opponents
were unable to convince the public, romantic visions often
obscure harsh reality. And so it was with Reagan's appeal to the
religiosity of the nation.

Religious belief systems provide one of the most fundamental
repositories for traditional values. Reagan recognized this fact
and naturally cultivated the support of religious conservatives.
Issues revolving around religion's place in the public schools
provided a ready vehicle for such cultivation. As candidate and
president, Reagan promised to support prayer, the teaching of
creationism, to denounce secular humanism, to endorse tuition
tax credits for parents who sent their children to private
schools, and to return "back to basics." The public schools,
where it seemed to some that traditional values had lost to the
onslaught of secular humanism, could provide one stage for the
return of America to those traditional values. Yet the religious,
cultural conservatism encouraged by Reagan's rhetoric too
frequently manifested itself in disturbing ways, as the following
case illustrates.

A few years ago, *The New Republic* published some interesting
correspondence. A California attorney had written the
Department of Education concerning the distribution of a
speech by a Department official, a speech that included a refer-

ence to the U. S. as a "Christian nation." The attorney, a non-Christian, stated that this blatant preference for the Christian religion upset him.  "The U. S. is not now—and never has been—a "Christian nation,'" he wrote, referring to appropriate passages in the Constitution.  He added that he felt "Christian Broadcasting Network agitprop," like the use of the term "secular humanism," threatened democracy.  In response, a Reagan appointee in the Treasury Department (a Christian activist who, through the Freedom of Information Act, monitored mail on Christian issues sent to the government) argued that the attorney's knowledge of the country's history and structure of government was "minimal at best," that we were, "indeed, like it or not, a Christian nation," that the "country was founded by Christians who were escaping the same kind of small-minded tripe you espouse" and that the framers specifically anticipated "those of your ilk who would try and abridge the very rights of freedom to worship guaranteed us by that document."  The Treasury employee went on to misinterpret the attorney's reference to secular humanism, closing with, "You are a truly amazing, but pathetic creature.  P. S. When you die, you will be giving account to Jesus Christ, your creator, who happens to be a Christian.  I hope you are prepared..."

Now this is frightening stuff!  While extreme, it is not atypical of the attitudes of those on the religious right who would return us to "traditional, *Christian* values"—including appropriate interpretations of the Constitution!  It appears to me that two aspects of this incident reflect basic issues that can be addressed in the schools.  First, implicit in the Christian activist's argument is a vague notion of some homogeneous "Christian" community in the past.  Similarly, the attorney's contention that the United States "has never been" a Christian nation implies a lack of understanding of the evolutionary nature of the Supreme Court's application of the principle of separation.  Thus, conflicting claims concerning the origins and development of our nation suggest that the schools need to foster a clearer understanding of the role religion has played in the nation's past.  Second, while claiming that the Constitution protected *his* beliefs, the Christian activist explicitly rejected any non-Christian beliefs that the attorney may have held. This aspect of our incident suggests the contemporary need for the schools to foster religious tolerance as a fundamental element of citizenship education. While the two roles for the school are complementary, I would argue that the first, informing students of the role religion has played in the nation's past, provides a basis for the second, fostering religious toleration as an element of citizenship education. Thus the public schools have a key role to play, but they are not doing so currently.

The typical exposure of students to religion and religious issues in the public schools is inadequate, and a variety of critics—from left and right—have made that point over the last several years. One of the most perceptive of these critics, however, does find a form of "religious indoctrination" in the schools—despite largely successful efforts to maintain separation. As Daniel A. Spiro (1989) has persuasively argued, rather than expose students to a serious and balanced treatment of religion and religious issues, public schools indoctrinate students in "American Civil Religion," a concept that Spiro describes as an amalgam of scientism, American nationalism, and a diluted Christianity. Scientism, according to Spiro, is an "exaggerated faith in the power of the natural sciences to explain social, psychological, or physical phenomena." It breeds a crude empiricism that fails to consider alternative explanations of reality. (I would suggest that, in the simplistic nature of its presentation, "scientism"—as Spiro describes it—at least fails to provide students with any serious consideration of how knowledge is created). American nationalism, or "Americanization," is fostered through a process of political indoctrination that extols dominant political, economic, and social institutions, without critical examination of the values that underlie them or serious consideration of competing perspectives. In the absence of alternative viewpoints, argues Spiro, many students "blindly adhere to the majority's values." The Christianity to which students are exposed is presented as the dominant religion in the early American experience and a source of strength to American heroes. Its association with school holidays—in the absence of the celebration of other religions' holy days—fosters an identification of Christianity with "the full, wholesome life." Proselytizing is rare, yet given the schools' attempts to maintain separation, serious treatment of principles underlying Christianity—or any other religion, for that matter—are absent. The result, according to Spiro, provides students with a picture of Christianity as a religion of uplift, and a "source of hope and joy, without severely restricting their daily actions and beliefs."

The net effect of the "indoctrination" of students in American Civil Religion has been, I fear, to contribute to what historian Michael Kammen (1989) has called "highly selective, sentimental, and sanitized versions of American history...a severely simplified vision of how we came to be the society we now are." A closer study of the history of religion in this country can help combat this simplistic picture while it provides a much more adequate background for both understanding the evolutionary nature of Supreme Court decisions concerning religion in the schools and fostering toleration as an element of citizenship education.

Let us consider, for example, the religious impulse behind reform during the antebellum period of American history. Limitations of space do not allow a thorough study, but the elements I will highlight are suggestive. If, then, students are exposed at all to the connection between religion and the reform impulse, it is simply to the idea that some reformers' religious beliefs motivated their efforts. For example, students might read that Charles Grandison Finney reflected the evangelical Christian roots of some anti-slavery sentiment when he argued, "Let Christians of all denominations meekly but firmly come forth, and pronounce their verdict, let them clear their communions, and wash their hands of this thing, let them give forth and write on the head and front of the great abomination, SIN!" Such a brief exposure, it appears to me, fosters that view of Christianity as a part of American Civil Religion that Spiro criticizes. Yet a closer study of religious benevolence in the antebellum period gives us a much broader and different picture.

The second quarter of the nineteenth century was characterized by tremendous dynamism in American society, not only as people moved West, but also as industrialization and urbanization began, people moved from farm to city, and hundreds of thousands of immigrants arrived from Western Europe. While "the Age of Jackson" was seen by many as an era of expanding opportunities, "others," argued historian Clifford Griffin (1957), "feared new forces in American life, worried about political and social upheavals, and deplored new moral standards. To many of those who could not accept the changing America, evangelical Protestantism seemed an excellent means of keeping the nation under control." In an attempt to identify the motives of those actively involved in religious benevolence, Griffin studied the managers of societies such as the American Home Missionary Society and American Bible Society. While motivated on one level by Christian benevolence, the idea that "certain persons, having received God's sanctifying grace, were obliged to extend to all men the means of obtaining that grace," and the belief that most of the people in the U. S. were living in sin, the managers saw it as their duty to make sinners "realize their evils, to persuade them to repent, and thus to help God's saving work."

Yet on another level, argued Griffin, these managers, drawn from the nation's conservative, social elite, shared a host of political, economic, and social concerns. The rise of Andrew Jackson frightened them. They associated Jackson with licentiousness and misrule and identified his political base as the religiously destitute West. Conversion of Westerners through the efforts of missionary and tract societies could lead to correct political behavior; that is, the election of religious men who would rule wisely. Christianity could promote general economic stability. Poverty was disturbing, yet hard work was the way to improve the lot of the poor, not socialistic communities or unionism. Perhaps most frightening to the managers, however, was the host of new immigrants—especially those who were Roman Catholic. Many flooded the eastern cities, where they were associated with social unrest—mobs, riots, and crime. Scripture could provide sources of control: the Bible would show the poor their rights and duties and develop in them "whatsoever is honest, and pure, and of good report." In sum, argued Griffin, the religion propagated by the benevolent societies could be made an effective means of controlling a seemingly chaotic society.

Interestingly enough, a number of proponents of public education joined the evangelical managers in their fear of the excesses in society. One such—at least in his early writing—was Horace Mann (Thomas, 1965; Perkinson, 1976). "The mobs, the riots, the lynchings, perpetrated by the men of the present day, are perpetrated, because of their vicious or defective education when children." Note the similarities in reasoning, as Mann called for an educational crusade:

> Let the intelligent visit the ignorant, day by day, as the oculist visits the blind mind, and detaches the scales from his eyes, until the living sense leaps to light...Let the love of beautiful reason, the admonitions of conscience, the sense of religious responsibility, be plied, in mingled tenderness and earnestness, until the obdurate and dark mass of avarice and ignorance and prejudice shall be dissipated by their blended light and heat.

For advocates of common schooling like Horace Mann and Henry Barnard, the essence of education was moral training—Protestant, Christian moral training.

Yet what did the recipients of all this attention think of the reform aimed in their direction? The Irish Catholic immigrants, in particular, would have nothing to do with it. Rejecting the assumption of perfectibility animating religious benevolence, the Irish manifested, instead, "a deep-rooted pessimism about the world and man's place in it" (Handlin, 1970). For them, religion was a source of solace, but in preparation for the after-life. As Oscar Handlin pointed out, "reform [the Irish Catholics believed] was a delusion inflating men's sense of importance, distorting the relative significance of earthly values, and obscur-ing the true goals of their endeavor—salvation of the eternal soul." The institution essential to salvation was the Roman Catholic Church, thus anything that threatened the Church or its authority was rejected out of hand. Not only did the concept of a common school, run by the state, undermine the authority of the Church in the education of children, it also—given the distinctly Protestant cast found in its rationale, curriculum, and instructional materials—directly threatened the Church's teach-ings.

It should not be surprising that, given the relative simplicity of naturalization, the Irish in antebellum America soon turned to the ballot to defend their culture and beliefs. In turn, reports of the growth of their voting strength alarmed Protestant advocates of reform. Historian Clifford Griffin summarized their concern:

> In Ohio, said a report, to curry favor with Catholic voters, would-be politicians opposed the Bible, Tract, and Home Missionary societies and thus threatened to leave the people in darkness, a prey alike to demagogues and priests. The Reverend S. E. Miner reported from Madison, Wisconsin, in 1845 that Catholics were steadily becoming more influential and that already they had "crouching whining politicians" as servants. In 1852 the Reverend George Sheldon, Bible Society agent in Indiana, advised the national managers to urge upon both Whig and Democratic nominees for school superintendent the use of the Bible in common schools. But Sheldon thought that with their Catholic allies the Democrats, who did not favor the Bible in schools would win. Democrats, Sheldon averred, did obeisance to "Romanists and Infidels...The Romanist with the infidelity they carry with them, have the balance of power between democracy [the Democratic Party] and Whigery..."

In this passage, Griffin early identified what more recent historians have described as a major source of political party alignment: ethno-cultural and religious differences. Lee Benson's study of New York politics (1961) found that religious groups with "Puritanical" moral values and ways of life emphasizing piety, sobriety, propriety, and thrift tended to vote for the Whigs. The Irish Catholics, many German churches, and other non-Puritanical groups—especially over local political issues like temperance and school reform—thus found their outlet for political expression in the Democratic Party. Ron Formisano's study of Michigan (1971) found essentially the same divisions. "Native evangelical Protestants voted heavily anti-Democratic (Whig, Liberty, or Free Soil)... Catholics disproportionately supported the Democrats. Most polarized, perhaps were evangelical Protestants and foreign Catholics." Similar divisions characterized party politics until the age of Bryan.

Thus historians have argued that one aspect of the antebellum reform impulse was founded in cultural conservatism, was expressed in evangelical Christianity, threatened an even more

conservative Christianity, and thus formed one basis for political party alignment during the course of the century.  While still
not a complete treatment of religion during the period—some
historians have emphasized how moral reformers released a
romantic perfectionism that undermined conservatism, and
others still have studied in greater detail the anti-Catholicism
and, later, anti-Semitism among evangelicals—thus far richer
treatment of religion does two things.  It shatters any image one
might have of some monolithic "Christianity" in the nation's
past, and it provides a basis for understanding why the Supreme
Court—that institution responsible for maintaining the principles upon which our body politic is based—has taken the
reasonable positions it has concerning religion in the schools.

In the matter of our "Christian past," to which Christian past
do our contemporaries refer, that of the evangelical Protestants
or that of the Irish Catholics?   Which was more Christian?
(Orestes Brownson, a Catholic, argued that a *Christian* Protestant was, to the Catholic mind, simply a contradiction in terms.)
They obviously did not agree on Bible reading in the schools.
Whose Bible would be acceptable to both groups?   In fact,
controversy over the possibility of Catholic children using the
authorized Catholic Bible during reading exercises in Philadelphia public schools led to bloody riots in that city in 1844!  It is
no wonder that—to escape Protestantism—Catholics largely
withdrew from the public schools and created their own system.

In the matter of interpretation of the First Amendment's two
religious clauses ("Congress shall make no law respecting an
establishment of religion, or prohibiting the free exercise
thereof..."), the Court has chosen to promote, in Jefferson's
phrase, a "wall of separation" between church and state.  While
I leave the debate over original intent to others, it appears to
me that one of the most fundamental reasons for the success of
our American experiment has been that the Constitution has,
indeed, been a "living" document—through amendment and
interpretation.   Through its interpretations of the religious
clauses, the Court has attempted to develop an operational
understanding of the principle of separation (*Lemon v. Kurtz-
man*, 1971).   As Garry Wills (1990) has argued, "No other
government in history had launched itself without the help of

officially recognized gods and their state-connected ministers. It is no wonder that, in so novel an undertaking, it should have taken a while to sift the dangers and the blessings of the new arrangement, to learn how best to live with it, to complete the logic of its workings." The Court's understanding has evolved against a background of religious diversity and conflict. Issues of Bible reading and prayer in the schools do not pit wholesome Christian-types versus unwholesome atheists of "secular humanists." Rather they are issues that reflect a history of political conflict among Christian denominations themselves, with the potential for even greater conflict in the more pluralistic society of today.

It is important that the schools foster an understanding of these developments. Such an understanding provides one aspect of citizenship education. Another is the affirmation of freedom of conscience as a basic right worthy of defense by all citizens. If religious liberty is to be protected, it must protect the liberties of minorities as well as majorities, the freedom of conscience of all religious groups—as well as those who profess no religion. Religious differences will remain, and they will contribute to political differences,but "to be an American" must mean to recognize within our civic discourse the right to freedom of conscience.

# References

Benson, L. (1961). *The Concept of Jacksonian Democracy.* Princeton: Princeton University Press.

Formisano, R. (1971). *The Birth of Mass Political Parties: Michigan, 1827-1861.* Princeton, Princeton University Press.

Griffin, C. (1957, December). "Religious Benevolence as Social Control, 1815-1860," *Mississippi Valley Historical Review,* XLIV, pp. 423-444.

Handlin, O. (1970). *Boston Immigrants.* New York: Atheneum.

Kammen, M. (1989). "History Is Our Heritage: The Past in Contemporary American Culture," in Paul Gagnon (ed.) *Historical Literacy*. Boston: Houghton Mifflin.

Perkinson, H. (1976). *Two Hundred Years of American Educational Thought*. New York: David McKay.

Spiro, D. (1989, June). "Public Schools and the Road to Religious Neutrality," *Phi Delta Kappan*, Vol. 70, No. 10, pp. 759-763.

Thomas, J. (1965, Winter). "Romantic Reform in America, 1815-1865," *American Quarterly*, Vol. XVII, No. 4, pp. 656-681.

White, J. (1988). *The New Politics of Old Values*. Hanover: University Press of New England.

Wills, G. (1990). *Under God: Religion and American Politics*. New York: Simon & Schuster.

# Chapter XI

# Educational Reform: What have been the effects of the attempts to improve education over the last decade?

Joe L. Kincheloe

Douglas J. Simpson

# Joe L. Kincheloe

The introduction to this book documented the struggle within the right-wing to formulate a coherent reform of education in the 1970s, 1980s, and 1990s. In this chapter I will explore a few of the effects of these reforms and the larger visions which drive them. The late twentieth century re-constitution of Manifest Destiny is central to our understanding—the educational reform of our era is based on the story of Western superiority, American superiority in particular.

All levels of education from elementary schools to the university have been profoundly affected by the reactionary reforms. The curriculum and mission of all schools, William Bennett argues, must be grounded on a clear vision of the common culture. Bennett's common culture finds its roots almost exclusively in European and patriarchal soil (Kimball, 1990, p.4). It assumes the moral superiority of the Western tradition and contends that any questioning of this superiority is tantamount to intellectual treason (Reitz, 1988, p.6). Thus, teachers in "reformed" systems who call for a democratization of curriculum in a way that draws upon a variety of individual and cultural experiences are not simply guilty of inappropriate pedagogy— they are the Benedict Arnolds of education.

As conservative editor Roger Kimball writes, "the word multicultural and its variants have become code words for an approach to the humanities that is in effect anticultural" (Kimball, 1990, p. 63). In the name of patriotism the reforms exclude the languages, cultures, and histories of subordinate groups as important aspects of school life (Giroux, 1989, p.175). While employing the language of democracy and inclusivity, reform leaders claim to possess the one true faith. The advocates of a curriculum which draws on a variety of cultures and traditions are portrayed as heritics, apostates who have forfeited their right to speak by stepping outside the Great Tradition. Bennett, Kimball, and Allan Bloom know what constitutes the Truth—indeed, like all those who are privy to "the Truth" they become fundamentalists, in this case educational fundamentalists, who degrade the Western tradition by sanctifying it. Those who oppose us, the right-wing reformers contend, simply don't understand our history—a seriously flawed change in light of the historical grounding provided by the advocates of a culturally diverse curriculum (Bloom, 1987, p. 56).

In one of the more bizarre defenses of the spirit right-wing educational reforms, Allan Bloom attempts to defend ethnocentrism. It is natural, Bloom writes, to not only prefer one's own way but to think it superior. Men (sic), Bloom continues, must be ethnocentric in order to preserve their families. We cannot be loyal if we do not consider our country, our culture, our people better than all others. To insure this loyalty a culture develops myths. Thus, the role of school in an industrialized culture is to perpetuate these myths of superiority. The problem of getting along with those who are different from us is secondary to our desire for "oneness" with our own people, our own way of life. Narrowness, he concludes, is not incompatible with the health of individuals or a nation—indeed, openness is the great sin which leads to the dissolution of a culture. For a nation to succeed its citizens must see themselves as chosen people, individuals with a special place in the cosmos. Schools grounded on such principles of reform promote a blind love which lays the groundwork for the unthoughtful embrace of militarism and imperialism. "New World Orders" structured on such worldviews do not differ too much from the failed visions of past world leaders commonly referred to as tyrants (Bloom, 1987, pp. 36-37).

Thus, educational reform becomes a key step in a larger right-wing political restructuring. Schools are the guardians for the Western way of life—much in the same spirit that segregated schools in the South of the 1950s were the guardians of the "southern way of life." Schools provide the ideological justifications for the right of the West to *mandate* the "New World Order" (as it is "superior" after all) and to institutionalize the attitudes necessary for the industrial discipline which leads to increased productivity. As Bloom concludes in his *The Closing of the American Mind*: "this is the American moment in world history, the one for which we shall forever be judged. . .The fate not only of freedom but philosophy. . ." rests in the hands of American schools (Bloom, 1987, p.6). Thus, the White Man's Burden emerges in a 21st century form with educators joining hands with our leaders in convincing the heathen of the superiority and thus the rightful dominance of the West.

Those who point to the problems with these images of America, these reactionary goals for education argue that one of the fundamental characteristics of the American experiment has been its commitment to diversity and possibility. This commitment carries with it the necessity of an informed, open conversation about the meaning of diversity as it applies to our everyday life, our institutions, education in particular (Simon, 1989, p. 146). Thus, within this context self-criticism and national self-reflection are virtues; within the new context created by the conservative reformers, self-criticism is an impediment to an adoration of the American way of life. When opponents of the right-wing reformers employ a democratic criticism of the historic race, class, and gender oppressions of the Western heritage, the reformers charge that America is faced with a war against the existence of our culture (Kimball, 1990, p. xii). Attacking those who are concerned with issues of social justice, James J. Kilpatrick writes, "those who love our Western inheritance had better get off their rumps and fight" (Kilpatrick, 1991, p. 8A).

What seems interesting here is that with the spate of literature issued by the right-wing about the coming fight over the Western tradition, very little has been written to answer the charges of the democratic critics. The conservative reformers never ask: are the questions about the failures of the Western tradition legitimate? The "Great Tradition" is rarely problematized. Even issues involving the human cost, the underside of post-Englightenment science, the Cartesian separation of mind and matter with its accompanying restriction of introspection (both individual and social), or industrialization and its commodification of both the human spirit and the environment are shielded from critical analysis. We once had standards for separating the civilized from the uncivilized, the protectors of Tradition contend, but the advocates of multiculturism and diversity have even tried to erase these boundaries. Those who value the unique contributions of the many cultures of the world are charged with a crass "primitivism" —a romantic sentimentalization of "primitive" cultures. Never addressing the question, can the West learn from these so-called primitive cultures?—the right-wing reformers merely ridicule the inquiry (Tuttleton, 1987, p. 47).

I am uncomfortable with the view of students implicit in these larger assumptions about the reform of schooling. Young people are not intrinsically valuable, youth culture is not something to be understood and appreciated for its creative and humanistic potential. Students are entities to be manipulated to fit the industrial, military, and/or ideological needs of the state. To accomplish such a task youth must be taught to accept "traditional values," i.e., a particular view of humanness in line with a particular interpretation of the Great Tradition. "Good students" with "good attitudes" are those who willingly embrace these values. Right-wing reformers are bolstered by scientific studies which correlate these traditional values with school success. Of course, students with these values tend to succeed—schools as they have come to exist reward on many levels students with these particular types of values. Thus, these values and the personality types they promote become the standard which the reformers attempt to impose on all schools and all students. Students who display other characteristics such as skepticism, the propensity to question, and a quest for creative individuality are seen as lacking in good character. Such students are portrayed as dangers to the nation who must be convinced of the superiority of conformity to the monolithic description of character and tradition (Simon, 1989, p. 137). The conservative reformers hold a Calvinistic view of students which regards them as sinners until they are "saved" by exposure to our "traditional values."

The vision of teachers implicit in the right-wing reforms is also disturbing. Teachers are wimps—passive creatures who do what they are told, who feverishly avoid any challenge to mainstream values or perceived injustice. Attempts to teach higher levels of thinking, new ways of seeing, more sophisticated consciousness are repudiated by reformers fearful of any form of experimentation. The reforms of the last decade have ushered in an educational Dark Age. The Reagan business-fundamentalist-Western Traditionalist axis has rendered

creative pedagogy an evil, if not at times Satanic, act. It is virtually impossible in the last years of the twentieth century for
teachers to speak of a socially-contextualized, expanded
consciousness without an onslaught of criticism (Giroux and
McLaren, 1989, p. xix).

The deskilling of teachers has been a central feature of the
Reagan-Bush reforms of the 1980s and 1990s. We see its highest expression in the teacher-proofed curriculum which sepa-
rates a broad understanding of educational purpose from the
everyday task of teaching. Caught in the bureaucratization of
the conservative reforms, teachers are reduced to technicians
who carry out specific directives from the state. We can take at
least some solace in the realization that top-down reforms do
not work (Ferguson, 1980, p. 310). Education cannot be
reformed by decree. No educational idea can survive unless it is
understood inside-out by the teachers who implement it. The
spirit of the reform must be a part of the teachers' lives, a part
of their belief systems if the reform is to work. While the right-
wing reforms will make short term gains and will dominate
particular schools and school systems, they will not achieve any
final triumph. The conservative reformers are too uncomfortable with *empowered teachers*—teachers who are in control of their
own professional lives, who have a voice in the development of
curriculum and the governance of the school, who reflect upon
the ideological precepts that are implicit in the reforms that
affect their everyday lives. Only empowered teachers will make
any lasting impact on the form education takes in this society.

No doubt, the conservative reform movement of the Reagan-
Bush era has made a profound impact on the nature of schools,
their goals and purposes. The stories the reformers tell about
the world, the Western tradition, the nature of success, and the
mission of America have convinced many of the logic of their
educational vision. But the disguise cannot last; the exclusionary policies are dynamically obsolescent, as marginalized groups
slowly begin to compile and publicize their own stories. The
stories teachers tell about the bureaucratization and unprofes-
sional treatment they face daily will be heard. And when they
are, the right-wing house of educational cards will collapse.

# References

Bloom, A. (1987) *The Closing of the American Mind.* (NY: Simon & Schuster).

Giroux, H. (1989) "Educational reform and teacher empowerment." In H. Holtz, et.al., *Education and the American dream.* (Granby, MA: Bergin & Garvey).

Kilpatrick, James J. (1991) "Western values under attack." *Evening Post* (Charleston, South Carolina) February 8, p. 8A.

Kimball, R. (1990) *Tenured radicals*, (NY: Harper and Row).

Reitz, C. (1988) "Bennett, Bloom, and Boyer: toward a critical discussion." Paper: S.W. Community Colleges Humanities Assoc. Kansas City, MO.

Simon, R. (1989) "Empowerment as a pedagogy of possibility." In H. Holtz, et. al., *Education and the American dream* (Granby, MA: Bergin & Garvey).

# Douglas J. Simpson

## Preliminary Remarks

On the surface, the question, What have been the effects of recent attempts to improve education?, appears to be a rather forthright request for a relatively simple answer. What, in other words, has resulted from the myriad of reports, discussions, and bills regarding the improvement of education? Unfortunately, the answer is not as straightforward as one might hope. Instead, answers are, at least in part, contingent, complex, and equivocal. Caveats abound when interpreting data and reported changes. Even the formulation of hypotheses is fraught with difficulty. The question before us, therefore, needs to be approached cautiously. Likewise, answers need to be viewed as incomplete, suggestive, and tentative.

On the other hand, it is reasonable for a person to want to know if the recent demands and legislation concerning education reform have resulted in significant and positive outcomes. Before we proceed further, it is important that we pause to clarify several difficulties with our question. These difficulties stem, in part, from the fact that the educational reform movement has been propelled by forces with different, competing, and conflicting aims. This point is critical both to understanding the underlying reasons for educational reform and to recognizing the difficulty of answering our question.

## The Expectations of Reformers

An analysis of reform literature of the 1980s leaves the impression that reformers are not always discussing the same problems, goals, interventions, and outcomes. Many reformers believe schools are failing to reach a rather obvious, at least to them, instructional goal, i.e., preparing graduates for employment. The work force of the nation, it is argued, is increasingly unable to complete basic tasks and compete successfully with the personnel of many other technologically-advanced countries. Consequently, American businesses are losing ground in the world market. Many Americans are so poorly educated that they are not qualified for even entry-level jobs. They cannot read, write, and compute, much less function independently as

employees.   One question of paramount concern for these
reformers is:  Has educational reform produced better prepared
workers for society?

Other reform endeavors are prompted not for economic and
employment reasons, but because some critics think students
should be knowledgeable of or possess particular historical,
geographical, literary, scientific, and mathematical information
and skills.   Some of these reformers are basically concerned
with high school graduates being reasonably well-educated
persons.   High school graduates, so they believe, are so far
removed from an ideal conception of an educated person that
one is justified in worrying about how poorly educated youth
will negatively impact important societal and democratic functions and institutions.   Critics of this type are concerned that
the quality of life in the country is deteriorating as fewer people,
proportionately speaking, understand, appreciate, and live a life
that is well informed.  Conversely, others are troubled that high
school graduates are not well prepared for collegiate studies,
and that these graduates do not have an understanding of the
fields of inquiry which enables them to grapple intelligently with
the issues raised in universities.  Eventually, the quality of life
will suffer, they argue, because universities cannot do their jobs
well and, correspondingly, university graduates will be less
capable of addressing the social, scientific, economic, and political challenges that face the nation.  While some of the reformers who share this orientation have a parochial Western focus,
there are others who possess a global view of the goals of
schooling.

Similar critics of schooling are largely concerned with having
a sufficiently large populace of knowledgeable, clear-thinking
citizens to preserve democracy in the country and, ideally, to
extend it in the world.  Youth, some contend, who lack a knowledge of history, government, politics, so forth, cannot possibly
understand—much less preserve—democratic values.  Thus, the
political foundations of the country, they believe, are at risk.
Among the many questions that need to be addressed for this
general group of critics is:  Have the reform efforts cultivated
better-educated persons who can use their developed abilities to

function as intelligent college students, informed citizens, and productive human beings?  A more pedestrian concern for some of these critics is:  Have schools become more successful in passing on a storehouse of information about Western culture to students?

Other educational critics stress the democratic importance of reform from a different perspective.  They may concur with the notion that democracy is dependent upon a knowledgeable populace, but they contend that democracy is connected to education in other respects.  Democracy not only needs to be preserved, it needs to be refined and extended to others in this country, especially to economic and ethnic groups who have not traditionally shared materially in the benefits of the country. Critics reason that if the proportion of the educationally and economically disenfranchised continues to grow, then the democratic fabric of society will be destroyed.  Likewise, they argue that it is contrary to the best democratic traditions to ignore the educational needs of large segments of society. Consequently, these critics want another set of questions answered, including the following:  Have education reform efforts positively affected the educational, political, and economic status of minority groups?

Still other reformers think the national crises of violent crime, child abuse, drug consumption, urban poverty, teenage pregnancy, and AIDS are related to inadequate education. They want an education that will cultivate caring, reasonable, thoughtful, and healthy citizens.  They want schools to produce students who reflect upon the consequences of their behavior before they act, who choose future opportunities rather than present gratifications, who value consciousness more than chemically induced states, who pursue humanitarian ends rather than egocentric goals, and who control their feelings and behaviors for the emotional, physical, and intellectual well-being of themselves and others.  Perhaps an overriding question for this group is:  Have educational reform efforts successfully cultivated students who choose and behave thoughtfully and ethically?

**The Clarification of Problems**

The previous discussion makes it clear that the question, What have been the effects of recent attempts to improve education? may be interpreted in at least four major ways: (1) Has educational reform produced better prepared workers for society? (2) Has educational reform cultivated better-educated persons who use their developed abilities to function as intelligent college students, informed citizens, and productive human beings? (3) Has educational reform positively affected the educational, economic, and political status of minority groups? and (4) Has educational reform successfully cultivated students who choose and behave thoughtfully and ethically?

These four questions are frequently reduced to a series of simplistic questions, such as: (1) Are universities producing better prepared teachers? (2) Do high school graduates know more mathematics and science than in 1980? (3) Have ACT and SAT scores been raised around the country? (4) Have school districts effectively addressed the dropout problem? (5) Are teenage pregnancy and drug consumption less prevalent?, (6) Are standardized achievement test scores higher? and (7) Are higher percentages of African Americans, Native Americans, and Hispanics graduating from high school and university?

Diverse reform expectations and responses not only present problems of focus and function, but they make it extremely difficult for researchers to ask and answer operational questions on a grand scale, e.g., What have been the effects of recent attempts to improve education? So the direction of reform efforts, the magnitude of reform plans, and the actuality of reform undertakings are major problems for anyone who attempts to assess the outcomes of educational reform. The most he or she may be able to hope for is a general conclusion based on a synthesis of information related to specific questions. Further, it is important to recognize that many positive changes occurring today had their origins in practice that predates the current reform movement. Thus, it is likely that credit for current educational progress in particular areas should not be attributed to the reform thrusts of the 1980s, e.g., research regarding effective teaching and effective schools was commenced a decade or so earlier.

Likewise, it is important not to confuse several other issues surrounding educational reform. For example, a *stimulus* for change does not necessarily *cause* an educational outcome. Human beings, students and educators, are not machines who respond in prescribed ways after objectives are established. Parents, administrators, teachers, and volunteers cannot *force* students to learn. Legislators and administrators cannot *compel* teachers to teach in a prescribed fashion.

Moreover, it is worth recognizing that the effects of educational reform can be both negative and positive. The negative outcomes that are being discussed by some include a lowering of teacher morale as policies and practices are forced upon the profession, a higher attrition rate for teachers as their responsibilities increase and support remains inadequate, a rise in dropout rates for students when they are required to take courses for which they are ill-prepared, a lowering of higher-order thinking skills as elementary skills are blindly pursued, and the production of less effective teachers as ill-informed teacher education legislation is implemented. These negative effects, although more important than most of the positive changes being reported, are largely ignored because the focus of this study is upon so-called positive changes.

**The Accomplishments of the 1980s**
At this juncture, several claims appear appropriate. These claims need to be made in spite of the limitations of psychometric instruments and data, the ambiguities of key concepts, and the problems previously mentioned. The first assertion is that there is no convincing evidence to support the conclusion that a single positive outcome—regardless of the goal identified—wanted by national educational critics has materialized during the 1980s. No major, sweeping positive change affecting the nation as a whole has occurred in K-12 schools as a result of educational reform efforts initiated during the 1980s. In fact, the same claim about states, cities, and school districts can be made. No state, major city, or large school district in the nation has made any fundamental improvement in schooling. No marked advancements have been made and sustained in achievement test, SAT, and ACT scores anywhere in the coun-

try. The children of poor, minority, and rural families are not better educated in important ways today than they were before the reform movement started. Businesses and corporations are not hiring significantly better prepared high school graduates than they were a decade ago. Colleges, as a rule of thumb, are not admitting better prepared students in larger numbers. Democratic institutions and values are not any more safe today than they were in 1980 as a result of our preparing greater numbers of informed, rational, and ethical citizens.

A second claim is that it is irrational, from one perspective, to have expected major national, state, city, and district changes to have occurred. The irrationality of this expectation results from a major shortcoming of the reform movements. It is illogical to expect schools by themselves to completely overcome the consequences of cocaine babies, maturational lags, inadequate health care, malnourished children, family poverty, stimulation deprivation, cultural mores, peer values, and delinquent behavior. The educational crisis today is not an isolated phenomenon but is part of the larger social, familial, and value crises that defy a simple solution, i.e., better schools. Better educators and schools are only a part of the solution. We need better families, communities, politicians, agencies, and corporations. We need people with radically altered value systems, i.e., people who truly place the education of children and youth above less worthwhile endeavors. While no excuses from educators can be tolerated, if we are to succeed in the present mission of dealing ethically with all children, no resources can be withheld from them. No reasonable, knowledgeable person—even though a reevaluation of priorities and a reallocation of existing school funds is essential—can conclude that educators have the support and resources they need to effectively educate students. Nor can that person conclude that schools are as effective as they could be if educators and policymakers acted intelligently and courageously upon the best available educational thought and data.

A third claim is that it is unreasonable to expect organizations as structured, traditional, bureaucratic, sterile, regulated, political, standardized, and defensive as schools are to deal adequately with chronic and pervasive learning problems in a brief period of time. Superficial change is all that can be expected as long as pressure for change comes largely from the outside. Improvements of a consequential nature cannot be made when leaders do not agree on which goals they should pursue or pursue dead end objectives, e.g., raising basic skills scores. Substantial progress will come only when those who are primary pedagogical providers—teachers, counselors, principals—are meaningfully involved in the planning and pursuit of educational reformation for each school. Modest and dispersed improvements in school attendance patterns, achievement test scores, elementary skills, teacher salaries, minority graduation rates, teacher morale, parental involvement, and business/ school partnerships will only result in a moderately changed workforce, citizen, college student, society, and nation. In fact, these kinds of improvement, which are not rare, could have been the focus of this essay. Slight improvements, while welcomed, are manifestly unacceptable, however, if we intend to meet the social, economic, and political needs of the country. With almost 50 percent of the nation's youth dropping out of high school, graduating as functional illiterates, or being classified as poorly educated, we cannot be satisfied with anything less than a radical conversion of key societal institutions.

## The Prospects for the Future

Even though dramatic improvements in the aforementioned areas have not occurred in the 1980s, we should not necessarily conclude that our efforts have been wasted. Several reasons lead us to be hopeful about the future. First, there are small projects around the country where unusually exciting advances are being made. These successes, often pilot programs, are providing invaluable information regarding the most appropriate ways to prepare future teachers for urban schools as well as for practicing principals and teachers to meet the needs of all students and teachers. The Houston Teaching Academy, for instance reveals valuable information about preparing teachers for urban schools.

Second, research, that is accumulating provides invaluable information about educating students who are most likely to profit the least while they are in school. In particular, valuable research is being conducted in urban schools.  The experiences at Randolph High School in Harlem and South Mountain High School in Phoenix illustrate this kind of urban school success. In addition, there is evidence that cooperative endeavors at the district and state levels are or will be successful.  New Haven, Connecticut, for instance, beginning in the late 1960s and continuing to the present, has gradually transformed many of its schools through parent-school partnerships.  Michigan has the opportunity to lead the nation in cooperative endeavors among universities, school districts, communities, and corporations to ensure that every child is properly educated.  This unprecedented cooperation among businesses, public schools, and universities is encouraging.  Many are realizing that the failure of society to properly educate all children is not a simple economic issue, but instead, is a complex moral and political concern.  Likewise, the efforts going into the study of effective schools, effective teachers, and effective administrators, are assisting teacher educators as they prepare their students. These efforts are resulting in a growing body of knowledge that may be used to transform how many departments and colleges of teacher education view teacher preparation and, thereby, how schools should operate.  There also appears to be a growing realization that the way many schools are organized, managed, and operated is antithetical to sound professional judgment.  Schools, as many are presently functioning, are neither places for reflective educators nor inquiring students. On the contrary, many schools either refuse or are not allowed to abandon the ineffective organizational and pedagogical patterns that treat the teachers and students as mindless subjects of the whims, ideologies, policies, and practices of the educational and political establishment.

The bottom line in this regard seems to be that we are currently in possession of a great deal of the research information, experiential understanding, and educational models that are necessary to educating students.  What, then, must occur in the 1990s if we are to be successful in educating children and youth?  While there are not any simple solutions to our complex social and school problems, a number of generalizations can be made.

First, an intelligent understanding of the available research information by current teachers and administrators is important. The task of disseminating information and getting educators to act upon the data will not be an easy task. Many teachers are skeptical of research findings because of the way the information has been mindlessly interpreted and autocratically prescribed at state and district levels.

Professional development and deregulation on a grand scale, then, are necessary if we are to change the practices of many in the current education force.    Professional development, however, cannot take the form of rigidly dictating and evaluating the behavior of teachers. Teachers and administrators need the freedom to make professional judgments about research in the field.    Legislated, mandated, and detailed instructions to superintendents, teachers, and principals will not result in the cultivation of independently functioning citizens, employees, and educated persons for society.    Educators need to be prepared as autonomous professionals and then held accountable for developing educated people.    Forcing them to perform like assembly-line workers will only aggravate teaching and learning problems, not produce people who see themselves as lifelong learners.

Second, the future teachers and administrators that are in colleges and universities need to be prepared in the light of the present and developing knowledge base.    Present-day teacher educators in some, perhaps many, cases are not current in regard to research about effective teachers, principals, superintendents, and schools. Nor do some recognize that the current crises are real. Consequently, these professors of education are not preparing students in view of a critical interpretation of the available research.    Departments and colleges of education, therefore, must update themselves if they are going to contribute significantly to solving the problems of schooling. In this realm, colleges and universities have to provide the incentives and the resources for teacher education units to advance to the cutting edge of the profession. We can no longer afford to have underfunded, neglected teacher preparation programs. Nor can we afford large numbers of teacher educators who know little or nothing about the daily operation of urban schools, the cultures of minority students, and how to teach to the needs of the disenfranchised.

Third, existing structural, organizational, union, and bureaucratic arrangements at state and local levels need to allow for the intelligent application of what is presently known and the intelligent pursuit of the unknown. State laws, district policies, teacher contracts, and school practices need to be altered in many instances in order to facilitate an informed transformation of districts and schools into effective centers of learning for all students. Likewise, school districts must learn to be less defensive and more open to input from and involvement by parents, businesses, and universities.

Fourth, schools and teacher preparation programs will need additional resources if they are to achieve the educational success that is essential for an educational renaissance in the country. In order to be effective on a large, district-wide scale, many more community and business volunteers will have to be enlisted. The commitment, contrary to what we may wish, must be viewed as a long-term one. The New Haven project started in the late 1960s and is still in the process of changing the entire school district. Further, financial resources are needed if science laboratories in elementary, middle, and high schools are going to be built or modernized. New classroom facilities and equipment are badly needed in many districts. Additional teachers, counselors, and social workers for schools with large numbers of at-risk students are needed if noteworthy change is to occur in a decade or less.

**Concluding Remarks**

Although there are observers who still deny that our nation is at risk from political, social, and economic perspectives, it is becoming increasingly clear that America is in serious danger of disappearing as an example of democracy. Policymakers, business leaders, community leaders, and classroom teachers recognize that if we are to meet our educational, economic, and political crises—our human crises—we must prepare more effective teachers, redesign our schools, commit more resources, and change our priorities and values.

# References

Alsalam, N. (Ed.). (1990). *The condition of education, 1990* (Vol. 2). Washington, DC: U. S. Government Printing Office.

Applebee, A. N., Langer, J. A., Jenkins, L. B., Mullis, I. V. S., & Foertsch, M. A. (1990). *Learning to write in our nation's schools: Instruction and achievement in 1988 at grades 4, 8, and 12.* Princeton, NJ: Educational Testing Service, The National Assessment of Educational Progress.

The Association of Teacher Educators. (1986). *Visions of reform: Implications for the education profession.* Reston, VA.

Collison, M. (1990, September 19). "Average score on ACT was unchanged in 1989-90; Scores of many minority students rose slightly." *The Chronicle of Higher Education*, p. A39.

Dodge, S. (1990, September 5). "Average score on verbal section of '89-90 SAT drops to lowest level since 1980; Math score unchanged." *The Chronicle of Higher Education*, p. A33.

Fenstermacher, G. D. (1990, Spring). "Which master will schools serve? Taking multicultural education seriously." *The Smith Project for Substance Abuse Education*, pp. 3-4.

Galambos, E. C. (Ed.). (1985). *What works in in-service education programs for teachers?* Atlanta, GA: Southern Regional Education Board.

Goldberg, M. F. (1990). "Portrait of James P. Comer." *Educational Leadership, 48,* (1), 40-42.

Goodlad, J. I., & Keating, P. (Eds.) (1990). *Access to knowledge: An agenda for our nation's schools.* New York: College Entrance Examination Board.

Hawley, W. D., Rosenholtz, S. J., Goodstein, H., & Hasselbring, T. (1984). "Good schools: What research says about improving student achievement." *Peabody Journal of Education, 61*, (4).

The Holmes Group. (1990). *Tomorrow's schools: Principles for the design of professional development schools.* East Lansing, MI.

The Holmes Group. (1986). *Tomorrow's teachers.* East Lansing, MI.

Houston, W. R. (Ed.). (1990). *Handbook of research on teacher education.* New York: Macmillan.

Koretz, D. (1986). *Trends in educational achievement.* Washington, DC: Congressional Budget Office.

Langer, J. A., Applebee, A. N., Mullis, I. V. S., & Foertsch, M. A. (1990). *Learning to read in our nation's schools: Instruction and achievement in 1988 at grades 4, 8, and 12.* Princeton, NJ: Educational Testing Service, The National Assessment of Educational Progress.

Linn, R. L., & Dunbar, S. B. (1990). "The nation's report card goes home: Good news and bad about trends in achievement." *Kappan, 72*, 127-133.

*The Michigan partnership for new education.* (1990). East Lansing, MI: Michigan State University.

The National Academy of Education. (1984). *Improving education: Perspectives on educational research.* Pittsburgh, PA.

The National Commission on Excellence in Education. (1983). *A nation at risk.* Washington, DC: U. S. Department of Education.

The National Governor's Association. (1986). *Time for results: The governors' 1991 report on education.* Washington, DC.

Ogle, L. T. (Ed.). (1990). *The condition of education* (Vol. 1). Washington, DC: U. S. Government Printing Office.

Quality Education for Minorities Project. (1990). *Education that works: An action plan for the education of minorities.* Cambridge, MA: Massachusetts Institute of Technology.

Raywid, M. A., Tesconi, C. A., & Warren, D. R. (1984). *Pride and promise: Schools of excellence for all the people.* Westbury, NY: American Educational Studies Association.

Reynolds, M. C. (Ed.). (1989). *Knowledge base for the beginning teacher.* Oxford: Pergamon Press.

Sarason, S. B. (1990). *The predictable failure of educational reform.* San Francisco, CA: Jossey-Bass Publishers.

Schwartz, T. (1990, June 11). "Making the grade: Principal Lottie Taylor's extraordinary success in Harlem." *New York*, pp. 37-47.

Sergiovanni, T. J. & Moore, J. H. (Eds.). (1989). *Schooling for tomorrow: Directing reforms to issues that count.* Boston: Allyn and Bacon.

Staff. (1990, June). "Annual state dropout rate for 1988-89 is 6.1%." *Texas Dropout Information Clearinghouse Forum*, p. 1.

Staff. (1990, Summer). "Final year of TEAMS results published." *Texas Education Agency Research Briefs*, pp. 2-3, 10-11, 16.

Staff. (1990, June). "Moonlighting survey shows decade of teacher change." *Advocate*, pp. 10-11.

Staff. (1990, September 5). "The nation." *The Chronicle of Higher Educational Almanac*, pp. 3-28.

U. S. Department of Education. (1987). *What works: Research about teaching and learning.* Washington: DC.

Wittrock, M. C. (Ed.). (1986). *Handbook of research on teaching* (3rd ed.).

# Chapter XII

# Education as a Political Issue: What's missing in the public conversation about education?

**Peter McLaren**

**Dennis Carlson**

# Peter McLaren

We live at a precarious point in time in which relations of subjection, suffering, dispossession and contempt for human dignity and the sanctity of life remain at the center of our social existence. Emotional dis-location, moral sickness and individual helplessness remain a ubiquitous feature of history. Our much heralded form of democracy has become, unbeknownst to many Americans, subverted by its contradictory relationship to the very object of its address: human freedom, social justice, and a tolerance and respect for difference. In the current historical juncture, discourses of democracy continue to masquerade as disinterested solicitations, and to reveal themselves as incommensurable with the struggle for social equality. The reality and promise of democracy in the United States has recently been invalidated by the ascendency of new postmodern institutionalization of brutality and the proliferation of new and sinister structures of domination. This has been followed by an ever fainter chorus of discontent as the voices of the powerless and the marginalized grow increasingly despondent or else are clubbed into oblivion by the crackling swiftness of police batons.

Although pain and suffering continue to pollute the atmosphere of social justice in the United States in alarming proportion to previous decades, the dream of democracy and the struggle to bring it about has taken on a new intensity, as recent events in Eastern Europe attest. In its unannounced retreat in the United States over the past decade, democracy has managed to recreate power through the spectacularization of its after-image, that is, through image management and the creation of national myths of identity primarily through the techniques of the mass media.

The prevailing referents around which the notion of public citizenry is currently constructed have been steered into the ominous direction of the social logic of production and consumption. Buyers are beginning to culturally merge with their commodities while human agency is becoming absorbed into the social ethics of the marketplace. Social impulses for equality, liberty, and social justice have been flattened out by the mass media until they have become cataleptically rigid while postmodern images threaten to steal what was once known as the "soul."

Given the current condition of end-of-the-century ennui and paranoia, we have arrived at the zero-degree reality of the kind that once only graced the pages of surrealist manifestos or punk fanzines.  Andre Breton's "simplest Surrealist act"—firing a pistol into a crowd of strangers—is no longer just a contemporary symbolic disruption of the grudgingly mundane aspects of everyday life or a symbolic dislocation circulating in avant garde broadsheets.  It is precisely in this current North American historical conjuncture that people *are* really shooting blindly into crowds:  at children in hamburger establishments, at employees and employers in factories, at teachers and class-mates in schools, and at female engineering students in univer-sity seminar rooms.  In some urban settings, children are murdering other children for their status-line foot gear— not to mention the lurid reality at L.A. 'drive-bys'.  In New York City, manufacturers of bullet proof vests are starting special fashion lines for toddlers and elementary school children who might accidentally absorb stray bullets from homeboy dealers in pumps, ten dollar gold tooth caps and who carry customized AK 47 assault rifles.  The guns are not fashion accessories — yet. But gas masks are.  New York celebrity fashion designer, Andre Van Pier, has recently announced a new spring fashion line based on the theme of "Desert Storm."  It will attempt to capture the "Gulf War look."  Fashion accessories revealed include neon-colored camouflage pattern, canteen purses, and gas masks slung renegade-chic over the shoulder.  A major New York manufacture of baseball cards has revealed a new line of Gulf War cards that are supposed to be "educational."  Of course, included are photos of the major American military hardware and portraits of the generals but the only item repre-sented from Iraq in this educational collection is a "scud" missile.

Today's social ugliness that makes the bizarre appear normal is no longer just a (white, male) surrealist fantasy or proto-surrealist spin-off, or a Baudrillardean rehearsal for a futureless future.  This scenario *is* the present historical moment, one that has arrived in a body bag—unravelled and stomped on by the logic of a steel-toed boot. Serial killer Ted Bundy has donated his multiple texts of identity to our structural unconscious and *we are living them.* A funky nihilism has set in; an aroma of cultural disquiet. There is a yearning for a comfortable apocalypse accompanied by forms of everyday life where salvation is unnecessary because chaos is always sublime and morality is frictionless in the age of MTV. Feelings of despair about the global condition have gone high-tech: We can not eroticize our depression and rearrange and reterritorialize our feelings by plugging our central nervous system in to the electromagnetic spectrum via tv waves and charting out our lives according to designer moods.

The erosion of the American dream has forced today's youth to occupy, if not a dystopian parody of *The Cosby Show,* then paracriminal subcultures of sardonic nihilism focussing on drugs and violence, apotheosized in movies like *Clockwork Orange* and *Colors.* Corporate rock's celebration of the subversion of adult authority gives its youthful listeners the illusion of resistance but not a language of critique or hope. It works to produce a politics of pleasure but simultaneously functions as a form of repression and forgetting—a motivated social amnesia and forced disavowal of the nation's complicitousness in racial demonization and colonialism.

The New Right has used the media effectively (and affectively) not simply to transform gangsters or actors into politicians through the services of high-tech image consultants, but even more impressively, to seduce Americans to retreat into cultural nostalgia and social amnesia as a way out of this postmodern era of retreat and despondency (many students I teach are already feeling a nostalgia for the Persian Gulf War as it was ideologically produced through CNN). At the same time the New Right has, through foreign and domestic policies shaped by the heritage of imperialism, helped the U. S. flex its global muscles in Grenada, Panama, and Iraq, setting the stage for a renewed patriotic zeal and construction of the postmodern national subject. Kellner (1990) notes that, under the control of multinational capital, the media have effectively served as ideological mouthpieces for Reagan/Bush disinformation and have helped to forge a conservative ideological hegemony.

Kellner (1990: 219) writes:

> It is a historical irony that the 1980s marked the defeat of democracy by capitalism in the United States and the triumph of democracy over state communism in the Soviet bloc countries.  At present, the "free" television media in the United States are probably no more adversarial and no less propagandistic than *Pravda* or the television stations in the Eastern European countries.  Hence the very future of democracy is at stake—and development of a democratic communications system is necessary if democracy is to be realized.

Largely because of the way in which the media function to shape and merchandise morality and to construct certain forms of citizenship and individual and collective identities, our understanding of the meaning and importance of democracy has become impoverished in proportion to its dissolution and retreat from contemporary social life.  In the current historical juncture of democratic decline in the United States, ideals and images have become detached from their anchorage in stable and agreed-upon meanings and associations and are now beginning to assume a reality of their own.  The world of the media is one that splinters, obliterates, peripheralizes, partitions and segments social space, time knowledge, and subjectivity in order to unify, encompass, entrap, totalize and homogenize them.  What is missing from the educational debate is the way in which capitalism is able to achieve this cultural and ideological totalization and homogenization through it ability to insinuate itself into social practices and private perceptions through various forms of media knowledge (see Grossberg, 1988).

Ironically, today's increasingly "disorganized" capitalism has produced a gaudy sideshow that has managed to promote a counterfeit democracy of flags and emblems—one that has managed to harness the affective currency of popular culture such that the average American's investment in being "American" has reached an unparalleled high the likes of which has not been seen since the years surrounding the post WWII McCarthy hearings.  The question that needs to be asked is: How are the subjectivities (experiences) and identities of individuals and the production of media knowledges within popular culture mutually articulated?

What isn't being talked about in today's educational debate is the desperate need within our schools for creating a media literate citizenry that can disrupt, contest, and transform media apparatuses so that they no longer have the power to infantilize the population and continue to create passive, fearful, paranoid, and apolitical social subjects (McLaren and Hammer, 1991).

George Gerbner (1989/90) and others have pointed out that American television viewers are accepting a distorted picture of the real world "more readily than reality itself." Television reality is one in which men outnumber women three to one, where women are usually mothers or lovers, rarely work outside the home, and are natural victims of violence. It is a reality where less than ten per cent of the population hold blue collar jobs, where few elderly people exist, where young Blacks learn to accept their minority status as inevitable and are trained to anticipate their own victimization (they are usually portrayed as the white hero's comic sidekick or else drug addicts, gang members, or killers). It is a world in which 18 acts of violence an hour occur in children's time programs. Violence in television demonstrates the social power of adult white males who are most likely to get involved with violence but most likely to get away with it. It also serves as a mass spectacle reflecting the allocative power of the state. And this is occurring in a country that in 1990 reported the largest number of rapes against women in its history and a prison incarceration rate of Blacks that exceeds that of South Africa. A country where rich Angelenos are hiring private police, where the wealthy neighborhoods display signs warning (Armed Response!) and where security systems and militarization of urban life are refiguring social space along the lines of the postmodern film, *Bladerunner*.

What educators need to realize is that George Bush's New World Order cannot be realistically achieved without creating a new moral order at home first (and that means in the classrooms and the living rooms of the nation)—one that refuses to challenge the received truths or accepted conventions that have provoked the current crisis of history and identity. So far Bush has been successful in reproducing a moral order in which young people are able to resist being motivated to enter into any logic of opposition through counterpublic spheres of cultural resistance.

It is sadly pathetic that the "education president" has invested more in the intelligence quotients of its weapons of war than in those who are growing despondent inside of the walls of the nation's schools.    While politicians self-righteously decry the retrenchment of the conservative "hard-liners" in the Soviet Union, they fail to see the ideological affinities among their own political positions; incredibly, they see their own conservative position as somehow more enlightened and the policies they support immune to the possibility that they could contribute to social ill.   This has blinded them to the ways in which the dominant social order continues to shut the colonized out of history—even in this so-called era of interculturalism and growth of poly-ethnic and poly-lingual communities.

Missing from the debate over public education is a serious examination of the way in which contemporary forms of schooling reproduce national images of citizenship modelled on the John-Wayneing of America and captured in the renumerative cliches,  Rocky Balboa's "Go for it!" and Clint Eastwood's "Go ahead.   Make my day!" which adorn the discursive fountain head of United States bravado culture.   These slogans have become cultural aphorism that reveal a great deal about the structural unconscious of the United States—slogans that constitute a combination of insurance company rationality, the politics of Sunday School charity drives, and the patriarchal, xenophobic and militaristic logic of terror (both Ronald Reagan and George Bush have referred to "Go ahead, make my day!" during their time in office).   When Clint Eastwood delivered "Go ahead, make my day!" in the movie, *Sudden Impact* (made during the Reagan presidency), he is daring a black man to murder a woman so that he (Dirty Harry) can kill him.   As Michael Rogin (1990) has pointed out, Dirty Harry is willing to sacrifice women and people of color in the name of his own courage.   Reagan had made women and Blacks  his targets by destroying their welfare-state tax benefits—an act he was defending when he dared his detractors to "Make my day!"  George Bush made the black criminal and white rapist of *Sudden Impact* into the figure of Willie Horton, as he attempted for the first time to organize American politics around the ominous image of interracial rape (Rogin, 1990). Rogin brilliantly articulates the use of movies such as *Rambo* and *Sudden Impact* as a form of political spectacle which operates as a form of social amnesia (1990, p. 107).

The kind of curriculum focus needed in today's schools is one that actively contests the historical amnesia created by contemporary cultural forms found in the mass media. Students should be invited to explore why they identify with Dirty Harry and Rambo, and begin to historicize such an identification in the context of the larger political and social issues facing the country.

It should come as little surprise that public opinion among those groups most advantaged by wealth and power is more supportive of the public school system and current reform efforts than those disempowered on the basis of race, socioeconomic status or gender. For those very populations that will be increasing in the coming decades—African Americans and Latino youth—the conditions in this country's school systems have appreciably worsened. Groups actively lobbying for minority positions on issues dealing with race, social and welfare concerns, are now being labelled within the conservative agenda by spokespersons such as Diane Ravitch, Roger Kimball, William Bennett, Lynne V.B. Cheney and others as "ethnocentric" or "separatist." Within this rationality, the call for diversity is sanctioned only when the converging of diverse voices collapses into a depoliticized co-existence based on capitulation to the hidden imperatives of Eurocentrism, logocentrism, and patriarchy. Those educators and students who refuse to genuflect before the Western cultural tradition and regard it glowingly as the apogee of cultural and political achievement are branded as perverse, ignorant and malicious sophists who have "defiled reason" (Kimball, 1990; see also Ravitch, 1990). What this ideological position effectively does is sound an alarm for the impending demise of white culture: "If white people have any pride in their heritage, now is the time to act because your history is under assault!" This clarion call for white authenticity embalms the past for people of color and shrouds their histories in the thinning strands of the moral and social consciousness of a nation plagued by social amnesia.  It also shrouds domination in a white sheet of race, class, and gender purity by exiling questions of racism, sexism, homophobia, and class oppression.

On the other side of the educational debate we have a population that has been taught to think so extravagantly about success and power being pushed even closer to the dream of cultural and moral salvation.  This dream has taken shape in Allan Bloom's colonial imagination where an "imperialist nostalgia" for the former grandeur of the empires of the center transforms itself into an inveterate fear of the unwashed masses.  Bloom's highbrow petulance over *declasse* academics wanting to teach courses on popular culture translates for public schools into educational initiatives towards a national curriculum designed to maintain American "standards" in the world of international market competition (in other words, to maintain a uniform identity defined by Europe's demonization of the darker skinned populations—one that pits the Anglo "I" against the dark, forbidding "Other").  Bloom's reaction against the transdisciplinary character of much of what is occurring in recent literary theory and its capacity to reterritorialize the structure of academic discourse is really a form of pining for the loss of the authority of and consensus on the meaning of Greek and Roman Antiquity and collapse of late-Victorian highbrow academic dilettantism.

In the effete paradise of Bloom (which, of course, consists of Victorian salons and Tudor libraries populated by white bourgeois males and *belles lettristes* from Ivy League schools) the non-Western thinker becomes the debased and inverted image of the hypercivilized metropolitan intellectual.  In other words, both non-Western knowledge and the uncultivated thought of the masses become, for Bloom, a primitive non-knowledge that serves as a conduit to savagery and barbarism—a descent into hell, reason's Negative Other.  Bloom's collision of empires of consciousness (the radiantly civilized high culture of hellenism of which Bloom himself is a prime representative and the dark, primitive culture of the mob) occurs in a theatre of the Western mind (whose doors are being forced shut by the incursion of unholy thought into American culture) where a fantasy narrative is played out that is common to many bourgeois male academics and one in which the hegemony of the universalized and eternalized language and tropes of the colonizer makes it easier to script: Euro-American civilization is keeping the grandeur of the savage at bay in the name of Truth, and is morally policing the borders of that dark continent of the psyche where female sensuality remains unmediated by the realm of ideas and where the violence of the "blood-male" remains untempered by reason and the rule of law. For Bloom, both these savage verities of sex and violence must be cruelly trussed rather than cossetted by the Western mind.

What educators like Bloom fail to understand is that our schools are failing large numbers of minority students precisely because too much emphasis is already being placed on trading in on the status of one's cultural capital. Ironically, those students who populate urban settings in places such as New York's Howard Beach, Ozone Park, El Barrio, etc., are likely to learn more about Eastern Europe in contexts designed by *soi-dissant* metropolitan intellectuals than they are about the Harlem Renaissance, Mexico, Africa, the Carribean, or Aztec or Zulu culture. The sad irony is that test scores based on the information filtered from the Western canon and bourgeois cultural capital are used to justify school district and state funding initiatives. The reality of schooling is that U. S. society is comprised of differentially empowered publics and mainstream schooling ensures that those publics already enjoy most of the power and privilege in such a society will continue their advantage for succeeding generations. In this way, intergenerational continuity is ensured: working-class students get working-class jobs; affluent students get the kind of employment that will advantage their life chances and those of their children.

Cultural literacy spokespersons such as E. D. Hirsch have recently reduced literacy to a cultural thesaurus to be memorized by students aspiring to become active, engaged citizens. Yet when culture is despairingly viewed as a storehouse of dead facts, a time capsule of frozen memories detached from historical context, then the concept of difference, when applied to issues of race, class, gender, age, sexual preference, or disability, can be absorbed into what I call "dead pluralism." Dead pluralism is what keeps at bay the need to historicize difference, to recognize the hierarchical production of systems of difference in whose interests such hierarchies serve, and to acknowledge difference as a social construction forged within asymmetrical relations of power, conflicting interests, and a climate of dissent and opposition.     The "pluralism" that supposedly already undergirds our so-called multicultural society in the vision of Ravitch and Kimball is one that is based on uncoerced consensus, interracial and intergenerational harmony and zero-degree public unity—a perspective shrouded in the lie of democratic ubiquity.     When Ravitch and Kimball call for pluralism over separatism they are really buttressing the status quo against disempowered minorities seeking social justice.

The real danger facing education is not simply the refusal of the general public to recognize its embeddedness in relations of power and privilege at the level of everyday life, but rather the fact that the public prefers to act as if there exists few—or no—such political linkages.     The danger is not an apathetic nation, nor a cynical one but rather the ability of the public sphere to exist relatively uncontested.     Why?     I believe that it has to do with the ability of the larger public sphere to mobilize desire, and secure the passion of the public, and the relative inability of progressive educators to analyze the social, cultural, moral and political implications of such an ability.

Another area of concern that relates to the ability of the schools to create a passive, risk-free citizenry is the ability of schooling to conflate citizenship values based on characteristics of nationhood and Christianity.     The question not being asked in the current debate over education in this country is how nationalism and religion work together in debilitating ways to construct racist formations within the wider citizenry.     For instance, self-righteous Christians who are making such an issue of curriculum censorship should be confronted by an educational system committed to curricular practices that examine the relationship among religion, nationalism and racism in our schools.

Citing the work of Alan Davies, David Seljak (1991) explores the various ways the figure of Christ has been constructed geopolitically that have had consequences for the way in which certain races have been viewed. For instance, students should be invited to examine The Germanic Christ (a combination of Lutheran pietism, romantic German nationalism and modern pseudo-scientific theories of racial purity and genetic superiority), the Latin Christ of France (a figure that embodies French nationalism, aristocratic resentment against the post-revolutionary bourgeois, classical Catholic anti-Judaism), the Anglo-Saxon Christ of the United Kingdom and Anglo North America (The United States and English Canada) which includes the incarnation of social Darwinism and the Aryan myth, the Afrikaaner Christ (Calvinist categories of double predestination and sphere sovereignty which through distortion came to justify the color dualism and racial segregation of later apartheid ideology). Students should also be invited to examine how the figure of Christ is being reconfigured in Latin America within the theology of liberation as a means of working for the empowerment of oppressed groups. Students should also be invited to examine the role Christianity has placed in the development of homophobia and violence against gays and lesbians (Sears, 1987). Religion plays an important role in the life of Americans and students should be given the opportunity to examine both the enabling and disabling effects of religious ideology in the shaping of future generations.

Needed for the coming decade is a critical pedagogy that is able to provide conditions for students to reject what they experience as a given. A pedagogy that includes a sharpened focus on the relationship among economies of capital investment, political economies, moral economies, economies of 'free' expression, sexual economies, economies of belief and identity formation and the construction of desire and formation of human will. Needed is a pedagogy of discontent and of outrage that is able to contest the hegemony of prevailing definitions of the everyday as the "way things are." A pedagogy that refuses the hidebound distinction between prosaic expression and popular culture, between art and experience, between reason and the imagination. We need a critical pedagogy in our colleges of education that can problematize schooling as a site for the construction of moral, cultural, and national identity, and emphasize the creation of the schooled citizen as a form of emplacement, as a geopolitical construction, as a process in the formation of the geography of cultural desire.  Teaching in our schools must be transformed into acts of dissonance and inter- ventions into the ritual inscription of our students into the codes of the dominant culture.  It must promote structured refusals to naturalize existing relations of power.  And finally, it needs to help create subaltern counterpublics.

Also needed is a curriculum that has as its focus of investiga- tion the study of everyday, informal, and popular culture and how the historical patterns of power that inform such cultures are imbricated in the formation of individual subjectivity and identity.  Pedagogy occurs not only in schools but in all cultural sites.  The electronic media is perhaps the greatest site of peda- gogical production that exists—you could say it is a form of perpetual pedagogy.  In addition to understanding literacies applicable to print culture, students need to recognize how their identities are formed and their "mattering maps" produced through an engagement with electronic and other types of media so that they will be able to engage in alternative ways of symbolizing the self and gain a significant purchase on the construction of their own identities and the direction of their desiring.  It is in such an investigation that teachers and students become transformed into cultural workers for self and social emancipation.  I am calling for a pedagogy of critical media literacy that is linked to what Paul Willis (1990) has referred to a "grounded aesthetics" designed to provide students with the symbolic resources for creative self and social formation in order that they can more critically re-enter the vast, uncharted spaces of common culture.

I am suggesting that students need to make critical judgments about what society might mean, and what is possible or desirable outside existing configurations of power and privilege. Students need to be able to cross over into different zones of cultural diversity and form what Trinh T. Minh-ha (1988) calls hybrid and hyphenated identities in order to rethink the rela- tionship of self to society, of self to other, and for deepening the moral vision of the social order.  This raises an important question:  How are the categories of race, class, gender, sexual preference shaped within the margins and centers of society, and how can students engage history as a way of reclaiming power and identity? The critical media literacy of which I speak is structured around the notion of a politics of location and identity as border-crossing (see Giroux, in press; McLaren, forthcoming). It is grounded in the ethical imperative of examining the contradictions in U. S. society between the meaning of freedom, the demands of social justice, and the obligations of citizenship on the one hand, and the structured silence that permeates incidents of suffering in everyday life (McLaren, in press). The politics of difference that undergirds such a critical literacy is one in which differences rearticulate and shape identity such that students can actively refuse the role of cultural servant and sentinel for the status quo in order to reclaim, reshape, and transform their own historical destiny.

# References

Giroux, H. A.  (in press).  "Border Pedagogy and the Politics of Postmodernism", in Peter McLaren (Ed.) *Postmodernism, Postcolonialism and Pedagogy*, Albert Park, Australia: James Nicholas Publishers.

Giroux, H. A. & McLaren, P.  (in press) "Leon Golub's Radical Pessimism", *Exposure.*

Giroux, H. A. & McLaren, P.  (1991)  "Radical Pedagogy as Cultural Politics", in Donald Morton and Mas'ud Zavarzadeh (Eds.) *Theory/Pedagogy/Politics*, Urbana and Chicago: University of Illinois Press, pp. 152-186.

Gerner, G.  (1989/90) "TV vs. Reality", *Adbusters, 1*, p. 12.

Grossberg, L.  (1988) *It's A Sin*, Sydney, Australia: Power Publications.

Hammer, R. & McLaren, P.  (1991) "Rethinking the Dialectic", *Educational Theory, 41*, pp. 23-46.

Hochschild, A. R. (1983) *The Managed Heart*, Berkeley: University of California Press.

Kellner, D. (1990) *Television and the Crisis of Democracy*, Boulder, San Francisco, Oxford: Westview Press.

Kimball, R. (1991) "Tenured Radicals", *The New Criterion, 9*, pp. 4-13.

Minh-ha, Trinh T. (1988) "Not You/Like You: Post-Colonial Women and the Interlocking Questions of Identity and Difference", *Inscriptions, 3/4*, pp. 71-77.

McLaren, P. (forthcoming) *Radical Pedagogy: Postcolonial Politics in a Postmodern World*, London and New York: Routledge.

Ravitch, D. (1990) "Multiculturalism", *The American Scholar, 59*, pp. 337-354.

Rogin, M. (1990) "'Make My Day!': Spectacle as Amnesia in Imperial Politics", *Representations, 29*, pp. 99-123.

Sears, J. T. (1987) "Peering into the Well of Loneliness: The Responsibility of Educators to Gay and Lesbian Youth", in Alex Molnar (Ed.) *Social Issues and Education*, Alexandria, Virginia, Association for Supervision and Curriculum Development.

Seljak, D. (1991) "Alan Davies on Racism", *The Ecumenist, 29*, pp. 13-14.

Willis, P. (1990) *Common Culture*, Boulder: Westview Press.

# Dennis Carlson

If, as Michel Foucault suggests, power and knowledge are inseparable, then curriculum may be studied in terms of the power
relations it constitutes and by which it is constituted.[1] Furthermore, since power is always *about* something, that is, always
deployed strategically to advance a particular project, the
curriculum may be studied as an apparatus of power deployed
within educational sites to reconstitute power in some interests
rather than others, to advance one social project rather than
another. Finally, since curriculum constitutes relations of
power, it cannot but artificially be separated from the organization of the schools which structures curriculum use. This all
implies that curriculum reform involves much more than
merely changing the knowledge that students learn. It also
involves changing the way teachers' work is organized and the
way schools are organized and operated, and for what purposes.

In what follows I want to examine the discourse and practice
of urban school reform over the past several decades—a period
Ira Shor has characterized as the "conservative restoration."
This examination will focus on the power relations that have
shaped the schools and are embedded with the malformation of
class, race, and gender oppression.[2] I argue that because
reforms have not addressed the roots of crisis in urban schools
or countered the inequalities that generate conflict and resistance among various groups, "basic skills" reforms are undermined by their own set of contradictions and crisis tendencies.
Finally, such a perspective on the curriculum and urban school
crisis directs our attention to the role the schools *might* play in
reconstructing power relations consistent with democratic–
progressive movements organized around agendas of "equity,"
"justice," "community," and "workplace democratization." In
this regard I conclude with a few comments on the articulation
of an alternative, democratic–progressive discourse on urban
school reform.

### The Conservative, Bureaucratic State Discourse on Urban School Reform

Over the past several decades, a conservative, bureaucratic state discourse has articulated urban school reform around a "basic skills" or functional literacy" curriculum, performance and output-based program evaluation and instructional objectives, minimum competency testing, and the reorganization of urban school consistent with "effective schools" research findings. Most directly and overtly, the "basic skills" restructuring of urban schools around standardized testing and a skill-based curriculum has been a response to the changing character of work in post-industrial America, and it has participated in the construction of a new post-industrial working class. Prior to the 1960s, major urban school districts had enrolled a heavily white, ethnic, working class student population. General education and vocational programs prepared most of these students for clerical and trade union jobs in manufacturing that were available upon graduation, and a small college preparatory program was available for those who aspired to more. The jobs available to high school graduates in industry were often routine and unrewarding, but they paid relatively high wages and offered some job security. Literacy requirements often took a back seat to manual skills in these jobs, particularly for boys but also for girls. The progressive-era urban school curriculum participated in the pre-skilling and socializing of this industrial working class by teaching students how to cooperate and be "good" workers, and it emphasized manual labor, typing, and home economics skills which were more manual than mental in their orientation.

The changing character of work in post-industrial America was already becoming apparent by the 1960s when business and state leaders began to talk of a growing mismatch between the literacy skills of high school graduates and the literacy requirements of the new jobs in urban areas. Enrollments in vocational education programs and tracks were still relatively high, but graduates of these programs found fewer and fewer jobs waiting for them that required their particular skills.[3] As manufacturing moved to the Second and Third World, the "good" trade union jobs began to disappear, and they have been replaced by clerical, data processing, janitorial, and service

industry jobs.    The new entry-level jobs increasingly require
more in the way of basic reading (word and sentence decoding),
comprehension and direction-following skills.[4]   Workers frequently have to refer to sets of standard operating procedures
and record data on forms or punch it into a computer.   They
also need to be able to interact with clients and customers and
categorize customer data.   Thus they need generalizable literacy
skills and competencies of a certain minimal level (generally
defined at about the 9th grade reading level) that can be put to
use and adapted to a number of diverse work settings.   As D. W.
Livingstone has observed, education for this new, semiskilled
labor force

> ...entails instruction in general preparatory skills that are open - ended
> and can be built upon or refined in a range of work settings.   In other
> words, it means the creation of labor market entrants who will be
> increasingly technically adaptable and capable of mobility among work
> settings in response to rapidly changing workplace technologies. [5]

The urban school curriculum, in response to these changes, has
been reconceived in terms of the minimal language decoding,
comprehension, and processing skills that students "need" to be
"effective" workers in the new service industry, maintenance,
data processing, and "para-professional" fields.   Furthermore,
the form of the curriculum, by organizing students' work in
terms of direction-following and the routine production of
workbook and drillsheet "piecework," orients students to the
ways of working that are most typically associated with the new
urban working class jobs.   Many urban students are enrolled in
several remedial basic skills courses to help them pass minimum
competency tests, and also are placed in low ability group
classes that emphasize basic skills over subject area knowledge.
    While the urban school curriculum has been reconstructed by
bureaucratic state reform initiatives around "basic skills," urban
schools have not, after several decades of reform, been able to
achieve even the very limited objective of "certifying" that their
students are "functionally literate" by the time they graduate,
and they have not been able to keep much more than half of all
socioeconomically    disadvantaged    students    in    school    long
enough to graduate.   In 1989, it was still possible for the New
York Times to warn of an "impending U. S. jobs 'disaster' with a

"work force unqualified to work" and with "schools lagging far behind needs of employees."[6] Like the Vietnam War and the "war on poverty," the war on illiteracy and the drop-out problem in urban schools has become bogged down, and it offers no light at the end of the tunnel.

Why is it that corporate and state reform initiatives in urban education have not been more successful in ensuring that socioeconomically disadvantaged students learn the literacy skills the "need" for gainful employment in the new working class? Several factors need to be considered. First, because the basic skills curriculum is highly rationalized and regimented, it contributes to student motivation problems rather than improves them. As more and more students are enrolled in basic skills courses, where instruction is organized around routine drillsheet and workbook, "seatwork" and rounds of standardized pre- and post-testing, teachers may have to lower work demands on students even more in order to reduce conflict and keep students from dropping out. Second, not only is a "basic skills" curriculum lacking in intrinsic motivation, it fails to hold out much for urban students once they leave school. Students are exhorted to stay in school, work hard to pass minimum competency tests, graduate, and then have a chance at one of the new service industry or data processing jobs that are available to urban high school graduates. However, the new working class jobs are low paying with little room for advancement, they offer little in the way of job security or health benefits, and workers may have to work six or more hours a week at various jobs merely to maintain their families above the poverty line. Subsistance on public welfare may seem a better option that works for many who face the prospect of entry into this working world, and for welfare subsistance a high school diploma is not required. Given the growing disparities of wealth and power in America, with fewer "good" jobs available, it may become increasingly difficult to "sell" a "basic skills" education to urban students in the years ahead.

To this point, I have limited my comments to an analysis of the urban school crisis and curriculum reform that relies upon a political economic and class theory of schooling. However, urban school reform also has participated in racial power relations and dynamics in ways that are related to class but have a somewhat independent development. Racial minorities were in the 1960s reclaiming America's inner cities, and traditional white working class and middle class neighborhoods were disappearing at a rapid rate as suburbanization accelerated. To some extent racial minorities were drawn to urban areas by the new service industry and jobs which many working class white males refused (at first) to take. Minorities had been effectively excluded from the trade union movement throughout the 1950s and white working class males continued in the 1960s to enjoy a relatively privileged status, although that status was threatened as the "good" unionized, industrial jobs began to disappear very quickly in the 1970s. The new post-industrial working class thus was initially constituted along heavily racial lines, and many new low-skill and semi-skilled jobs were readily available to minorities in urban areas. Aside from economic considerations, African American and Hispanic people were drawn to America's major urban areas because they were seeking "space" within a highly oppressive society—space to assume control of their own institutions, and thus reclaim those institutions from the control of a repressive white power structure.[7] The hope was that once minority peoples became an electoral majority within a given geographical space, they could use their power to make public institutions serve new emancipatory purposes by empowering minority communities.

The state-sponsored "basic skills" reform movement, in these terms, has had the effect of overriding local control of the schools at a time when poor African American and Hispanic peoples were becoming the numerical majority in urban America. State-mandated minimum competency testing, all of the bureaucratic regulations associated with "aligning" the urban school curriculum with the new basic skills test, the growing financial dependency of urban schools on the state (resulting from chronic fiscal crisis in urban America and particularly in urban schools), and the growing threat of a direct state takeover of "failing" urban school districts have had the effect countering efforts by African American and Hispanic communities to "reclaim" urban schools. The local school board members,

superintendent, and other local school leaders may be minorities, but so long as urban schools have to teach to the state test
and adhere to a myriad of state funding guidelines and procedures, local or community control of urban schools is more
formal than substantive or real.  To challenge these curricular
and educational power relations, African American and
Hispanic groups will need to move beyond formal democratic
control of local school boards to reclaim involvement in
substantive rather than merely technical educational decisions,
and this implies challenging the "basic skills" model of bureaucratic state control.

Finally, the conservative, bureaucratic state discourse on
"basic skills" and urban school reform participates in gender
power relations in the school.  Most obviously, basic skills
curricular reforms have taken for granted a bureaucratic and
hierarchical chain of command in urban schools that rigidly
subordinates women teachers (particularly elementary teachers)
to male administrators.  However, it is not merely a case of
individual male administrators dominating individual female
teachers.  Even when women have been "promoted" from the
corps of teachers to the ranks of administrators, it has generally
been because they have learned how to speak a patriarchal
discourse that is taken as the norm—a phenomenon that might
be referred to as the "Thatcherising of women administrators.[8]
It is this patriarchal discourse that is involved in the construction of the dominant models of school reform.  As Michael
Apple observes:

> The very program of rationalizing all important social relations in our
> major institutions is, in fact, pre-eminently a masculine discourse...Such
> a hierarchical conception is not neutral.  It disenfranchises alternative
> concerns for human relations, connectedness, and care. [9]

In education, the "teacher-proofing" of the curriculum, which
has been advanced through "basic skills" reforms, also has been
based on the masculine presumptions that teachers are not
intelligent or intellectual enough to be seriously involved in
important curricular decisions, that they need to be told exactly
what to do, and that they prefer leaving important decisions to
administrators.[10]  Basic skills reforms have also been consistent

with a patriarchal structuring of power relations in education because they take for granted a rigid bifurcation of administrative and teaching roles within an asymmetrical power relationship, and because they privilege a technical rather than discursive or dialectic rationality. Consequently, teacher support for "whole language," "cooperative learning," and other progressive approaches to curriculum and instruction that hopefully return power to teachers and students to construct the curriculum through discourse, practice, and self-reflection, represent a threat to continued patriarchal hegemony in the discourse on urban school reform. In the meantime, teachers' lack of support for performance-based "teach to the test" approaches to basic skills instruction undermines the effectiveness of top-down reforms.

I have suggested some of the ways that urban school reform during the basic skills era has served to organize class, race, and gender power relations in urban schools in highly inequitable ways. The increased centralization, bureaucratization, and rationalization of curriculum and instructional decision-making has not, consequently, been a "neutral phenomenon." However, while state officials have been relatively successful in "selling" or legitimating a basic skills reform agenda by appealing to broad public support for high standards and more "accountability" in education, the conservative reform agenda has not solved or even ameliorated the basic problems that beset urban schools.

## Toward a Democratic-Progressive Discourse on Urban School Reform

Over the past several decades of the "conservative restoration," progressive opposition to the bureaucratic state reform discourse has remained largely fragmented and politically marginalized. Liberal groups have exerted some influence on policy-thinking, but little on actual policy-making. Liberal discourse has advanced concerns over "equity" and "excellence," supported a curriculum organized around "higher order" literacy skills, a college preparatory curriculum for all students, emphasized the need to professionalize teachers rather than deskill them, personalize instruction rather than regiment it, and called for a decentralization and debureaucratization of authority through some form of "site-based" management.[11] These have been important concerns, and they provide some basis for struggle in response to concrete reform proposals sponsored by the conservative, bureaucratic state. However, for a number of reasons liberalism has failed to "deliver" fully on its promises, even when liberal politicians have gained control of the state, and this has to do with a failure to take on certain "hard" questions about whose interests are served by the current system of structured inequalities and what it will take to fundamentally change the way power is arranged and distributed in schools.[12] In moving beyond these limitations in liberal discourse, without abandoning its insights, let me briefly suggest several elements of a democratic-progressive discourse in education that help us better address the crisis in urban schools and reconceptualize urban school reform in ways that move beyond the current impasse.

First, while a democratic-progressive discourse would move beyond a "human capital" or economically functional analysis of the curriculum, with its presumption that what is learned in schools must bear a rather direct functional relationship to current economic "needs," it would not completely reject economic or workplace considerations in curriculum decision-making. On the contrary, some relationship *should* exist between school work and work in other important institutional sites in society, since education serves to initiate individuals into the "productive" work of building culture and objectifying experience in useful ways. Marx argued that people make themselves and culture through work: "What they [humans] are, therefore, coincides with their production, both with *what* they produce and with *how* they produce."[13] This suggests the importance of preparing students with the discursive skills and capacities associated with non-alienating, self-enhancing, productive work within the context of the democratization of the workplace.[14]

Second, while the conservative state discourse has organized a discussion of the urban school curriculum around the notion of "functional literacy," and while the liberal discourse has emphasized "higher order" literacy skills (generally corresponding to the higher rungs of Bloom's taxonomy), a democratic-progressive discourse would reconceptualize the curriculum around notions of "critical literacy." This latter notion suggests a capacity for discursive reflection on one's own identity formation with a culture characterized by struggle and change along a number of axes, including class, gender, race, sexuality, etc.[15] In urban schools, students need to learn how to critique the discourses and practices that keep them subordinated and reflect on their own role in the social construction of inequalities. For teachers, critical literacy education implies a reconceptualization of the pedagogic roles. Henry Giroux writes that teachers need "to undertake social criticism not as outsiders but as public intellectuals who address the social and political issues of their neighborhood, their nation, and the wider global world."[16] They must engage themselves, as well, in the struggles of their students to articulate their own voices and construct identities.

Third, beyond a reconceptualization of students' work, and in order to make such a reconceptualization possible, a democratic-progressive discourse would imply a restructuring of teachers' work and the organization of the school consistent with workplace democratization. This would imply drastic changes in the way schools are organized and how educational decisions are made that shifts substantive decision-making power from bureaucratic state officials to local communities, schools, and classrooms. Workplace democratization may be consistent with some aspects of "site-based management." however, it goes beyond most such plans in that it advances a real democratization of decision-making in urban schools and communities rather than merely bureaucratic decentralization of authority within a system that continues to be overwhelmingly under the control of bureaucratic state and central office officials.

Finally, a democratic-progressive discourse would focus our attention on the need to link-up educational theory and practice with social and cultural movements. Social movements involve a collective rearticulation and reappropriation of cultural meanings and values in advancing particular agendas for changing the distribution and use of power in society. They arise out of contradictions within existing power relations and institutional structures and offer a way of moving beyond current crisis tendencies. To ward off crisis, dominant groups in education have become quite adept at crisis management and "muddling through" from one crisis to another. However, should the various groups which have been disempowered by basic skills reforms (in ways that are related to their class, gender, and race) articulate their different concerns as part of a common movement to challenge bureaucratic state discourse and practice in education, it might yet become possible to build a new democratic-progressive "voice" and movement for change that looks beyond crisis management and mismanagement towards crisis resolution.

# Footnotes

1   Foucault, M. (1980). *Power/Knowledge: Selected Interviews and Other Writings, 1972-1977.* In Colin Gordon (ed.). New York: Pantheon Books.

2   Shor, I. (1986) *Culture Wars: School and Society in the Conservative Restoration, 1969-1984.* Boston: Routledge & Kegan Paul.

3   Gray, K. (1991, November 6) "Vocational education in high school: A modern phoenix?" *Phi Delta Kappan, 72,* pp. 437-445.

4   Levin, H. & Rumberger, R. (1986) *Educational Requirements for New Technologies.* Palo Alto: Stanford Center for Educational Research.

5   Livingstone, D. W. (1985, January) "Class, educational ideologies, and mass opinion in capitalist crisis." *Sociology of Education, 58,* p. 8.

6   Fiske, E. (1989, September 25) "Impending U. S. jobs 'disaster': work force unqualified to work." *New York Times,* p. 1+.

7   Lefebvre, H. (1979) For Henri Lefebvre, spatial conflict entails the appropriation of space by marginalized groups from its capitalist spatial organization see "Space: social product and use value." In J. W. Freiberg (ed.). *Critical Sociology: European Perspectives,* p. 293. New York: Irvington Publications.

8   Blackmore, J. (1989) "Educational leadership: A feminist critique and reconstruction." In J. Smyth (ed.). *Critical Perspectives in Educational Leadership.* New York: Falmer Press.

9  Apple, M. (1986) *Teachers and Texts: A Political Economy of Class and Gender Relations in Education*, p. 142. New York: Routledge & Kegan Paul.

10  Freedman, S. (1988) "Teaching, gender, and curriculum." In L. Beyer & M. Apple (eds.). *The Curriculum: Problems, Politics, and Possibilities*, pp. 204-218. Albany: SUNY Press.

11  As examples of the liberal discourse in education see:
The Carnegie Foundation for the Advancement of Teaching Reports (1986)  *A Nation Prepared: Teachers for the 21st Century*.  New York: Carnegie Forum Task Force on Teaching as a Profession.
The Carnegie Foundation for the Advancement of Teaching Reports (1988) *An Imperiled Generation: Saving Urban Schools*. Lawrenceville, NJ: Princeton University Press.
Sizer, T. (1984) *Hoarce's Compromise: The Dilemma of the American High School*. Boston: Houghton-Mifflin.

12  Grubb, W. N. & Lazerson, M. (1988) *Broken Promises: How Americans Fail Their Children*. Chicago: University of Chicago Press.
Gintis, H. & Bowles, S. (1988) "Contradiction and reproduction in educational theory." In M. Cole (ed.). *Bowles and Gintis Revisited: Correspondence and Contradiction in Educational Theory*, pp. 16-32. New York: Falmer.

13  Marx, K. & Engels, F. (1974) *The German Ideology, Part One*, p. 42. New York: International Publishers.

14  Davis, E. & Lansbury, R. (1986) "Democracy and control in the workplace: An introduction." In Davis & Lansbury (eds.). *Democracy and Control in the Workplace*, pp. 1-29. Melbourne, Australia: Longman Cheshire.
Shuler, T. (1985) *Democracy at Work*. New York: Oxford University Press.

15  McLaren, P. & Lankshear, C. (eds.). (Upcoming)  *Critical Literacy*. Albany: SUNY Press.

16  Giroux, H. (1990) " Rethinking the boundaries of educational discourse: Modernism, postmodernism, and feminism." *College Literature, 17* (2/3), p. 42.

# Chapter XIII

# Educational Visions: What are schools for and what should we be doing in the name of education?

Henry A. Giroux

Maxine Green

# Henry A. Giroux

American public education is in crisis. It is not an isolated crisis affecting a specific aspect of American society; it is a crisis that is implicated in and produced by a transformation in the very nature of democracy itself. This is not without a certain irony. As a number of countries in Eastern Europe move haltingly toward greater forms of democracy, the United States presents itself as the prototype for such reforms and leads the American people to believe that democracy in the United States has reached its penultimate form. The emptiness of this type of analyses is best revealed by the failure of the American public to actively participate in the election of its own government officials, to address the growing illiteracy rates among the general population, and to challenge the increasing view that social criticism and social change are irrelevant to the meaning of American democracy. But the failure of formal democracy is most evident in the refusal of the American government and general population to view public schooling as fundamental to the life of a critical democracy. At stake here is the refusal to grant public schooling a significant role in the ongoing process of education people to be active and critical citizens capable of fighting for and reconstructing democratic public life.

The struggle over public schools cannot be separated from the social problems currently facing this society. These problems are not only political in nature but are pedagogical as well. That is, whenever power and knowledge come together, politics not only function to position people differently with respect to the access of wealth and power, it also provides the conditions for the production and acquisition of learning; put another way, it offers people opportunities to take up and reflect on the conditions that shape themselves and their relationship with others. The pedagogical in this sense is about the production of meaning and the primacy of the ethical and the political as a fundamental part of this process. This means that any discussion of public schooling has to address the political, economic, and social realities that construct the contexts that shape it as an institution and the conditions that produce its diverse population of students. This perspective suggests making visible the social problems and conditions that affect those students who are at risk in our society while recognizing that such problems need to be addressed in both pedagogical and political terms, inside and outside of the schools.

Existing social and economic problems do not augur well for either the fate of public schooling or the credibility of the discourse of democracy itself as it is currently practiced in the United States. For example, it has been estimated that nearly 20% of all children under the age of 18 live below the poverty line. In fact, the United States ranks first among the industrialized nations in child poverty; similarly, besides South Africa, the United States is the only industrialized country that does not provide universal health care for children and pregnant women. Moreover, the division of wealth is getting worse with the poor getting poorer while the rich are getting richer. In fact, the division of wealth was wider in 1988 than at any other time since 1947. As Sally Reed and Craig Sautter (1990) have pointed out: "the poorest 20% of families received less than 5% of the national income, while the wealthiest 20% received 44%...1% of families own 42% of the net wealth of all U. S. families" (p. K5). At the same time, it is important to note that neo-conservative attempts to dismantle public schooling in this country during the last decade have manifested themselves not only in the call for vouchers, the development of school policy based on the market logic of choice, and attacks on education for cultural diversity, but also in the ruthless cutbacks that have affected those most dependent on the public schools, i. e., the poor, people of color, minorities, the working class, and other subordinate groups. The Reagan "commitment" to education and the underprivileged manifested itself shamefully in policies noted for slashing federal funds to important programs such as Aid to Families with Dependent Children, drastically reducing federal funding for low income housing and, in general, cutting over 10 million dollars from programs designed to aid the poor, homeless, and the hungry. At the same time the Reagan government pushed the cost of military spending up to $1.9 trillion dollars.

Within this perspective, the discourse of democracy was reduced to conflating patriotism with the cold war ideology of military preparedness, and the notion of the public good was abstracted from the principles of justice and equality in favor of an infatuation with individual achievement. Greed became respectable in the 1980s while notions of community and democratic struggle were either ignored or seen as subversive. Absent from the neo-conservative public philosophy of the 1980s was any notion of democracy that took seriously the importance of developing a citizenry which could think critically, struggle against social injustices, and develop relations of community based on the principles of equality, freedom, and justice. This should not suggest that as educational and cultural workers we have nothing to do but wallow in despair. On the contrary, as part of the struggle to reclaim schools as agencies of critical citizenship and democratic public life, educators need to develop a new language of critique and possibility. In what follows, I want to suggest four developments such a language might take as part of a project of linking the struggle over schools to a project of radical democracy.

**Reclaiming Democracy: The Missing Language of Schooling**
The problems facing secondary schools in the United States need to be reformulated as a crisis in citizenship and ethics. This suggests that the solution to these problems lies ultimately in the realms of values and politics, not in the realm of management or economics. Schooling is about the production of citizens and the responsibilities of citizenship represents an ethical compact that makes primary the language of community, solidarity, and the public good. Education for democracy cannot be reduced, as some politicians have suggested, to forcing students to say the pledge of allegiance, developing good work habits, or measuring citizenship competencies through standardized cultural literacy tests. Instead, educational reformers concerned with ethics and schooling need to address more fundamental concerns of purpose and meaning such as those implied in the questions: What kind of citizens do we hope to produce through public education? What kind of society do we want to create?

If educators are to take the relationship between schooling and democracy seriously, this means organizing school life

around a version of citizenship that educates students to make
choices, think critically, and believe they can make a difference.
It also means that educators need to affirm and critically inter-
rogate the knowledge and experiences that students bring with
them to the classroom; at the very least this means that educators need to affirm the voices, histories, and stories that provide
students with a sense of place, identity, and meaning.   In
addition, critical educators need to offer students the opportunity to engage in a deeper understanding of the importance of
democratic culture while developing classroom relations that
prioritize the importance of cooperation, sharing, and social
justice.   The primary purpose of schooling is neither commercial nor chauvinistic; we must reject the current conservative call
to make schools adjuncts or the cooperation or bastions of
Eurocentricism.   Progressives all across the country must
reclaim the importance of educating all students with the
knowledge, skills, and values they will need in a democracy for
the responsibilities of learning how to govern.   This means
organizing curricula in ways that enable students to make judgments about how society is historically and socially constructed,
how existing social relations are implicated in relations of equality and justice as well as how they structure inequalities around
racism, sexism, and other forms of oppression.   It also means
offering students the possibilities for being able to make judgments about what society might be, what is possible or desirable
outside existing configurations of power.

**Schooling and the Politics of Difference**
Students need more than work skills and information about
society, they also need to be able to critically assess dominant
and subordinate traditions so as to engage their strengths and
weakness.  What they don't need is to treat history as a closed,
singular narrative that simply has to be revered and memorized.
Educating for democracy and ethical responsibility is not about
creating passive citizens.   It is about providing teachers and
students with the capacities and opportunities to be noisy,
irreverent, and vibrant.  Such capacities are essential for creating the conditions necessary for dialogue, respect, and compassion to emerge as the organizing principles necessary for

sustaining a democratic society. Central to this concern is the need for students to understand how cultural, ethnic, racial, and ideological differences enhance the possibility for dialogue, trust, and solidarity. Difference must be analyzed and constructed within pedagogical contexts that promote compassion and tolerance rather than envy, hatred, and bigotry. The pedagogical imperative at work here is one that demands opportunities for students to be border crossers. That is, educators need to offer students the opportunities to explore cultural difference in historical and contextual terms that open up rather than shut down partiality, possibilities, and dialogue. As border crossers, students must engage knowledge as citizens of the world. Hence, they must be provided with pedagogical opportunities to engage the multiple references that construct different cultural codes, experiences, and histories. In this context, such a pedagogy offers students the opportunity to rewrite the discourse of diversity and difference through the process of crossing over into cultural zones that provide a critical resource for rethinking how the relations between dominant and subordinate groups are organized, how they are implicated and placed in relationships often structured in dominance, and what should be changed in such relations in order to promote a democratic and just society. Difference in this case does not become a marker for deficit, inferiority, chauvinism, or inequality; on the contrary, it opens the possibilities for constructing pedagogical practices that deepen the project of a critical democracy. Rather than precluding the possibility for broader forms of solidarity among different groups, a pedagogy and politics of cultural difference can be forged in social relations rooted in compassion, trust, and generosity. As such, difference becomes the basis for developing a broader discourse of cultural citizenship. In this case, difference does not become the basis for competition, but for organizing forms of cultural democracy that serve to enlarge our moral vision.

**Reclaiming the Radical Responsibility of Ethics**
At the same time it is important to acknowledge that the radical responsibility of progressive educators necessitates an ongoing analyses by students of the contradictions in American society

between the meaning of freedom, the demands of social justice, the obligations of citizenship and the accumulated suffering, domination, force, and violence that permeates various aspects of everyday life.  In part, this suggests acknowledging that the failure of ethical discourse in our schools is rooted, in part, in viewing learning and values as merely abstract and procedural problems.  The crisis in ethics is not about relativism; students are constantly subjected in mass society to the moral discourses of individualism, consumerism, and violence.  What is at stake is recognizing how one is shaped within ethical forms of addresses and what the implications in terms of practice mean for violating or enhancing the quality of public life.

Educators need to insert a concern for the concrete and social back into the language of ethics.  That is, moral education should be grounded in forms of learning that arise out of specific relations that connect the principles and practices of classroom life with the concrete struggles that inform community life and the dynamics of the wider society.  Students should be provided with opportunities to link classroom learning with social projects that allow them to read, listen, and see the histories, stories, experiences and pains of those who are excluded from the benefits of American society by virtue of their race, class, gender, or age.  By being given the opportunity through school projects to address fundamental inequalities in their communities and the wider society, students can begin to distance themselves from being implicated in power relations that are oppressive.  But moral discourse as it is being formulated here is not based on simply the refusal to engage in relations structured in domination, or on the passive learning of particular rights, but on an active and discriminating participation in democratic public life.  I will conclude by taking up this issue in more detail.

Recognizing democracy as a moral ideal implies an ongoing struggle to reconstruct human experience in the realization of such principles as freedom, liberty, and fraternity.  Within this context, learning must be grounded in the ethical imperative to both challenge the prevailing social order while simultaneously providing the basis for students to deepen the intellectual, civic, and moral understanding of their role as agents of public formation. At one level, this means that the school curriculum must be more attentive to the issues, problems, and histories that construct the experiences of their students and the political and moral density of everyday life. At another level, this suggests that schools need to reconstruct their relations with the communities that they allegedly serve. Schools need to reach out into these communities and learn about their traditions and struggles, share power with the parents who live in them, and use their resources to empower not only dominant members of the community but also those individuals and groups that are generally excluded from school life. Progressives need to situate the meaning and purpose of schooling within a broader theory of social welfare and cultural democracy. At the very least, this means that educators can work to insert the idea of the public back into schooling and in doing so be able to defend their responsibilities as public servants by referencing and critically engaging the principles that shape their view of schooling and society *within* rather than outside of the principles and practices of a critical democracy.

**Teachers as Public Intellectuals**
Teachers and other cultural workers need to redefine their roles as engaged and transformative intellectuals. In opposition to dominant views of teaching defined through accountability schemes that deskill teachers while simultaneously reducing them to the status of clerks and technicians, progressives need to reclaim the role of teachers put forth by John Dewey, C. Wright Mills, Paulo Freire, Miles Horton, Maxine Greene and others. In this view teachers are seen as engaged and transformative intellectuals who combine vision, conception, and practice. This suggests providing teachers with the conditions they need to produce curricula, work productively with outside social agencies and community people, and exercise a notion of leadership that combines a discourse of hope with forms of self and social criticism. Teachers and other cultural workers dedicated to reforming all spheres of educating as part of a wider revitalization of public life need to raise important questions regarding the relationship among knowledge and power, learning and possibility, social criticism and human dignity, and how these

might be understood in relation to rather than in isolation from those practices of domination, privilege, and resistance at work in the larger society. This is essentially a question of not only what people know but also how they come to know in a particular way within the contexts and constraints of specific social and cultural practices. Teachers need to become public intellectuals and engaged critics capable of resurrecting traditions and memories that provide new ways of reading history and reclaiming power and identity in the new interests of creating a democratic society that affirms difference, justice, equality, and freedom. Not only does this suggest that educators develop a vision that enables rather than dismantles the possibility for critical citizenship, it also suggests that educators make connections with other cultural workers in order to form alliances, create critical public cultures, and collectively struggle for work conditions which enable them to function and engage as principled educators.

Recent events in Eastern Europe have often been interpreted to mean that America's legacy of democracy has reached its penultimate expression in the resurgence of democratic revolutions abroad. In actuality, the struggle for democracy is never over, and the complacency and indifference to the language of democracy as it is often expressed in the United States signals an important reason for educators to once again reclaim the language of schooling as an ethical and political imperative. If democracy is not to fall victim to a growing ethnocentricism, individualism, and consumerism, at the very least educators and others can work together to develop a political and ethical discourse that provides a rationale for students and others to comprehend democracy as a way of life that consistently has to be fought for, struggled over, and rewritten as part of the practice of critical citizenship.

# References

Reed, S. & Sautter, C. (1990, June). "Children of Poverty: The Status of 12 Million Young Americans," *Phi Delta Kappan*, pp. K1-K11.

# Maxine Greene

Education, as both concept and undertaking, is in continuing tension with the institutions called schools. Education, after all, has to do with engaging live human beings in activities of meaning-making, dialogue, and reflective understanding of a variety of texts, including the texts of their social realities. Growing, becoming different, becoming informed and articulate: all these are involved in the project called education, a project that must be chosen by persons intentionally and cooperatively involved in learning to learn. Schools, speaking largely a transitive language, were established to work upon the young from without, to shape the raw material of human nature (as Horace Mann saw it) into the forms required by a society caught in material pursuits, divided by class and gender and color boundaries, fragmented in commitments to values and to faith. Control was demanded, along with what was called "voluntary compliance" with the laws of righteousness and with (illegible though it often was) the dominant ideology. That meant agreement with meritocratic arrangements; it meant stratifications even in classrooms. For a long time, there was a general acquiescence with hierarchy and distinction because of the promises continually offered: promises of equity, upward mobility, a chance at pecuniary success. Immigrant parents, poor parents, dislocated parents could not but accept the goal of accomodating to market demand.

There were, of course, signs of alienation from the beginning, stirrings of discontent. Not all were specifically oriented to schooling; but many, like the critiques of the socialist Robert Owen and Frances Wright, or of the Catholic reformer Orestes Brownson, struck directly at those dimensions of the system the common school was invented to serve. We might say the same of some of the great Black leaders like Frederick Douglass, Sojourner Truth, and Dr. W. E. B. Dubois. We might summon up the voices as well as of women protesting subordination and exclusion within and outside society's dominant institutions. Out of these and other articulations of discontent, like many of those that followed after in the 20th century, we might work forward to an educational vision appropriate to a nation so poorly served by the metanarratives of progress, so entangled in its own myths at a moment of erosion and decline.

Avoiding both functionalism and determinism, we see schools defining themselves variously in different regions of the country and, indeed, in different localities. Schools in homogeneous communities (in the Cumberland mountains, in the midwestern prairies, on lakeshores and northern peninsulas) are likely to transmit the codes and value patterns that have sustained particular groups sometimes over generations. What Pierre Bourdieu calls "cultural reproduction" has taken place in such schools, sometimes on the basis of a shared investment in "cultural capital," on the model of the early common schools. Factory closings, failures on the farms, the impacts of technology, the effects of media and popular culture have often created great gulfs between what the schools believed they were "for" and what changing communities required if they were to survive. Mark Twain's steamboat plowing down the river in *The Adventures of Huckleberry Finn* still provides a fitting metaphor for what happened and what is happening today. Huck and Jim, having been swept south by the current, are waiting for the fog to lift when they hear the steamboat pounding along. "She aimed right for us," says Huck. "Often they do that and try to see how close they can come without touching; sometimes the wheel bites off a sweep, and then the pilot sticks his head out and laughs, and thinks he's might smart." In all that indifference and impersonality, with her furnaces blazing and her steam whistling, "and as Jim went overboard on one side and I on the other, she came smashing right through the raft." It is not only the violence and carelessness of technology that has overwhelmed the face-to-face community represented by Jim and Huck. It is the lack of anything like an empowering education that renders them so powerless once they reach the riverbanks, so vulnerable to hypocrisy and mystification and greed. Huck has been taught the skills and pieties of a slave society in school. He has felt "cramp'd up" by it all, perhaps especially by the norms of a society that sold children away from their mothers, decorated houses with genteel sentimental sketches, allowed gun-toting landowners to listen to sermons on brotherly love on Sundays across the land. But he has not been helped to interpret in such a fashion that would bring him in contact with a community of restless ones, those trying to transform. At the end, he refuses to be "sivilized"; and he can only "light out for the territory ahead," territory long closed. Still, there is a vision in the making, as we shall see, a kind of vision that might lead to the enfranchisement of boys and girls like Huck, a trust in the meanings to which they give voice, the shaping of a critical community.

Huck has, to a degree, been schooled and been miseducated by what he could bear to learn. There are other examples in the 19th century literature: Herman Melville's Bartleby who could not cope with a walled-in, commercial society where free choices were inefficient and unacceptable. He could only survive (at least for a while) by repeating "I prefer not to," by becoming a living negation of what schools were intended for—and with no recourse but death. His employer, whose story it is, experiences a moment of fraternity; but, in the midst of the bustling city, in the law offices of Wall Street, he can find only lifelessness and barriers. There is Edith Wharton's Lily Bart, schooled perhaps, but ending with the feeling of being a mere cog in a machine or "of being swept like a stray uprooted growth down the heedless current of the years." Here, too, there is the intimation of a vision. Lily, "rootless and ephemeral, mere spindrift of the whirling surface of existence, without anything to which the poor little tentacles of self could cling. . . And as she looked back she saw that there had never been a time when she had had any real relation to life." She has lived from house party to house party, bridge game to bridge game, loan to loan in a burgeoning New York; and nothing binds her to "the mighty sum of human striving." So is it with Edna Pontellier in Kate Chopin's *The Awakening*, another woman schooled to passivity and thoughtlessness, caught (she is convinced) between the "soul's slavery" of domesticity and a future of promiscuity. In some terrible way fixated, she swims out to sea with images of her far-off childhood in mind, all future possibilities closed.

The stories in and out of imaginative literature are multiple: stories of schooling standing in the way of educating, of critical consciousness, of legitimate awakenings. Of course, for those sometimes called the "fortunate fifth," for suburban children and wealthy children, the schools have built upon the cultural capital brought in by the students. They have used the investment to produce the inventors and discoverers and bankers and superintendents and military men even Horace Mann had seen emerging from the schools. The irony has been that resources made available to suburban and exurban schools have allowed them to institute enriched curricula, interdisciplinary studies, arts and humanities experiences. Here, too, school people have felt themselves able to "afford" an encouragement of critical thinking, problem-solving, field work of various kinds. Here, where a tracking system reaches a kind of grim apotheosis, schooling and educating now and then mesh.

In the declining cities, where calls for equality contest with calls for more child-centering in the schools, where structural disintegration threatens the very survival of the young, efforts to restructure by involving more of those affected in the schools themselves now and then become educative in the deepest sense. Parental involvement, "family groups" within the schools, outreaches into community, journal keeping and field research, bilingual experiences, experiential learning: all become indications of what can be done and should be done if we are serious about educating the young. They open towards possibility, in fact, because they ground learning in situated life. They release the young to tell their stories, to "name" the world they hope to transform. This occurs, as is well known, in the Foxfire schools, in Central Park East in New York City, in various schools represented by the "network" for democratic education. Whether or note they depend upon tests to determine their "success," they nonetheless offer evidence that committed people working in small communities can make schools habitable, stimulating, sustaining—and sometimes resistant to a society that too obviously does not care.

The signs point to a lack of care where poor and minority children are concerned, as does the erosion of financial support since the beginnings of the Reagan administration. The Reaganite stress on deregulation, privatization, uniform standards, and technical norms had, it turned out, an almost immediate and malign effect on schools. The so-called "reform" reports, beginning to emerge in 1983 and following after a period of shallow preoccupation with behavioral objectives, competencies, and the rest, focused on measurable achievement. More often than not, the inability to achieve, or to show evidence of "higher cognitive skills," was blamed upon the child, usually the poor child or the child's family. She/he was not read to; not enough time was spent on homework; American youth lacked "background knowledge," there was insufficient "cultural literacy."

The decade saw a convergence of end-of-the-world warnings of a decline in technological dominance and economic competitiveness with laments about what 17-years old did not know, what teachers could not do on their own, what relativism and immorality and banality were doing to national greatness and national pride. The young were repeatedly spoken of as human "resources," with obvious implications that they were to be grist for the market, for the nation's technocratic mills. It was made clear enough in a number of the reports that those who could not master the skills required, those who could not adjust to the new technologies could not expect to be supported by public funds. Little mention was made of the fact that the actual future for thousands of the young was to be found in the service industries, in places where the deskilling process was at work, as in hamburger shops and supermarkets. Not expected to use their capacities or to develop new potentialities in a society where energies were to run down narrower and narrower channels, they were scarcely thought of as *persons* to be educated. When the Department of Education issued a monograph called "What Works" early on in the decade, presumably showing what research was contributing to education of the young, they left a general impression of the most sterile pragmatism. Incurious about the newcomers in society, disinterested in the suppressed talents and energies distributed through the country, obsessed by the raw-edged individualism associated with *laissez-faire*, federal bureaucrats and certain academics came together to fashion a myth about a rejected golden age. Below the surface of what they were doing and saying was a call for a conformist, untroubled, unquestioning, stratified society. People would be lulled by the media into becoming passive audiences while they were being attacked for what they did not know. Their own stories, their own meaning structures would be scorned and set aside, as education was reread to mean a return to some absolute, to a realm accessible mainly to the well-to-do.

The great popularity of books like Hirsch's *Cultural Literacy* and Bloom's *The Closing of the American Mind* is not to be attributed to any conspiracy. Hirsch's book speaks out of a conservative dread of fragmentation in what was never the kind of "language community" Hirsch speaks of preserving. Moreover, the discrete pieces of information that compose the "knowledge" ostensibly necessary for any kind of "excellence" in this country are arbitrarily selected from what seems to be an objectively existent body of concepts and facts. Calling for an emphasis on content (officially selected), oversimplifying and actually distorting the work of Rousseau and Dewey in order to condemn and emphasis on "process," Hirsch offers a kind of reassurance to those troubled by the profound changes in our culture. Not only does there exist a dependable body of knowledge, he says; we can overcome the great rifts and uncertainties in our society by identifying a specific content and thereby make sure that the young are equipped for the economic demands of the "modern" world.

Bloom, in contrast, is mainly concerned with elite young people. They become the exemplars for him of what is happening in a society he believes is being corrupted by feminism, rock music, the persisting spirit of the Sixties, and German philosophy. Challenging all that along with banality and lack of commitment, he asks even the humblest among us to look upwards, to fasten our small wagons to a Platonist star, to a universal notion of the Good (not to speak of the True and Beautiful). Diversity, perspective, situatedness, plurality: all are cancelled out by this elementary kind of classicism that appeals so much to those who are fearful of youth, of the new music, of racial harmony, of questioning and unrest.

These books and many other books and articles following in their wake are today focusing on the evils of "multiculturalism," on changes being made in the traditionally male and Eurocentric canon. Moreover, they have invented a new scare term called "P.C." which is being used to silence increasing numbers of people and keep others in their places. The initials stand for "politically correct," now attached to what is called a posture of indoctrination and intolerance on the part of a radical few. Unfortunately (and significantly) those working to make "P.C." a cure for relativism and radicalism and multiplicity are beginning to focus on far more than inclusion in the curricula, the introduction of Women's Studies and Black Studies, the rewriting and reconsideration of texts. On some level in tune with those who intend to make the schools more than ever before training grounds for the "Deltas" who will presumably make up the majority in the post-industrial society, these conservatives try to cloak themselves in the mantle of esoteric, almost priestly scholars. They present themselves as guards of the House of Intellect against the barbarians in the garden. Never have the engines of economic power installed themselves so shamelessly and obviously in the inner halls of that House. The irony, of course, is that the House is ancient and probably sinking into the ground. Here and there, the sunlight hits a window-pane, or a branch strikes against a sagging door. It may be ready to be brought to a new life if the need and restlessness of this country can be recognized again, if enough people have the courage to ask themselves what they should be doing in the name of education.

Pursuing a vision, deeply aware of the war just ended, the war that scars everyone of us, I can only think of what education should be in terms of a refusal of what that war entailed. First, there was the assumption of the value of the "technological fix." If our technology is powerful enough, it can solve all problems; and value questions must be held irrelevant when the "fix" is in sight. Technology, of course, in the case of the Gulf War, signified the most powerful destructive machines yet seen in history. It made possible a distancing, a terrible depersonalization that infected most of those who paid heed with what Albert Camus called "plague." Indifference, distancing, lack of responsibility, a making living beings into things—or "targets," or diagrams. Dr. Robert Lifton would describe what happened as an almost fatal psychic numbing. Coupled with that was a use of language to distort, disguise, deny. We all recall "collateral damage," "sortie," "take out"; and many of us still shudder at the sound of "victory," given the circumstances of the war. None of this, of course, is intended to defend or justify the brutal actions of the leader of Iraq. All of it argues, however, for an ability to hold opposing and sometimes contradictory ideas in mind at the same time. All of it argues powerfully for the use of imagination, at least in the posting of alternative possibilities. Surely, there are alternatives to mass killing, to fires, to withholding of the basic goods human beings need to live.

Considering all that, I can only shape an education vision that demands moral judgment when it comes to the uses of technology, and the learning of self-reflectiveness when it comes to the kind of thinking described as technical rationality. To speak of moral judgment today, however, is to remind ourselves of the ways in which significant moral values are grounded in lived life and realized when persons choose them in their coming together, in the making of face-to-face communities. The shaping of narratives, the telling of stories help persons to identify their moral purposes, to orient themselves to some vision of what they believe to be decent and good and right. So does the gathering together in classrooms and corridors to play together, to sing together, to make decisions together that affect all involved. There must be moments for recognition, moments for face-to-face encounters among the diverse newcomers in our schools. It is when spaces open among them, when their diverse perspectives are granted integrity that something they can hold in common may begin to emerge. It requires imagination; it requires involvement with the arts and the personal presentness the arts invite. It demands, as well, the identification of deficiencies in the world around (the addictions, the illnesses, the abandonments, the devastations) and a shared effort in some manner to repair. It is when this occurs that values are created, that persons with diverse backgrounds can come together. Camus talks in his novel about how important it is, in time of pestilence, to take the side of the victims. I can imagine no vision more important than a vision of transformation for the sake of fighting plague.

Giving what we see—the neglect, the cold carelessness, the rampant greed—it will take outrage if we are to succeed in education. It will take a new kind of hope, a new shaping of possibility, a new venture into the unpredictable. But, then, utopias are never predictable. We can only choose ourselves for something caring and humane and daring. We can only choose ourselves for something caring and humane and daring. We can only begin.

# List of Contributors

**Clinton B. Allison** is Professor of Education in History of Education, University of Tennessee, Knoxville. He is an expert in the history of southern education, having published numerous articles on the topic. His latest publications include a chapter in *Curriculum as Social Psychoanalysis* (State University of New York Press, 1991) and *The Past and the Present: Issues in American Educational History* (Lang-forthcoming).

**Kathleen Berry** is Associate Professor at the University of New Brunswick, where she teaches literacy and drama. She taught both elementary and secondary school over a period of fifteen years. Author of *Creative Curriculum: The Mythological Roots* (World Council of Curriculum and Instruction, 1990) and her forthcoming book, *Thinking and Acting Critical in Non-critical Schools: Misbehaving in a Behavioral World* (Lang-forthcoming), (with Shirley R. Steinberg).

**Deborah P. Britzman** is Assistant Professor in the School of Education and Human Development at the State University of New York at Binghamton where she teaches courses in multicultural education and supervises secondary English education. She is author of *Practice Makes Practice: A Critical Study of Learning to Teach* and recent articles in *The Harvard Educational Review* and *Curriculum Inquiry*.

**Dennis Carlson** is Assistant Professor of Education at Miami University (Ohio). A student of urban education, Carlson has published numerous articles on the critical analysis of power relations within educational contexts. His "Teachers as Political Actors" published in the *Harvard Educational Review* is a highly-regarded example of the application of critical social theory to the analysis of the institutional and social roles of teachers.

**Dalton B. Curtis, Jr.** is Director of the University Studies Inter-disciplinary Program at Southeast Missouri State University where he also teaches history of education, philosophy of education and European history. He is a co-author of *Lives in Education*, a book of biographical essays on the history of educational thought and practice. He also has published articles on Jacques Maritain and the Social Reconstructionists.

**Henry A. Giroux** is Professor and Renowned Scholar in Residence in the School of Education and Allied Professions at Miami University, and Director of the Center for Education and Cultural Studies. He is the author of *Ideology, Culture, and the Process of Schooling*; *Education Under Seige*; *Teachers as Intellectuals*; *Schooling and the Struggle for Public Life*; *Popular Culture, Schooling and Everyday Life*; *Postmodern Education: Politics, Culture and Social Criticism* and most recently, the editor of *Postmodernism, Feminism, and Cultural Politics: Redrawing Educational Boundaries*.

**Andrew Gitlin** is Associate Professor of Educational Studies, University of Utah. He has taught and published in the areas of curriculum, critical theory, and teacher education. His major areas of interest include the effects of school structure on teachers' work, evaluation, and school reform. His most recent book is *Teacher Evaluation: Educative Alternatives*, (co-authored with John Smyth).

**Robert P. Green, Jr.** is Professor of Education at Clemson University where he teaches social sciences methodology, instruction, and curriculum development. As a former social studics teacher, Green is a consultant to several publishers and the author of many articles on social studies education. He is the co-author of the educational foundations text, *American Education: Foundations and Policy* (with J. Walker and E.J. Kozma).

**Maxine Greene** is the William F. Russell Professor of Philosophy and Education at Teachers College, Columbia University where she teaches social philosophy, aesthetics, and the Arts and American Education. Her latest book is *The Dialectic of Freedom* (Teachers College Press). In addition to many articles, she is the author of *The Teacher as Stranger, Landscapes of Learning,* and *The Dialectic of Freedom.*

**Madeleine R. Grumet** is Dean of the School of Education of Brooklyn College, City University of New York. She is a curriculum theorist who brings phenomenological, psychoanalytic, literary, and feminist studies to research in education. Her book *Bitter Milk: Women and Teaching* (1989) is a study of the relation of our reproductive projects to epistemology, curriculum, and pedagogy.

**Walter P. Gutierrez** is Counselor in the Center for Educational and Cultural Advancement at the University of Wisconsin-Parkside. He is a former Spanish teacher, and has also worked extensively in minority student retention at the university level.

**Eleanor Blair Hilty** is Associate Professor of Education at Kennesaw State University. She has written several articles on moonlighting teachers. Her forthcoming book is entitled *Political Dimensions of Educational Psychology: Learning in Critical Perspective* (Lang).

**Harvey J. Kaye** is the Ben and Joyce Rosenberg Professor of Social Change and Development and Director of the Center for History and Social Change at the University of Wisconsin-Green Bay. Kaye is author of *The British Marxist Historians* (1984) and *The Powers of the Past* (1991); and, with K. McClelland, the co-editor of *E.P. Thompson: Critical Perspectives (1990).* He is currently working on the question of intellectuals and the development of a popular democratic historical memory, consciousness and imagination.

**Joe L. Kincheloe** is Professor of Education at Clemson University. He is the author of *Understanding the Impact of the New Right on Education, Getting Beyond the Facts: Teaching Social Studies in the Late Twentieth Century, Curriculum as Social Psychoanalysis: Essays on the Significance of Place* (with William F. Pinar),

*Teachers as Researchers:  Qualitative Paths to Empowerment, The Stigma of Genius:  Einstein and Education* (with Shirley R. Steinberg and Deborah J. Tippins), *The Politics of Teacher Thinking* (Bergin and Garvey, forthcoming), and *Critical Vocationalism: Connecting Cognitive and Vocational Education* (Lang, forthcoming).

**Magda Lewis** is Assistant Professor and member of the graduate faculty at Queen's University, Kingston, Ontario where she teaches feminist theory, issues in social class, gender and race in education and qualitative research methods.  Her publications, most recently in the *Harvard Educational Review*, reflect her long and active interest in feminist politics and pedagogy.  Presently she has two book manuscripts under way, concerning issues of feminist pedagogy in the classroom and the experiences of women in the academy.

**Cameron McCarthy** is Assistant Professor of Education at Colgate University.  A leading scholar of race and curriculum theory, McCarthy has published important articles on media criticism and racism.  His theory of non-synchrony involving the ambiguous construction of racial identities has proven to be an important development in the study of racism in educational contexts.  He is the author of *Race and Curriculum* (Falmer Press, 1991).

**Peter McLaren** is Associate Professor of Educational Leadership and Renowned Scholar-in-Residence, School of Education and Allied Professions, Miami University, Ohio. He is author of *Cries from the Corridor:  The New Suburban Ghettos* and *Schooling as a Ritual Performance*.  His book, *Life in Schools* was named by the American Educational Studies Association as one of the most significant books on education for the year 1989.  Forthcoming publications include *Paulo Freire:  A Critical Encounter* (Routledge) and (with Colin Lankshear) *Critical Literacy:  Radical and Postmodern Perspectives*.

**Janet L. Miller** is Associate Professor in the Department of Curriculum and Teaching, Hofstra University.  Her teaching, writing, and research interests include curriculum theory, feminist studies, qualitative inquiry, and critical and collaborative forms of teacher research. In addition to many articles in these areas she recently published *Creating Spaces and Finding Voices: Teachers Collaborating for Empowerment.*

**Clara Ann New** is Assistant Professor of Teacher Education at the University of Wisconsin-Parkside. She is a former teacher in the Milwaukee Public Schools. Her areas of interest are multicultural curiculum, early childhood education, and expectancy behaviors in achievement for black males in urban schools.

**Joseph W. Newman** is Professor of Educational Foundations at the University of South Alabama, where he was voted Outstanding Professor in 1986 and Outstanding Scholar in 1991. He teaches social foundations and multicultural education and the history of American education. He is author of the textbook, *America's Teachers: An Introduction to Education* (1990, Longman). He is author of a chapter in *Curriculum as Social Psychoanalysis* (State University of New York Press, 1991).

**Jo Anne Pagano** is Associate Professor in the Department of Education at Colgate University. She has written extensively in the fields of curriculum theory, teacher education and feminism. Drawing upon feminist psychoanalytical theory and literary criticism, Pagano has provided a unique perspective on the educational enterprise. Her latest work is *Exiles and Communities: Teaching in the Patriarchal Wilderness.*

**William F. Pinar** is Professor of Education at Louisana State University in Baton Rouge. He is the editor of *Contemporary Curriculum Discourses* (Gorsuch Scarisbrick, 1988) and (with Joe L. Kincheloe) of *Curriculum as Social Psychoanalysis* (State University of New York Press, 1991). He is the co-editor (with William M. Reynolds) of *Understanding Curriculum as Phenomenological and Deconstructed Text.* The founding editor of *JCT: An Interdisciplinary Journal of Curriculum Studies*, Pinar helps organize the yearly Conference on Curriculum Theory and Classroom practice held at the Bergamo Conference Center in Dayton, Ohio.

**E. Wayne Ross** is Assistant Professor of Education at the State University of New York at Albany where he teaches courses in social education and curriculum theory. His numerous publications reflect a research focus on the influence of social and institutional contexts on teachers' practice and reflective thinking in teaching and teacher education. His book, *Teacher Personal Theorizing: Connecting Curriculum Practice, Theory and Research* (co-edited with Jeffrey W. Cornett and Gail McCutcheon) is forthcoming.

**Douglas J. Simpson** is Dean of the School of Education, Texas Christian University. Simpson has brought an educational philosopher's perspective to the study and reform of teacher education. His book, *The Teacher as Philosopher*, combines his scholarly interests in educational philosophy, teacher education, and the purposes of schooling.

**Christine E. Sleeter** is Associate Professor of Teacher Education at the University of Wisconsin-Parkside. She has published articles on multicultural education, race, social class and gender issues in education. Her books include *Empowerment through Multicultural Education*, and (with Carl Grant) *Making Choices for Multicultural Education, Turning on Learning*, and *After the School Bell Rings*.

**William Stanley** is Chair of the Department of Curriculum and Instruction at the University of Delaware. Having published numerous important articles in social studies education, Stanley has brought the insight of critical social theory to the analysis of the purposes of social studies education. His recent work in social studies education has focused on the implications of postmodernist social theory for the field.

**Shirley R. Steinberg** developed the "In-Process Collective" which employs dialogue and social drama in a constantly evolving format. She is the co-editor (with Joe L. Kincheloe) of the new Peter Lang Series, *Democratic Advances in Modern Education* and is author of *The Stigma of Genius: Einstein and Education* (with Joe L. Kincheloe and Deborah Tippins-forthcoming) and co-author of *Thinking and Acting Critical in Non-critical Schools: Misbehaving in a Behavioral World* (with Kathy Berry, forthcoming, Lang).

**Susan R. Takata** is Associate Professor of Sociology at the University of Wisconsin-Parkside. Her most recent publication is "Who is Empowering Whom? The Social Construction of Empowerment" in *Empowerment through Multicultural Education* (ed. by Christine Sleeter). She has published numerous articles on criminology, law, race and ethnic relations.

**Rodman B. Webb** is Professor of Social Foundations of Education at the University of Florida. Webb is well-known for his work in teacher efficacy and qualitative research. His book, *Qualitative Research and Education: Focus and Methods* (co-edited with Robert R. Sherman) (Falmer, 1990) is an excellent introduction to qualitative research studies in education.

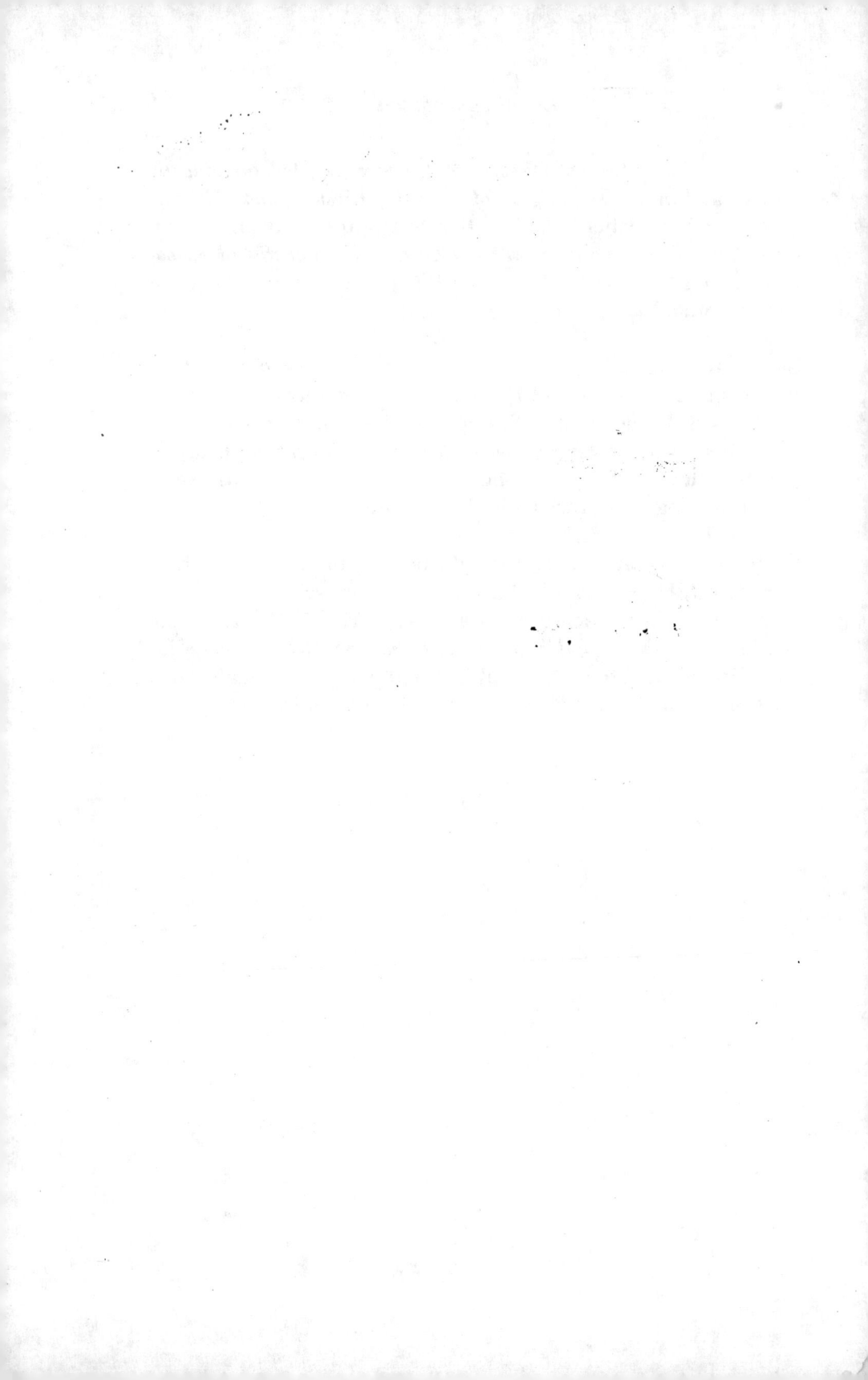